JAMES SALERNO,

BOXER

A TRUE STORY

BY
JOHN GREENBURG

ACKNOWLEDGEMENTS

I wish to thank the Salerno family and all the people I interviewed while writing this book. In addition, I want to thank Butch Flansburg, his lovely wife Kathy and Steve Canton, who are the three permanent board members of the Florida Boxing Hall of Fame. They were very encouraging and supportive of my efforts. Most of all, they headed the organization which gave James credibility by inducting him into their Hall of Fame.

"SHOW ME A HERO, AND I WILL WRITE YOU A TRAGEDY"
- F. SCOTT FITZGERALD

The night of August 1, 1999 was hot as usual in Jacksonville, Florida. A new month had just begun, but time was quickly ticking away for a tall white male in his late thirties. He had no idea how few minutes remained in his life as he effortlessly climbed the stairs to the second floor of the Comet Apartments in the Murray Hill section of the city. The bounce in his step was a clue that he had once been a well conditioned professional athlete who had experienced more than his share of triumphs and moments in the limelight. Now, he was reduced to very brief euphoria offered by the crack pipe. After reaching the second floor, he turned to walk toward apartment number twelve. He had been told that a drug dealer he owed a large sum of money to would be waiting for him to work things out in a peaceable way. Suddenly, a boy no more than thirteen years old called out to him. All the kid said was, "Salerno?"

The tall man answered, "Yes." In the dim light, he didn't notice that the boy was holding a .22 caliber hand gun. There was no more conversation. The kid fired once. Salerno shouted, "HELP, HELP, I'VE BEEN SHOT!" He fell backwards, landed hard on the back of his head and died.

Even though the shooter was very young, it was still a murder committed by a cold blooded hired killer. No one would have shot James Salerno out of anger because no one ever hated him. He had been a sensitive, loving, generous and compassionate man his entire life. When it came to race, he was truly color blind. He would give anyone the shirt off his back. He came to the aid of anybody who asked for his help. In his own way, he was out to save the world. He was always trying to help anyone he hung out with to become better persons, even the crack cocaine addicts whom he spent his last days with. He knew no strangers and wanted everyone to be his friend. All of these good qualities eventually proved to be fatal flaws because he wore rose colored glasses which blinded him to the dark side of life and made him as vulnerable as a newborn babe.

As sensitive, loving, generous and compassionate as he was, it was amazing that he became one of the most talented boxers who ever walked the face of the earth. When he was thirteen, the great Muhammad Ali took him under his wing. Anyone who saw him perform in the ring as a teenager predicted that he would be a Caucasian version of Ali. At the age of seventeen, he had won twenty straight fights and appeared on Good Morning America. Legendary promoter Don King called him "my Great White Hope." When he didn't fulfill his promise, he slipped from the public eye and everyone asked, "Whatever became of James Salerno?" This book supplies the answers.

INTRODUCTION

Boxing is the oldest of all sports. Evidence has been found that pugilism was practiced by the ancient Sumerians more than 3,000 years B.C. Pierce Egan, an Englishman who lived from 1772 to 1849, is acknowledged as being the first boxing historian. Egan referred to boxing as "the sweet science of bruising." Essayist A. J. Liebling shortened the term to "the sweet science," a description of the sport which is still being used. Both Egan and Liebling wanted to make the point that boxing is more than a form of athletic competition. It requires physical stamina and mastery of techniques to such a degree that they become second nature, but it is ninety percent mental. It is full of poetry and drama. It is, in truth, an art form. The best teachers of boxing believe that it is an excellent means of learning life skills.

Liebling was of the old school, and he saw nothing good about the marriage of his beloved sweet science with television. In 1951 he wrote,

The immediate crisis in the United States, forestalling the one high living standards might bring on, has been caused by the popularization of a ridiculous gadget called television. This is utilized in the sale of beer and razor blades. The clients of the television companies, by putting on a free boxing show almost every night of the week, have knocked out of business the hundreds of small city and neighborhood boxing clubs where youngsters had a chance to learn their trade and journeymen to mature their skills. Consequently, the number of good new prospects diminishes with every year, and the peddlers' public is already being asked to believe that a boy with perhaps ten or fifteen fights behind him is a topnotch performer. Neither advertising agencies nor brewers, and least of all the networks, give a hoot if they push the Sweet Science back into a period of genre painting. When it is in a coma, they will find some other way to peddle their peanuts.

James Salerno was a product of television. He became enthralled by the sweet science from watching Muhammad Ali on the small screen. His legend was fueled by an appearance on ABC's Good Morning America when he was seventeen and had already fought twenty professional bouts. As a result of his being interviewed by Hugh Downs, he received duffel bags of fan mail from all over the world. He became known as "The Mouth of the South," thanks to the medium of cable television. Many of his fights were carried by ESPN, HBO, Sports Channel America and the USA Cable Network.

James always put on a show in the ring and he gave the viewers even more with his priceless post fight interviews. The first time I ever saw him in action was on an ESPN telecast from Nashville, Tennessee that featured expert analysis from Al Bernstein. James was matched against a local fighter whose full time job was in law enforcement. The lawman had earned a reputation as a knockout artist and relied on his dynamite right hand to carry him to victory. Salerno gave him a bitter dose of reality by administering a boxing lesson in the process of winning the fight by a technical knockout.

He made short work of the boxer from Tennessee, but the fight was only the prelude to the real show. Once James was given the microphone, the Mouth of the South went into high gear. He gave praise to God, thanked his mother and father for all they had done for him and gave credit to his veteran trainer, Jimmy Williams. Once those obligations were taken care of, he parked his humility at the door. He claimed to be the "Real Italian Stallion" and the "Master of Disaster." He challenged Dwight Braxton, the defending world light heavyweight titleholder, by boasting that he would "turn the Camden Buzz Saw into the Camden Bus Boy." He talked tough, but he seemed capable of backing up his words.

James Salerno was one of his sport's all time characters. He once said to his mother, "Momma, I get up in the morning and look in the mirror. Each time I think, 'I'm good enough, I'm smart enough and doggone it, people love me.'" He didn't win every fight or capture a world title, but he was always fun to watch and even more fun to listen to. More often than not, he backed up every boast. Jimmy Williams said, "James was a rarity; a white boy who fought like a black man." Hall of Fame referee Bryan Garry worked several of his bouts and said of Salerno, "James had balls… big balls."

Without question, the man was unique; the greatest boxer who never won a world title. This is not just my opinion, it is a fact. James has been inducted into the Florida Boxing Hall of Fame.

His story begged to be written, and I feel privileged to have been given the task. I traveled from one end of the Sunshine State to the other in order to learn as much as I could about his turbulent life, and I discovered many facets to his complex personality. The final stop on my quest was the little town of Wewahitchka, whose claim to fame is the Tupelo honey produced there.

The name of the town is an Indian word for "water eyes," a term most fitting for the occasion. As I sat with James' parents, Sal and Joanne Salerno, and his uncle and aunt, Joe and Jean Salerno, we shared bittersweet moments. Tears welled up in our eyes as we went over the tragic parts of his life, but we also shared laughter as we talked about the humorous things James had done. It was an emotional rollercoaster for his family members, and it is our hope that the pain and work involved will be worth it. We believe that even if only one life is changed in a positive way because of James' story, the cost will be justified. His life ended tragically at the age of thirty eight, but he is a true legend of the sweet science... and legends never die.

ASSORTED FLAVORS
BY
JAMES SALERNO

WRITTEN WHILE HE WAS PERFORMING RAP MUSIC AS "ITALIAN ICE"

The battle is never between black and white

But between the forces of wrong and right

Pointing to statistics and reading from a chart

Just draws the people further apart

We are all precious and colorless in God's sight

And told by our consciences to do what's right

God gave us all a personal choice

But some parents speak in a prejudiced voice

In order for their kids to do what they're taught

They will be put on a path to being trapped and caught

Seeing someone of a different race

Used to put a frown upon my face

Should a white be with a black or a black with a white?

Just turn to the Bible and see what's right

Never does it say to label another

Because their skin is of another color

It will hurt future generations

To be without God and one nation

Kids learn hatred. You know that's the truth

We must teach them while they are in their youth

Under one roof we all can stay

And teach our babies a better way

We've gotta start now and get it underway

Or we'll all be in trouble on judgment day

To all the dominant males: Don't forget what the Man said

"If you think you are great, then be the servant."

Table of Contents

PART ONE
THE SALERNO FAMILY'S
EARLY YEARS

HOW JAMES' PARENTS MET

Whenever I begin to write someone's life story, I try to learn about their up-bringing, and this includes how their parents met. I unearthed this information about James' mom and dad during my first day in Wewahitchka. Sal Salerno felt the best way to use our time together was to play hours of family videos that had been converted to DVD from spliced together Super 8 footage. Sal was way ahead of the curve when it came to documenting the various milestones in his children's lives. He shot an enormous amount of Super 8 film at a time when few parents were doing so, and he took pains to preserve it. Without question, his family was very important to him.

As Sal and I sat in a living room dominated a huge flat screen TV, he made no objections when I interrupted the session by asking, "How did you and your wife meet?"

He responded by telling me about what went on during 1959. It was a time when the Cold War was in high gear and America's military leaders were concerned about unmanned aviation devices called "drones." They were convinced that the Soviets had them and were about to use them against us. A facility had been set up for tracking drones at Cape San Blas in the Florida Panhandle, a location bordered by the pristine waters of St. Joseph Bay and the Gulf of Mexico.

Sal had recently been discharged from the U.S. Air Force. He was working at Cape San Blas for International Telephone and Telegraph (IT&T) using the same equipment he had been trained on during his enlistment. It was a very good job for the twenty four year old native of Brooklyn, New York that included not only a generous salary but also per diem. He could live on his expense money and bank practically all his regular pay.

Sal spent some of his money on a stylish automobile. He paid $1,500 cash for a brand new 1960 Pontiac Bonneville at a time when a loaf of bread cost twenty cents. It had the most powerful V-8 engine offered, and the name Bonneville possessed a magical charm back then. It would be a useful tool for achieving his ultimate goal of meeting and marrying a beautiful woman. Sal was blessed with artistic talent, and he painted a unique gold stripe down the middle of the maroon automobile that made his Pontiac a sure fire chick magnet.

The way Sal told it, he was on a double date with a co-worker and two local girls. They had decided to take a drive on one of the large beaches the area is noted for and find a romantic spot to park. Their plans fell apart when the tide washed in and the Pontiac sunk in the sand just deep enough to prevent the car from starting up. There was no danger of drowning, but the foursome had no idea what they were going to do.

After an hour and a half went by, a black man driving a logging truck came along. This was a fantastic stroke of luck. The Good Samaritan stopped for them, attached a chain to the rear bumper of the Bonneville and pulled the car out of the sand. He also agreed to tow the vehicle to the closest Pontiac dealer after Sal told him he was willing to pay for it. Sal and his three companions got into the car and braced themselves for a slow trip to the closest town.

Unfortunately, Sal and the truck driver made two mistakes. The first was that they attached a chain to the car's front bumper. Another complication was Sal's inexperience at sitting behind the wheel of an automobile that was being towed. The first time the truck made a sudden stop, he didn't react quickly enough and the front end of the Pontiac banged into the rear of the truck. It startled the truck driver as much as Sal, but they continued on. When they arrived at the new car dealer, the front bumper of the Bonneville had almost been completely pulled off and the classy paint job had been badly scratched up.

The nearest dealership turned out to be Wimberly Pontiac in Port St. Joe. It was a small store with only three cars in the showroom, but it was an efficiently run operation with a solid reputation for service. The business was a success because of a twenty one year old woman named Joanne, whose title was "office manager." This was back when it was an oddity for a woman to be running an auto dealership.

While he was telling me this story, Sal said, "I couldn't take my eyes off Joanne. She could have been in the movies." I asked him, "Who did she look like?" He replied, "She could have been Ava Gardner's twin."

When he first saw her, he thought his dreams had come true, but his hopes took a spill the next instant when he spotted the engagement ring she was wearing. Never one to give up easily, the recently discharged serviceman decided to do a little intelligence work. Sal struck up a conversation with one of the mechanics and asked, "Who's that good looking woman?" The mechanic replied, "Oh, that's Joanne. She's engaged to a guy named Beau. They've been going together for three or four years, but I guarantee she won't have that ring on long. They break up every couple of weeks."

The Pontiac Bonneville required a great deal of work to bring it back to like new condition, and Sal was left with a hefty bill that amounted to nearly half of what he had paid for the car in the first place. There were no such things as factory warrantees or extended insurance coverage for repairs back in those days. All that was offered by auto manufacturers were Applications for Assistance (AFA's) in the event a vehicle proved to be defective. Sal asked the gorgeous office manager to file an AFA for him. He didn't get any sympathy from the young but hardnosed businesswoman. She acted as though the good looking young man from the north was trying to get over on her and replied, "The company is not going to pay for it because it's your own fault. They cover things that are manufacturing defects. If you're ignorant enough to go out in the water, they're not going to pay for your stupidity." Sal ended up shelling out to get his Bonneville taken care of. Joanne was a little surprised at how well he took it. She didn't know Sal was so happy at having met his dream girl that he was able to take it in stride. The cost of fixing his car was of little concern to him. He wanted her.

Sal had fallen for Joanne in a big way. She didn't seem to like him, but he loved her just the same. He was willing to do whatever it took to become the man in her life. He decided to go back to Wimberly Pontiac a couple of weeks later under the pretext of having the dealer order a part. He insisted on dealing only with Joanne and left a four dollar deposit. She saw right through his ploy. She didn't even bother to order the part, held on to the money for a while and ended up giving him his four bucks back. Still, the charade was worth it to the ardent young man because he noticed that the engagement ring was missing from her finger.

It turned out that Beau was not Joanne's type after all. He was so low key and laid back that she sometimes had to check his pulse to see if he was still alive. Joanne was looking for a little more excitement and some fire. She also thought it would be interesting to have a man who had big ideas. Beau wasn't overly ambitious and content with his job at the mill in Port St. Joe. The biggest drawback to her hometown boyfriend, as far as she was concerned, was that the only things he seemed passionate about were hunting and fishing. After all, they were the most popular things to do in that part of Florida. Joanne had no interest in hunting trips or fishing excursions. She was not content being in a small Florida town. She loved to gamble, a pastime she had learned from her father, an expert stud poker player. She also had a desire to travel and live in a big city. Joanne was ready for something different, and Sal was a big change from any of the men she had ever known.

He was handsome. In addition to having a good job and artistic talent, he also possessed a fine singing voice. Another plus for him was that he was a devout Roman Catholic and never used profanity. Beau rarely went to the Baptist church that he and Joanne belonged to and like many rural males, cursed a blue streak when the need arose. She wasn't a hard shell Baptist by any means, but she felt that being religious was an important quality for a family man to have. Frugality was another quality about Sal that appealed to her. Even though he had spent money on a new car, she took note of the fact that he was practical enough to try to get an AFA to cover his repair bill and he had put away enough to pay cash. She decided to let him know that she was interested in him, but still play a little hard to get.

The next time he saw her, Sal tried to crack some jokes before asking her out, but she seemed to take his attempts at humor the wrong way. All she said was, "You must be one of those Yankees they warned me about." Just when he thought he was dead in the water, she added, "I'm going to a basketball game tonight with my girlfriend. If you want to see me tonight, come to the game. You can join us." He jumped at the chance and embraced the opportunity in hopes of eventually putting his arms around the southern beauty with the dazzling smile. He met Joanne and her friend at Wewahitchka High's assembly hall and they watched the game together. To this day, they still watch basketball games together. Beau showed up that night, but that proved to be no big deal. He quickly faded out of the picture, and that was just the opening Sal needed. He moved in quickly to win her hand.

OPPOSITES ATTRACT

At first glance, the southern belle and the New Yorker had very little in common. Joanne came from a large loving family. There were seven siblings and they all cared a great deal about each other. Her dad was working at the Bib Mill in Columbus, Georgia when he and her mother had married. They later moved to Abbeville, Alabama, and that was where Joanne was born in 1940. Her father had his fingers in different businesses and was always working, even during his vacations. He would scout for timber, buy it, send in a crew to cut it down and then sell it. He was a good provider and he was also very generous. He would budget his money so that each night he could afford to come home from work with treats or toys for each of his seven children. In addition, he bought groceries for his poor relations, even though they were lazy. Joanne's mom was also a wonderful parent. She kept a watchful eye on her children when they were little and truly nurtured them. She was a skillful seamstress and also took charge of the farm where the family lived, making sure that chores were done and the crops tended. With so many mouths to feed, the farm was critically important to the family's solvency.

Sal's background was very different. He came from a dysfunctional household. His family lived on New Jersey Avenue in Brooklyn. His mother, Nancy, was an alcoholic who went through nervous breakdowns. There were times when he went to wake her up and thought she was dead. In addition to her alcoholism, she had trouble keeping her anger in check. Nancy was less than five feet tall and cute as could be, but wouldn't take crap from anybody. She worked as a supervisor in a frozen food plant and was in charge of some strapping black women much bigger than her who weren't shy about using their sharp fingernails or fists. As rough as they were, they steered clear of Sal's mom and wouldn't dare give her any back talk. The petite Italian woman would turn into a hellcat if anyone crossed her.

To be fair about it, Nancy wasn't all bad. She had her good qualities. Like Sal's father, Agatino, she was a Roman Catholic and never used any profanity. She was an excellent cook. She was also a practical joker who thought it was hilarious to do such things as hide in closets and then jump out and scare people. This form of humor was passed on to her grandson, James Salerno.

Sal's dad was the complete opposite. His friends called him Al, but his children called him Poppy. He was a quiet, non-confrontational soul who smoked a pipe and was content with his job. He worked for a factory that made metal products and spent his entire workdays polishing items that came off an assembly line. The factory was in a terrible neighborhood, a manufacturing district where the sky always appeared orange from whatever was belching out of the plants. He drove his 1950 Ford to work at first, but the car was always getting broken into. He ended up taking the subway and carrying a switchblade knife at all times. Despite the dangers involved, he worked at that company for years, was never late, never absent and often spoke of how grateful he was to have the job.

The mother and father were always in conflict and it was inevitable that they divorced. The straw that broke the camel's back was when Nancy gave Poppy two black eyes during an argument. It was "her way, or you'll pay a physical price." Even though Catholics didn't believe in divorce, Al realized he could no longer be married to Nancy if he wished to continue living.

There were two children involved. Sal's only sibling was a brother named Joe who was three years younger. After the divorce, Sal's father moved out of the third floor flat, but not very far away. His new address was only fifty feet from the building where Sal, Joe and their mother lived. Sal would go back and forth between the two apartments, depending on the mood his mom was in.

Nancy soon remarried. Her new husband was named Tommy. He seemed like a decent enough sort at first glance, but he had a cruel sense of humor. He thought it was hilarious to pull a chair out from under a kid who was about to take a seat, causing them to land hard on their backside. Tommy and Nancy got along fine as long as everything was done her way, but when they fought it was strictly no holds barred. She once became so enraged at him that she unscrewed a leg from a coffee table and clobbered him with it. It only took eighteen stitches to close the wound.

Nancy displayed another of her quirks whenever a family member mentioned that they didn't like certain food. This would compel her to make them accept what they detested. An example of this occurred when Tommy absolutely refused to eat veal. Nancy handled that issue by preparing veal cutlets and telling him they were chicken. Her second husband believed her and in fact became so fond of her "special chicken cutlets" that he bragged to friends and relatives, "If you want to eat good chicken, you need to eat my wife's chicken." There was no in between when it came to Nancy. You either liked her or you didn't. You either went along with her or you hit the trail… and you might get hit hard in the process. It was no surprise that the thought of disobeying their mother never crossed the minds of Sal and his younger brother Joe.

The two boys grew up in a working class neighborhood with multiple ethnic groups. Talented people lived there, and that section of Brooklyn produced a celebrity. Sal grew up with the singer Steve Lawrence, who later formed a hit duo with his wife Eydie Gorme. Steve's real name was Sidney Liebowitz, and he was a year older than Salerno. They knew each because they both sang. Sal possessed a good tenor voice. He sang opera in some amateur productions, but never professionally. He was known as Sonny to his friends, and they often said to him, "Sonny, you're wasting your time. You should be in the Metropolitan Opera." Sal didn't look at it that way. Singing was fun for him and if he had tried to become a professional, it would have taken a lot of the joy out of it.

In discussing his high school years, Sal said,

I was not a great student in high school, but I was very good in track. The high water mark of my athletic career took place when I finished second in the New York City high school championships for the 110 yard hurdles. Even though I didn't win, I'll never forget the championship race held on Randall's Island. I was ahead of the field when I made the mistake of taking a peek over my shoulder to see if anyone was gaining on me. It was just a slight movement, but it was enough to allow another guy to get a step on me. In a 110 yard race, one step can mean everything. My grades were not very good, so I was not offered any scholarships to college. I didn't consider that a big loss because I already had a going business. By the time I was in high school, I was deeply involved with dealing in stamps, coins and other collectibles.

I asked him about the other young men he grew up with. He replied,

I had little in common with most of the guys in the neighborhood who were the same age as me. They spent their time drinking, smoking, hanging out in pool halls and popping pills. I didn't want any part of that. I was very much like my father in that I was non-confrontational and had an aversion to violence in any form. So, I chose to hang out with my brother Joe and his friend Billy. Joe and I were opposites. He would get mad and show his temper, but his anger would quickly pass and he did not hold grudges. I looked out for the two of them, and the three of us became very close. In fact, Billy was the person who got me interested in stamps, and for that I owe him an eternal debt. Stamps became my passion, and they have been very good for me.

Sal was capable of doing college work, but had little interest in formal education. His goal was strictly to get his diploma, and he accomplished that. After graduation, he joined the Air Force. As a result of the aptitude test he was given, Sal was assigned to a technical school and learned electronics. He was then sent to a unit that consisted of enlistees who had also scored high on tests. Sal said, "I got my second stripe right after basic training, but never rose above Airman Second Class. This was during the Cold War when rank was frozen."

The duties he was assigned resulted in his being surrounded by pilots. During his free time, he would take trips with his pilot friends to an Air Force flight school in South Carolina. Once the plane was in the air, they would let him take over the controls. While stationed at Keesler Air Force Base in Mississippi, Sal was selected for pilot training, which could have led to an assignment with the Strategic Air Command. It would have been quite an achievement because the Air Force had previously required their pilots to be college graduates. Sal chose not to take advantage of the opportunity. One factor was Poppy and Nancy's concern that he might be shot down, but the biggest reason was that he would have had to sign a contract requiring a fourteen year reserve commitment. That didn't appeal to him because he was looking forward to serving his hitch and then launching a career as a stamp dealer. He fulfilled his commitment, but before he could get his stamp business started, he obtained his well paying position with IT & T. He was willing to put his dream on hold for awhile because he was believed he was getting in on the ground floor of something big. It was a time when a young man with only a high school diploma and some technical training could make a very good living.

Joanne had been a very good student at Wewahitchka High, but after graduation, there was no money for college. One of her brothers worked in Port St. Joe, which was twenty miles away and offered the only jobs in that area. He had heard of an opening for a bookkeeper at the local five and dime store that was part of the Christo's chain. Joanne got the job and about a year later, she was hired to be the office manager at Wimberly Pontiac. She had been with Wimberly for three years at the time she met Sal. It didn't take him long to propose. Joanne accepted and presented him with a picture of her that she signed "To the Forever Love of my life."

MARRIAGE, THEN PARENTHOOD

As Sal and I discussed the early stages of his relationship with Joanne, he stated,

She was the answer to my prayers. From the time I first noticed girls, I dreamed of marrying a woman who was drop dead gorgeous, having children and then later enjoying grandchildren. Before I went to sleep at night, I would look over at a blank wall and try to fill that space with an image of what I thought the future Mrs. Sal Salerno would look like. I knew deep down she was going to be someone who would knock me off my feet. All that I really wanted in life was a beautiful wife, a home and a family, and I was lucky to get all three.

Sal was a true romantic, and his oldest son would turn out to be a great deal like him in that regard. Unfortunately, James never became as responsible as his dad.

Joanne was a prize catch; a rare combination of brains and beauty. She had been a homecoming queen at her high school, which was referred to by the locals as "Wewa High." She graduated with the highest grades of all the girls in her class. Sal said, "If she hadn't married me, I would have literally died."

I found it interesting when Sal said, "I truly believe that the biggest reason Joanne married me was my frugality" and then later mentioned that he gave her an engagement ring that was over one carat. It set him back $1,400, when a gallon of gas cost twenty five cents. Their dating began to follow a pattern. He would have her back to her parents' home by 10:30 P.M., but that wasn't the end of their evening together. They would sit in his Bonneville and become involved in deep conversations which lasted for hours. Her father would finally break things up around 1:30 A.M. by saying, "Joanne, you need to come inside."

The courtship wasn't all smooth sailing because Sal was pushy and Joanne was very fiery. They had more than their share of spats. One night, they got into such a heated argument that she threw the engagement ring away. Fortunately, they were at her house when she did it. Her father, her mother and her six siblings immediately began searching for the expensive piece of jewelry and after an hour or so, they found it. Everyone wanted to see them marry because they believed they would be good for each other.

Sal and Joanne were wed within three months of their engagement. There was a sense of urgency because Sal had just been told that he was being transferred to a project in Alabama. This created a problem for his parents because there wasn't enough time for them to make all the necessary arrangements and as a result, neither of them attended the wedding. The marriage ceremony was performed at St. Joseph's Church in Port St. Joe. Sal had insisted that their children be raised Catholic and Joanne converted from Baptist to Catholic before the wedding. Joanne's sister Jeanie also converted because she had fallen in love with Sal's brother Joe and they would eventually marry.

In order to smooth things over, the newlyweds spent their honeymoon at Nancy's and also visited Sal's dad at his place. Sal's mother and her second husband Tommy were living at the time in Levittown, a hamlet of Hempstead, Long Island. Amazingly, Joanne and Nancy really hit it off. Sal's mom taught her son's bride how to prepare Italian dishes, and the new bride showed a flair for that type of cooking. Nancy paid her daughter in law high praise when she said, "Joanne has become a very good cook… for a Baptist."

After their stay in New York, Sal and Joanne moved to Grove Hill, Alabama, which is near Mobile. It had a population of around 1,500. They rented a house and Joanne got a job working at the local courthouse, even though she had just become pregnant with James. Despite being a Yankee, and a New Yorker to boot, Sal got along very well with the local good ole boys. He had two things in his favor. His Bonneville was the hottest car around and he was married to a lovely lady born in Alabama. With those two things in his favor, he had to be all right.

Grove Hill was a pleasant place, but the closest hospital was twenty miles away in Jackson, Alabama, which was five times bigger in population. James was born in that hospital on July 12, 1961. Sal said, "I was told that Jackson, Alabama was also the birthplace of Joe Louis, the Brown Bomber."

I asked Sal, "Was James a big baby?" He replied,

He weighed ten and a half pounds at birth, which meant that he was a little larger than usual. James was six inches taller than me at his full growth and he was much taller than his siblings and his mother. We figured that his height came from his paternal grandfather's side of the family, although his uncles on his mother's side were over six feet tall. My brother Joe and I had a keen interest in boxing and closely followed the careers of Rocky Marciano, Archie Moore and other top boxers of the day, but to the best of my knowledge, nobody in either family ever did any boxing.

After a year or so in Alabama, Sal was offered a better position and more money by General Dynamics, and he went to work for them. The new job required that Sal and his family move back up north to New York. It was the first, but not the last time that the family would have to move. Sal always had high paying jobs that required frequent relocation.

The move to New York occurred after Joanne's sister Jeanie and Sal's brother Joe were married, and the two couples wound up sharing the same house. This also established a pattern. Throughout the course of their lives, both couples spent the majority of their years as neighbors. This was significant because while James was growing up, he spent almost as much time with his Aunt Jeanie and Uncle Joe as he did with his mom and dad. The couples remain inseparable. When I paid my visit to Wewahitchka, I discovered that Sal and Joanne live on the same street as Joe and Jeanie and there is only one house between the two couples.

Sal did all he could to provide for his family, and he had to make many sacrifices. In addition to all the relocations, he had to be on the road a great deal. When we were discussing this, Sal said,

I sent all my paychecks home. I lived mostly on travel expenses and per diem. I put myself on an allowance because of my family. My children were very important to me and I wanted them to enjoy every possible advantage. All I required was a place to stay and food, and all I ever wanted was for my kids to be happy.

Joanne was at home more than Sal, but she also worked. Both of them were committed to giving their children everything they might ever desire. They were making a good income, but in the process, found themselves unable to spend as much time with their kids as they would have liked. This is a problem that many of today's parents must face. In the case of the Salerno's, it had a huge impact on the way James Salerno turned out.

JAMES' EARLY CHILDHOOD

After viewing hours of Super 8 video converted to DVD of James Salerno as a little kid, I was struck by what a good looking youngster he was. He was a string bean, though, and no one could have predicted that he would have turned out to be a great boxer. As the videos moved from year to year, he always seemed to be tall for his age, but he never had the build of a typical boxer. Then again, when he fought professionally, he never looked like a fighter because he was lean, lanky and possessed film star looks.

Other than his appearance, what really set him apart from practically every boxing champion were the creature comforts he enjoyed as a child. Boxing is known as "the poor man's out;" a way for those on the lowest rung of the ladder to better themselves and obtain desired material possessions. The Salerno children did not fit that template. They never wanted for anything. The family lived in a four bedroom home in Winter Park, Florida that had a swimming pool, and they enjoyed lavish Christmases.

I was told that James had no physical health issues or vision problems. He had, in fact, inherited excellent peripheral vision from Sal. He was never into sweets and he never had any problems with his teeth, such as cavities or other issues. His only serious problem was one which did not show on the outside. His mother described it as "something in his head that wasn't connected properly." He was never diagnosed as having Attention Deficit/Hyperactivity Disorder (ADHD), but it is very likely that he was afflicted with it. No one knows for sure because little was known about it back then. Today, we realize that persons who suffer from that disorder are not physically or mentally ill. They are just other types of human beings. It has been said that having ADHD is like living inside a video game, in the sense that "everything is coming at you at once." Each sight, sound and sensation is a distraction. It is also much easier for a person with ADHD to learn from visual presentations rather than from textbooks.

James' ADHD issue first came to light when the family lived in Omaha and he was sent to a parochial school for the only time in his life. This was back in the late 1960's, when Catholic schools used iron fisted discipline and unquestioning obedience to get problem children's minds right. They were not the greatest places for kids who would today be considered special needs students. If a child happened to be left-handed, the good sisters would insist that they learn to write with their right hand. As far as the nuns who wore dangling rosaries and enormous crosses were concerned, James' problem was that he just didn't have any willpower. They would handle him by instilling discipline.

They didn't see things from the boy's point of view. He perceived what went on in the classroom as complete chaos. The only time during the school day when he could tune it out was recess. This created a problem because he found such comfort in that oasis he would lose track of time. When a nun would ring a bell to end the recess period, he would act as though he hadn't heard the bell and would continue playing. He was quickly judged by the good sisters as a terrible student and a troublemaker. They would whack his hands with rulers and make him stand out in the hall, but that didn't alter his behavior in the least. Finally, the Sister Superior in charge of the school had a meeting with Joanne Salerno and said, "James marches to his own music and he will have to do his marching somewhere else."

When I discussed this setback with his mother, she said, "After things didn't work out at the parochial school, we enrolled him in public school and he began attending Confraternity of Christian Doctrine classes every Saturday. He really hit it off with a Father Redmond and the priest took him under his wing." That helped a little, but didn't provide him with a better learning environment. He never really felt comfortable with formal instruction. Even as an adult, he occasionally found a book interesting, but the only one he spent a great deal of time reading was his Bible.

His ADHD continued to make school an overwhelmingly negative experience for him. He was capable of doing the work because his penmanship was pretty good and in his later years, he did quite a bit of writing. All of his written works were in cursive handwriting, though, and he never mastered using a typewriter or computer keyboard.

When he was in the classroom, his attention wandered and he didn't seem to listen well. He had a tendency to overlook details, and this made it difficult to complete assignments. The public school teachers didn't treat him as harshly as the nuns had, but he didn't fit in and began to be picked on by some of his classmates who had issues of their own. They were jealous of his being taller than them and so good looking. They didn't try to physically beat him up, but they called him "stupid" and a "ree-tard." They made faces at him and passed around unflattering drawings of him. These things wounded him deeply. In discussing this facet of his son's persona, Sal Salerno said,

James was sensitive to the emotional needs of others, as well as to the way people reacted to him. He seemed to overhear anything said about him, even if it were said softly. He had an innate desire to please and be accepted by total strangers, and he was always trying to make new friends. Before he became involved with boxing, he sometimes found this very difficult to do.

Another problem the boy faced was that Sal was often away on business and even when the father was at home, he was not the sort of dad who would help his kids with their homework. If his children had to do special projects, he loved getting involved with them, but he made sure they were done his way. One time, James had joined a Boy Scout troop in hopes of making friends. A contest was held for building model cars, so Sal carved a small car out of a piece of wood to help his son impress the other scouts. James entered it as his own work and won second prize. It helped the kid fit in, but Joanne was not pleased with the way things worked out. She said, "You were supposed to help him and guide him, not do the work for him." Sal had the best of intentions, but he soon realized that he couldn't fight the boy's battles for him. James desperately needed someone he could relate to, look up to and emulate. Help arrived from an unlikely source.

A great deal of the limited quality time James and his father shared was spent watching television together, and this led James to boxing. It all began one day when the boy was five. They were watching an ABC telecast of Howard Cosell and Muhammad Ali analyzing one of Ali's fights. James became enthralled by the heavyweight champion who was as quick with his quips as he was with his fists. From that day on, he watched Ali every chance he could. In recalling what happened, Sal said,

I truly believe that James saw what Ali was doing in the ring and said to himself, 'I can do that.' My oldest son had a very unusual quality about him. He had a photographic memory when it came to remembering any physical movements he observed. He could watch what you were doing and immediately pick it up. He was very talented at doing impressions. For this reason, he was able to emulate Muhammad Ali's boxing skills and outspoken personality. I believe that as time went on, my son created a separate personality for the outside world that he could put on like a mask. He also put a comedic spin on everything. This was something that was reassuring for him whenever he had to face disappointments, deal with strangers or was trying to get along with kids his own age.

The fact that a boy from a well to do background would feel kinship with a black man who came up the hard way is an example of the magic of sports.

Almost immediately, James asked for boxing gloves and a punching bag, and Sal gave him exactly what he requested. The boy made so much use of the items that it wasn't long before they became worn out, and the father replaced them right away. Ninety percent of the kid's free time was spent trying to master boxing skills.

Boxing calmed the internal chaos he experienced each day and gave him something which provided immediate feedback. He found that he was able to focus on it for hours. It was still his own little word, though, and he desperately craved a feeling of belonging to something big. Boxing would eventually provide him with a measure of what he was seeking, but that would be a few years away.

James first began working with punching bags while Sal was assigned to Stromberg Carlson's Rochester, New York office. He and Joanne had rented a home right off of a large park. They were content and planned on being there for a long time. In recalling that period, Sal said, "I always took my kids to the park across from our home and other family activities. We also adopted a dog. It was a white mixed breed with one black eye. We named him Knockout." When he told me this, I thought about how amazing it was that they chose the name Knockout. It was an omen of what the oldest child's future profession would be.

Fate stepped in a little more than a year later when Sal was assigned to install the telephone systems at Walt Disney World in time for the theme park's grand opening in October, 1971. At the time the couple relocated to Orlando, they had no idea how the move would radically alter the course of their oldest son's life.

LOVE THY NEIGHBOR

When the Salerno's first moved to the Orlando area, they lived in the George-town Apartments in the suburb of Pine Hills. After about a year, Sal used a V.A. loan to buy a four bedroom brick home on Tangerine Avenue in the Goldenrod development that was just north of Winter Park. It was a brand new neighborhood, and theirs was only the second house built there. This was in 1971 when James was ten. Both of his siblings were under five years old. Gina, who was born in Bayshore, Long Island, was five years younger than James. Matt was born in 1968 in Panama City, Florida. All three children had their own bedrooms. A couple of years after moving in, Sal was given a $5,000 bonus by his employer for reducing a troubleshooting guide from a book the size of a small telephone directory down to two pages. By then, the cost of a loaf of bread had risen to ninety five cents, but five grand was still a pretty substantial sum. Sal used the money to have a large swimming pool built in his backyard for his family to enjoy.

Both parents had good jobs that paid well but required long hours. Joanne took a management position with Jimmy Bryan Toyota in Winter Park. Bryan had gotten in on the ground floor of Toyota's success story by working for Jim Moran. Moran was a legendary Ford dealer in Chicago who was one of the pioneers in using television ads to attract customers. He was so proud of the service he provided that he named his dealership Courtesy Motors and became known as "Jim Moran, the Courtesy Man." When Toyota offered him the chance to become the brand's distributor for the entire southeast, Moran embraced the opportunity. It was a great move that resulted in his becoming one of the wealthiest auto dealers in history. Jimmy Bryan followed in Jim Moran's footsteps and became a household word in Central Florida because of his ever present television commercials.

Joanne Salerno fit perfectly into the mold of those two high powered executives. It should be noted that she was a pathfinder who, in some small way, contributed to women eventually playing major roles in the automobile industry. Within a relatively short time, she became the heart and soul of Bryan's dealership. There was a huge price to be paid for her success, though. Like Sal, she had to sacrifice by not being able to spend as much time with her children as she would have liked.

Even though she wasn't around as much as she would have preferred, Joanne was a wonderful influence on her oldest son, and James adored her. He was most attentive to his mom when she was home. He would spend a half hour massaging her feet that were sore from walking around all day in heels. He continued to do that even when he was in his twenties.

With such demanding work schedules, the Salerno's were fortunate to have Ernie and Judy Campbell as next door neighbors. The Campbell's occupied the first house in the subdivision and had moved into the neighborhood a month before Sal and Joanne. Ernie was in the U.S. Navy, stationed at the Naval Training Base near Orlando. He was not an officer, but everyone in the neighborhood thought he was because enlisted men normally couldn't afford to live in such upscale surroundings. The Campbell's could swing it because they were not only frugal, but masters at pinching pennies. Joanne Salerno did their taxes and would marvel at how well her neighbors were able to live on so little. She said to Judy, "How on earth are you able to live here and have a truck, a car and a boat on how little you make?" Judy replied, "I've heard that being cheap is the new way to becoming rich. You would be amazed at how well you can live by making every penny count." The Campbell's never ate out, watched every penny and let nothing go to waste.

Joanne and Judy became like sisters, and the Campbell's became close enough to Sal to call him Sonny. When I interviewed Judy Campbell, she spoke of how determined he was to have a tall pine tree in front of his home. She said,

He dug a hole in his front yard that was big enough to bury a car in. After he placed the tree in the hole, I told him, 'Sonny, that tree is not going to live.' He argued, 'Yeah, it will.' I said, 'No it won't because you do not have the north part of the tree facing north. When you transplant a tree, you have to do it so that it is in the same position as when it was growing.' Well, the tree died. That didn't faze him in the least. He dug up the big tree and brought in another monstrosity. He planted that one in the correct position, left the water dripping on it and it survived. It grew to be bigger than the house. It taught me a great deal about how determined Sonny was. Once he had a thought in his head, he would go after it, come hell or high water. He was just as determined about helping James to become a great boxer, once he saw how dedicated his son was.

The big pine tree enhanced the quality of life in the entire neighborhood. Sal decked it out each Christmas, and it was such an impressive sight that strangers would make special trips to Goldenrod to marvel at the Salerno's decorations.

Judy Campbell had a great deal to say about James' home life. She stated,

To be blunt about it, James was raised in a household that was not normal. Joanne worked very long hours. She left early in the morning and wasn't home until seven or eight o'clock at night. She was only off one day a week, and that was usually a Sunday. She relied upon me a great deal to look after her two youngest kids, Gina and Matt. I was able to easily do this because the Salerno's left the back door to their house unlocked, which gave me complete access to the premises. She often told me I was a godsend to her. I fed Matt and Gina breakfast many times and dinner almost every night. They usually ate their dinner with my kids. I also saw that those two children were bathed and ready for bed. Ernie and I loved having them. We had four sons and had always wanted a little girl. Gina became our daughter and Matt was a fifth son.

Each week, Joanne would spend her entire day off cooking. The food was the best stuff you could ever eat. Sonny's mother had taught Joanne how to cook Italian dishes, and she did a great job of it. She would make what they would call gravy and I called spaghetti sauce. She put chicken, pork chops, sausage and flank steak into the gravy. She also made special meatballs to put in it. Then she would make up stuffed pasta shells, put them in a container and store them in their freezer. All that had to be done for dinner was to thaw them out and heat them up. The food was absolutely yummy. She was always working late, so she'd tell me, 'There's stuffed shells in the freezer if you want to use them for dinner.' James, however, would never eat with me or my family. As a result, he seldom ate with his brother and sister.

The reason he didn't eat with them was because he was extremely independent and no one could control him. James did what James wanted to do. He didn't want to do anything bad, but he wouldn't mind me at all. If I got after him, he'd run across the street or run down the street because he knew I wasn't going to chase him. He was this way from the very first time I met him. At first, when I told Sonny about it, he would get mad at him. He called James' behavior 'stupid bullshit.' This shocked me because it was the first time I heard him use vulgar language. He also gave him a smack and boxed him around like any father would if they got mad at their kid back then.

Things changed radically when the boy was twelve years old. In recalling that year, Judy said,

One day, I told him to get his behind in my house and once again, he took off across the street. I didn't run after him, but I told Sonny about it when he came home. Sonny said, "Ah, just leave him alone. Don't mess with James. Just take care of

the other two. He's perfectly okay.' In my opinion, this made the situation worse. *The next time he misbehaved, James talked back to me. He said, 'I don't need no babysitter,'* then he ran into his house and locked himself in his bedroom. *I went up to the door to his room and told him to come out. He said, 'I ain't comin' out!' I was surprised that he wouldn't because I'm sure he knew that I wasn't going to whip him. I said, 'I'll just have a talk with your daddy.' He replied, 'Well, you go ahead.' That response nearly floored me. I wasn't used to kids talking to adults like that. None of my four sons would have acted the way James did, and Matt certainly didn't.*

Judy was in for another surprise that night when she told Sal about what his oldest son had done. In recalling what happened, she said,

I thought his dad would scold him, but he didn't. I was shocked even more when he said, 'Just don't mess with him.' So I said, 'Okay, I'm not gonna worry myself sick over it. He's your son.'

I don't want you to get the wrong idea. James was usually very pleasant and polite to me. I know he really liked me. When he turned pro, he always gave my husband and me tickets to his fights. The only issue between us was that I was very strict. He actually went around and told other people in the neighborhood that I was the Gestapo. He said to them, 'The Gestapo lives next door to me.' When I heard about it, I thought it was hilarious. The first time he called me the Gestapo to my face, I said, "It's because you don't want to mind me. I make my children mind me.' That was one thing about James. You always knew where you stood with him. Whatever he thought about you, he told you to your face. I guess he got that from his grandmother."

By the time he was twelve years old, the troubled boy had become devoted to boxing. People are just now discovering that the sweet science is a marvelous way for kids with ADHD to build self control and self confidence. It also teaches youngsters how to think and act for themselves, and individual initiative is something that should always be encouraged. In addition, it is an exacting sport which requires more physical movements in a shorter period of time than any other form of athletic competition. Action in boxing is immediate, and there is no time for separating offense from defense, as they are so closely connected. In fact, hyperactivity is an advantage for a prizefighter.

Boxing dominated James' every waking hour. He was building up his body and learning values through boxing, but as far as he was concerned, it was even bigger than that. He perceived it as a way to be accepted by others and even loved. He had material possessions, but he hungered to become somebody big. He wanted to be just like Muhammad Ali, a man people admired and listened to. The problem was getting from where he was to where he wanted to be. He couldn't learn what he needed to know simply by watching television or hitting the punching bags in his family's garage. Sal tried to help him all he could, but the boy needed an outside motivator who could teach him that a real man is someone people can depend on and who is always there for his friends. Luckily, he encountered not just one such man, but two.

PART TWO
BOB BARFIELD
AND JIMMY WILLIAMS

THE MEN WHO BUILT
THE FIGHTER

JAMES MEETS THE BARFIELDS

James first became involved in organized sports while his family was living in Pine Hills. It was one of the few times in his life when he participated in league competition other than boxing. He played for a peewee football team in the local Boys Club league. While on that team, he met Larry Barfield, who would become his closest friend. They were not teammates because James was two years older. Salerno was taller than most of the players, but despite his height advantage, he only played youth football for a couple of years. After that, his entire life became boxing.

Larry Barfield was living in Georgia when I interviewed him. In discussing the time they first met, Larry said,

It was kind of a funny situation because James' team was the Falcons and my team was the Broncos, and we were in different age groups. However, our jerseys were the exact same color. After we got to know each other, I had him come over and talk to a player from a team we were about to play. I said to the opposing player, 'Hey, this is our quarterback.' James was about 5' 8" or 5' 9" then, but he towered over those kids, and you should have seen the looks on their faces. I was trying to psych them out and it must have worked because we won the game.

James and Larry attended the same elementary school, and James was a couple of grades ahead of Larry. Their days together appeared to end during the summer after they first met when the Salerno's moved to Winter Park. Both became a little upset about the prospect of never seeing each other again.

About a year later, the Barfield's bought a home in the same Goldenrod subdivision that the Salerno's had moved to. Larry had no idea that he would be living so close to his buddy because the parents didn't know each other at that time. After his family had settled in, Larry was moping around because he didn't have anyone to play with. He was also worried about having to start out at a new school in the fall. His mom said to him, "Why don't you go out on your bike and ride through the neighborhood?" At first, Larry wondered if his mother knew what she was talking about. The subdivision was far from being completely built up and there were more construction workers around than residents. Streets were still being put in and most of them were unpaved. Nevertheless, he took his mom's advice and hopped on his bicycle. After pedaling no more than three hundred yards around the nearest curve, the boy was overjoyed to find James playing in front of the Salerno's new home. When he saw his old chum, Larry hollered, "JAMES!" Salerno responded with a big smile. Once again, life was sweet for the two boys.

One of the first things Sal Salerno did after moving into Goldenrod was install a heavy bag and a speed bag in his garage for his son, but the boy could only accomplish so much on his own. As mentioned before, the father wasn't home much and even if he were, James needed guidance from someone who was knowledgeable about boxing. Lucky for him, Larry's dad, Bob Barfield, had the knowhow and more important, the willingness to share his knowledge, experience and expertise.

BOB BARFIELD: INFANTRY FIGHTER, WAR HERO AND PROFESSIONAL BOXER

Bob Barfield was the first boxer who gave James Salerno any coaching. He also set a good example for the boy. Bob was only 5' 6" and around 130 pounds, but he was a true warrior. He had been an infantry fighter and a war hero. He had also boxed at both the amateur and professional levels.

Bob had grown up in an orphanage in the north part of Philadelphia, Pennsylvania and joined the Army in 1950 at the age of seventeen. He became determined to fight for his country after seeing a picture in a newspaper of an American GI who had been captured by the Chinese Communists. The infantryman's hands had been tied behind his back and he had been shot through back of the head. Barfield thought, "They can't get away with this."

Immediately after basic training, he was shipped out to Korea, where he grew up in a hurry. Bob was still only seventeen when he took a sniper's bullet in his right shoulder. By the time he was eighteen, Bob was a Sergeant First Class. It wasn't long after that when he performed his greatest acts of heroism.

Bob was assigned to the Seventh Infantry Regiment of the Third Infantry Division, the same division Audie Murphy, the most decorated American soldier in World War II, fought with. In June, 1953, Barfield's unit was ordered to hold a hill named Boomerang against a Chinese onslaught.

Boomerang Hill was not named simply for the shape of its rise. Prior to America's involvement in Korea, the Chinese had fought with Belgium for that land. Chinese forces had tried to take the hillock from the Belgians three times. Each time, they were repulsed. Chinese Communist troops tried to take it from the Third Infantry Division twice in nine days, and again they failed. As a result, the hill was named Boomerang because the Chinese kept trying to take it, only to get their butts whipped.

Bob Barfield and his fellow soldiers were there when the Chinese mounted their last desperate effort on June 14, 1953. They were subjected to over 17,000 rounds of mortar fire. That was terrifying enough, but the real horror began when the enemy attacked late at night. Their unit was overrun and they ended up fighting hand to hand in the trenches. This was probably the last instance of hand to hand combat during the Korean Conflict.

Men who have seen the horrors of war are often reluctant to share their experiences. I felt privileged when Bob spoke candidly to me about what happened. He said,

After two and a half hours of mortar fire, the barrage slowed dramatically. When I looked out of our badly damaged bunker, I gasped. Our trench line, which had been eight to ten feet deep, was now only three to five feet, and the sides were caved in. I could also see that some of the other bunkers were demolished. And downhill I could see hundreds and hundreds of Chinese soldiers charging up toward us. The scene was surreal. Both our artillery and the Chinese were firing flares. Our searchlights in the rear were also lighting up the sky. The Chinese infantry had taped flashlights to the barrels of their burp guns (machine guns very similar to AK-47's), the better to see in our trenches and bunkers. It looked like thousands of fire flies swarming up the hill. Even with all that light, it was hazy from the dust that had been kicked up by all the artillery the Chinese had thrown at us.

As the enemy continued pouring up the hill, we were dazed from the shelling; ringing ears, busted ear drums and not a few concussions. But as the artillery fire slowed and enemy troops approached, I turned to action. I could fight an enemy I could see. Adrenaline surged through my veins, and I got my men into position and firing on the Chinese. I made everyone fix bayonets. I had to go up and down the line, reposition what was left of my squad and redistribute ammunition, but we soon got effective fire on the Reds. Still, they kept coming.

They poured through the wire, across our mines and past our booby traps of white phosphorus and Claymores. We fired our final protective fires, artillery shooting variable time fused rounds which exploded several feet in the air and rained shrapnel down on those without overhead cover. Small arms, machine guns, mortars, recoilless rifles; we fired everything we had at them, and they still kept pouring in on us.

At one point, I saw Chinese in the trench line to my right. The South Korean troops in that section had obviously retreated. I picked up a BAR (Browning automatic rifle). I can't remember whose it was, but he was dead. I charged down the trench line, killing eight or ten Chinese. They kept swarming into our positions. Fighting had deteriorated into hand to hand combat. I ran back and forth, screaming at my guys and shooting every Chinese I came across. Several times, just by sheer numbers, they forced us back, but just as quickly we waded into them and forced them to retreat.

After the shelling let up a bit, I carried half a box of grenades around to redistribute and to check on my men. That's when I found Private Ford, a black soldier, and a South Korean soldier who served in our squad. They were wounded and laying in the trench. A relief column was coming through the trench line, and some other American soldiers were on top. I screamed for someone to help me with my two wounded. One soldier finally stopped and laid down his rifle, as if he were going to drop down into the trench and help. Instead, he just walked away, leaving his rifle laying there. I ran back to my bunker and shouted at one of my guys to come with me. He was pretty shell shocked. He just looked at me, shook his head and refused. I snarled at him, 'You're coming with me, or I'll shoot your ass.' He followed me out and we got Ford and the South Korean to the aid bunker. Ford was severely wounded and died five days later. I could never find out if the South Korean lived or died.

After I returned, I heard our lieutenant yelling. The tank on our right flank was withdrawing. Chinese soldiers who had poured in from the vacated South Korean positions were swarming all over that American tank. I grabbed Innocenti, who was my sniper, and a couple of others, and we charged into the Chinese troops. We killed several and repelled the rest. Then I quickly repositioned a machine gun, got a few other troops in position and began firing on the Chinese who were swarming the tank. We killed most of them and forced the remainder off our tank. Then, the lieutenant got artillery into the area and sealed off the front.

Our communications were completely out, and we needed help. Lieutenant Hotelling sent a runner, a guy named Red, back to the company command post to get it. When he reached the command post, it was empty. Apparently, everyone had been dispatched forward to the trenches. As Red started back up the hill, he encountered more Chinese troops. They fired on him and hit him in both legs. I heard him scream as he went down and ran toward him just as a Chinese soldier raised his weapon to kill him. I charged into the enemy soldier and bayoneted him in the neck. Then I carried Red back up to our trench line, which was safer than lying out in the open with Chinese all around. He was eventually taken to an aid station, but I don't know if he lived or died.

After I had carried Red to the trench line, I had no idea what time it was or even how long we'd been fighting. Just before daylight, I saw Lieutenant Hotelling standing on the edge of the now all but destroyed trench line, using his M-1 carbine as a club. Obviously, he had expended all his ammunition and grenades. Suddenly, a piece of artillery or mortar round exploded near him. I dropped to the ground, but when I got up, a couple of dead Chinese, missing arms and legs, lay there. Lieutenant Hotelling was gone. I ran over to where he had been standing. Inno-

centi was behind me. Looking around, we found him half buried upside down in the trench. As we began digging him out, five Chinese came running over toward us. I stopped digging and fired, killing all five. When we got the lieutenant out of the dirt, I could see that his right foot was dangling only by a piece of skin and ligaments. I found an empty bandoleer and applied a tourniquet to stem the flow of blood. The lieutenant outweighed me by almost a hundred pounds, but Innocenti and I supported him between us as we climbed out of the trench and started out for the aid station. The lieutenant had enough stamina to hold his right leg up all the way there. We had to stop and fight Chinese soldiers at least three times as we went downhill toward the medic. Each time, I laid the lieutenant on the ground in order to fire at the Chinese. To the best of my recollection, I shot most of them. Innocenti and I finally got the lieutenant to the aid station.

Lieutenant Hotelling and I didn't see each other after the battle and both of us thought that the other had died back there on Boomerang. We didn't learn otherwise until 1996. When we met, he reminded me of something I had long forgotten. He said that after I got him to the aid station, he asked me, 'Were you scared?' I replied, 'No sir, I have a guardian angel.' The proof of that was the fact that I didn't even get a scratch the entire night. The lieutenant lost his right foot and part of his right leg.

The Chinese lost over 2,000 men. One thousand two hundred fifty five Chinese were killed and 865 were wounded. We had 26 killed, 79 wounded and one man was taken as a prisoner of war. Out of fifty eight men in my platoon, only fourteen of us were able to walk off the hill the next morning. The trenches were nine feet deep before the battle, but when the fighting ended the next morning after five hours of carnage, the depth had shrunk to only two feet in some places because of the many bodies that had piled up.

Noted military historian John C. McManus wrote, "The Battle of Boomerang was one of the five most desperate battles ever fought by the Seventh Infantry Regiment and the actions of Sergeant Bob Barfield were among the top five bravest exploits in the history of the regiment."

It is interesting to note that during the nine day period when the Chinese forces attacked the Third Infantry Division, they lost 2,500 troops in two battles that consumed only eight hours of actual time. The Third Infantry, on the other hand, saw only 44 of their men killed in action, 152 wounded and one missing; for a total of 196 casualties. To put these statistics into perspective, the Chinese lost almost as many soldiers in eight hours of fighting as the U.S has lost during our eleven years of operations in the Middle East.

Bob Barfield further stated,

It was shocking to think that all the death and maiming was for a lousy hill that wound up being part of a no man's land after the truce was signed. My commander said that the Chinese wanted Boomerang Hill real bad. If they had taken it, they could have been able to observe activity deep into South Korea. At least we kept them from getting the observation post they so dearly wanted.

When the echoes of battle had died down, Barfield and his fellow soldiers learned a harsh lesson about the way medals and honors are handed out. Despite eleven affidavits attesting to his bravery, the gallant baby faced sergeant was not awarded the Congressional Medal of Honor. He was given the Silver Star instead. Though he knew in his heart he should have been accorded the highest honor, he was grateful for what he received. What really pissed him off, though, was the Seventh Infantry being denied the accolade it well deserved. In recalling what happened, he said,

When the battle was over, our regimental commander put us in for a Presidential Unit Citation. The recommendation was received at the White House and then was sent back to Battalion Headquarters for approval. The Battalion Commander disapproved it! It was said that he would not approve it unless he could also receive the reward. We did, however, receive the South Korean Presidential Unit Citation.

Bob did not learn he had been recommended for the Medal of Honor until 1998, forty five years after the Battle of Boomerang. The newfound knowledge inspired him to write his autobiography, Insufficient Evidence: From Orphan to Medal of Honor Recommendation. The book is still in print.

Barfield served three years in the Army, became a paratrooper and then served four years in the Navy. It was during his years in the service that he took up amateur boxing. During the 1950's, he participated in a memorable service boxing show at Camp Chickamauga in Beppu, Japan. Beppu was a hot springs resort city of 300,000 on the northeast coast of Kyushu and was 500 miles southwest of Tokyo. Bob was assigned to the 508th Airborne combat unit. They were housed in a walled camp within the city.

The camp was under the command of General William Childs Westmoreland, who later headed U.S. military operations during the peak years of the Vietnam War. The general was a native of South Carolina, the son of a prosperous textile manufacturer and a rabid boxing fan. His camp had a big match coming up, and Westmoreland was relying on the services of his light heavyweight,

J.D. Chapman, to assure his squad of victory. The commanding officer was faced with a dilemma because of a tragedy that occurred during the weeks leading up to the competition. Chapman, the talented light heavyweight, had caught his girlfriend cheating on him and stabbed the guy she was with. J.D.'s jealous rage resulted in his being sentenced to twenty years and placed in the stockade. When Bob related this story to me he said, "General Westmorland let him out just for that fight. He was certain that J.D. Chapman wouldn't try to escape, but he took a big chance that could have destroyed his military career. It just shows you how much the general loved boxing."

When he returned to civilian life, Bob went to work for the U.S. Postal Service. During his spare time, he fought professional bouts as a bantamweight limited to 118 pounds and in the lightweight class with a 135 pound limit. He became a pro at the advanced age of thirty two and was known as "The Fighting Mailman."

During our interview, he regaled me with the story of his first pro fight. It was a bantamweight bout staged in Melbourne, Florida, in which he fought another 118 pounder named Jose Rojas. Rojas was part of the stable of the legendary brothers Chris and Angelo Dundee, and he also happened to be a deaf mute. Barfield had no knowledge of Rojas' handicap until he showed up at the arena. When he learned about it, he asked the referee, "How in the hell will he know when a round is over?" The referee replied, "His corner bangs on the canvas hard enough to feel the vibration. He stops fighting when he feels the shaking."

Bob explained what happened by saying,

Rojas' handlers pounded on the canvas when the first round ended and that worked out all right. The same thing took place at the end of the second round. When the third round ended, I dropped my hands and started to go back to my corner. Damned if Rojas didn't drop down into a crouch and try to hit me with all he had in my stomach. Thank goodness he missed his target and the blow landed along my side, so I was better able to take the punch. I guess his handlers weren't pounding on the canvas hard enough. I complained to the referee, but he just shrugged his shoulders and told me to go back to my corner. I ended up losing a split decision. The moral of the story is that if you don't knock your opponent out, you leave yourself open to getting screwed. .

Despite his inauspicious beginning, Bob fought professionally for eight years, finally hanging the gloves up in 1973 at the age of forty.

He fought during a time when the going rate for a pro boxer in Orlando was one hundred dollars a round. Bob's most lucrative fights turned out to be unsanctioned bouts held during the late 1960's in Tampa's Ybor City. Barfield called them "black market fights." In recalling those days he said,

An Orlando real estate guy got me the fights. I was matched strictly against Cubans. The bouts were held in an abandoned food store. The first time I fought there, my brother brought along his camera and tried to take some Polaroids. A Cuban woman stopped us and shouted, 'NO CAMERAS! WE WANT NO CAMERAS!' It was obvious that whatever was going on was illegal.

It was an unusual setting for a prizefight. Each side of the ring being used was only fourteen feet long, which was about ten feet less than usual. There were chairs set up on both sides of the ring, which was all the way in the back of the premises. They intentionally set the ring up so that one side was right up against a wall. A visiting fighter had to be careful because if they got too close to the wall, the local talent would try to smash the visitor's head against it. Each bout was three rounds and I was paid $600 a fight. I fought eight times in that place. The spectators were all Cuban, and they were betting money like crazy. They were not only wagering on who would win the fight, but also whether or not a fighter would make it through the next round. It was like human cockfights. I was overmatched in every bout. The last time I fought there, I weighed 123 and was matched against a man who weighed 170. Somehow I managed to last the three rounds and pick up my $600.

Bob's most memorable bout was a direct result of his television set blowing up in 1968. He had a good, secure job with the Post Office in Parcel Post Relay and Collection. Unfortunately, he couldn't afford to just go out and pay $260 for a new Muntz 21 inch tabletop model color TV. It appeared that Barfield had a stroke of good luck when he received a phone call from Pat Currey, who was working as a matchmaker for the Dundee brothers in Miami Beach. By this time, Bob had a solid reputation as a pro, and a couple of his fights had been covered in Ring Magazine. Currey said, "Angelo wants you to fight Angel Lorenzana in the Miami Beach Municipal Auditorium the day after tomorrow." Bob was told that he would be paid $300. He was willing to take the fight, but this was during a typical hot Florida summer and he didn't want to drive his car all the way down there because it didn't have air conditioning. He told the matchmaker, "I don't have any way of getting there and back. If you pick me up in an air conditioned car and drive me back, I'll do it." Dundee's representative agreed to the terms.

Pat Currey had told Bob that his bout was being treated as a special fight to be held just before the main event and might not start until very late, so Barfield tried to make the task a little easier by requesting permission from the Postal Service to take the day after the fight off. He was denied permission, which made his schedule very tight, since his shift began at 5:00 A.M. Barfield's only hope of making it to work on time was if the earlier fights on the card ended quickly.

Luck was against him. All the earlier fights went the distance. As the night ended and the early morning hours drew near, Bob became so anxious about getting to work on time that he said "The hell with it" and told Currey to throw in the towel for him in the second round, regardless of how the fight was going. It was recorded as a victory for Lorenzana by knockout because there is no such statistic as "having to leave to go to work." It was only the first of Bob's disappointments that night. The next problem consisted of all the deductions that were taken from his purse. Among other things, he was charged for the use of a robe, for having his hands wrapped and for the use of a mouth guard. He was forced to use equipment supplied by the promoter because he had left Orlando in such a hurry that he didn't have time to pack all of his gear. Barfield's $300 purse shrunk to $75 after all the fees and expenses were taken out. When he entered the car that would take him back to Orlando, Bob discovered that the vehicle wasn't air conditioned. Fortunately, the long drive was during the early morning hours, but it was still muggy. He was dropped off at work, made it with thirty minutes to spare and had to work a full day with no sleep. Things could have been worse, though. At least he got off in the afternoon and was able to sleep until early the next morning. He also had enough money to buy a good used 19 inch black and white TV.

After he no longer competed as a pro, he continued to train on the heavy bag and speed bag he had installed in his garage. By then, his oldest son Robbie was sixteen years old and competing as an amateur. In addition, Larry Barfield, who was James Salerno's best friend, had a desire to get into the sport. In recalling those times, Bob said,

James came over to our house one day and told me he wanted to become a boxer. I started letting him hit the heavy bag, and I taught him how to work with the speed bag. He worked very hard at learning boxing skills, but he was anything but an overnight sensation. He was beaten badly in the first few amateur fights he had. The thing that impressed me most about him was that no matter how any of his amateur bouts turned out, he was always right back in the gym seeking to improve his technique. At that stage of his life, he wanted to be a great boxer more than anything else. I figured that if he kept at it, he would become good. I decided to introduce him to Jimmy Williams. Jimmy should be given all the credit for turning him into a great boxer.

James, himself, was in full agreement. In the years that followed, he often made it a point to remind everyone that "Jimmy Williams is the man who built the fighter I became."

JIMMY WILLIAMS: PROFESSOR OF PUGILISM

At first, Bob Barfield enrolled James in a boxing program conducted at the Naval Training Center in Orlando that was open to civilians. It didn't take long for Barfield to see that Salerno was way ahead of the other kids in that program and needed more advanced training. He then took James to the Orlando Sports Stadium. The stadium had its Boxing Club, which was an amateur program conducted by Jimmy Williams. It was a place where young boxers with potential were being developed into magnificent fighters, and it attracted both black and white youth.

When I interviewed Jimmy for this book, he was approaching ninety years of age and was still training and working the corner for professionals. He is one of the greatest teachers of boxing of all time. His accomplishments were recognized when he was among the first class inducted into the Florida Boxing Hall of Fame.

I spent several afternoons with the remarkable man. The first thing he said to me when I arrived at his residence was,

Life is a spectacular splash of colors, but too often we only see it in terms of black and white. You look at me and you see my color, but that's not me. That's the house I live in. Our bodies are like houses. A man lives in a house, but you don't know that man until he invites you into his home. Then you find out something about the inner man. You learn about his values and see if his house is in order. Welcome to my home.

Williams' approach to boxing evolved from his being multi talented, from possessing diverse interests and from having a thirst for knowledge. He had been a loose limbed professional dancer and drummer performing at New York's Cotton Club and Savoy Ballroom. He had also been a professional model, and he possessed fighting skills that enabled him to box at both the amateur and professional levels in the 147 pound weight class. He lived in Harlem for many years and formed friendships with both Sugar Ray Robinson and Robinson's legendary trainer, Robert "Pop" Miller. Jimmy went on to become a world traveler who acquired an impeccable sense of style and truly appreciated the finer things in life. He is a true renaissance man.

It might seem odd to conjure up an image of a combination boxer, dancer and fashion model. In truth, the seemingly disparate worlds are closer than most people think. The bloody bouts and broken noses of the boxing ring are not that far apart from the rarefied arenas where dancers, musicians and fashion models perform. In essence, it is all about rhythm, graceful movement, displaying poise, showing class and providing entertainment. Jimmy Williams said, "Muhammad Ali himself admitted that he was a dancer before he became a boxer. His boxing idol was Sugar Ray Robinson, whom I consider one of the greatest boxers of all."

Many experts agree with Jimmy. They say that, pound for pound, Sugar Ray Robinson was the greatest fighter of all time. He had 110 knockouts in the course of his career. Robinson won his first forty bouts, and twenty nine of the victories were knockouts. These statistics are important because the essence of boxing is to knock an opponent out and avoid leaving the final result in the hands of the judges.

Muhammad Ali once said of the legendary middleweight, "Sugar Ray Robinson was the greatest fighter of all time. I styled my dancing moves after him. He had a hard, hard punch and could back up and dance. He was a pretty fighter, with excellent rhythm. He's the only one who was better than me."

The style of dancing Sugar Ray Robinson learned and then passed along to both Muhammad Ali and Jimmy Williams came from a vaudeville tap dancer named Howard "Sandman" Sims.

Jimmy Williams knew the man well. He said,

Sandman was about ten years older than me. He was always at Ray Robinson's training camps to provide entertainment. You see, a fighter needs entertainment in order to keep his concerns about the upcoming fight from wearing on his mind. The Sandman carried sand in his pockets, and he would sprinkle it on the floor to amplify the sound of his steps when he danced. The closest thing today to the sound he made would be the DJ's who scratch vinyl records with a needle on a turntable. But that isn't close to the captivating rhythmic sound that Sandman produced.

Many people do not know what an enormous influence Sandman Sims had on great boxers and entertainers. He taught Sammy Davis, Jr. and Gregory Hines how to dance. Sugar Ray Robinson and Muhammad Ali learned the Sandman style of tap dancing. I also learned it and tried to pass it on to James Salerno, Larry Barfield and the other boys I worked with. Without question, James was the best of my fighters at doing what Sandman called his 'desert dance.' When I taught it James and the other kids, I called it the 'Sahara shuffle.'

Robinson was taught by Robert 'Pop' Miller. I was fortunate to have been able to study the sweets science under the tutelage of Sugar Ray and Pop, and both of them were dancers as well. Music, rhythm and dancing are all important ingredients for the black style of boxing.

Boxing and dance have a great deal in common. They are both grueling physical disciplines. The difference is that boxing is about inflicting pain, while dance hides the grim reality of pain beneath a veneer of beauty, form and finesse. The bruises, sprains and injuries dancers suffer go unseen, but they are there all the same. The fight fans see the pain that the boxers go through, but those watching dancers perform often fail to notice that they are exhausted at the end and their feet are destroyed. There is just as much violence demanded of dancers as people expect from boxers.

As a boxer, I fought against an opponent. As a dancer, a musician and a fashion model, I had to fight against an audience. Performing was just like a confrontation. I had to constantly surpass my last effort and display a great deal of virtuosity. I had to impress them. I had to repeatedly show that I was the best of them all. Whether performing as a dancer, a boxer, a drummer or a model, the will to win is the same. The musician, the dancer and the model all want win over the critics. The boxer wants to impress the judges and be awarded a decision. Any performer must face pressure and stress.

Jimmy was born in Leesburg, Florida in 1927. This was back during the years of segregation, and the only school available to blacks in that town was the Lake County Training School. Williams yearned for more than what was offered, and he didn't want to continue living behind what he called the "Cotton Curtain." He wanted to be in a place where he wouldn't feel restricted because of the color of his skin, so he left both the school and the town at the age of thirteen.

He headed for Asbury Park, New Jersey, a seaside community located on New Jersey's central coast. When Jimmy arrived there in the early 1930's, it was a popular thing to ride trains to the seashore. Tourists were drawn to Asbury Park's boardwalk and the imposing Berkeley-Carteret Hotel. He found work, first as a bus boy and then a waiter. He also worked at Ocean Grove, which was regarded as the "Queen of Religious Resorts." Millions of visitors would travel great distances to bask in the Victorian seaside splendor of that New Jersey destination location. They would also attend engaging, extroverted religious ceremonies. Starting with Ulysses Grant, many presidents vacationed there, as well as world heavyweight boxing champions James J. Corbett and Max Baer.

Jimmy said,

I came to New Jersey with some southern blacks who were 'following the sun.' They would work up north until September. When fall came, they would go back down south. I, on the other hand, went up to Harlem.

His new life in Harlem was a tough life in a big city. He was a fighter, but as he said to me, "I survived with a soft philosophy." He explained that statement by saying,

My mother gave me moral strength. That's why I never got in trouble in New York. I was never in jail. I could have taken what might have appeared to have been the easy way out and become part of the criminal element, but I looked for the best place where I could fit in. I tried dramatics, music, dancing, modeling and boxing. Learning how to fight began for me as a way of protecting myself from the gangs who would try to pressure me to do their dirty work.

I learned the right way to box by joining the Salem Crescent Athletic Club and becoming involved with organized amateur boxing. I also learned a great deal by competing in bouts arranged by the Police Athletic League and the Catholic Youth Organization. Both the PAL and CYO would block off the streets and conduct supervised boxing shows on the pavement. It was through those two organizations that I met Sugar Ray Robinson. I joined a street club he had formed called The Slicksters. Today, we would call it a mentoring program. It changed the course of my life.

Ray Robinson encouraged me to stop by Billy Grupp's Gym on 116th Street, where he himself trained, and he made me feel at home there. For a time, I would watch the man train every day. He was poetry in motion. Everything he did was class. He even jumped rope with style and class. They would clap Anchors Aweigh and he would do his rope work to the rhythm of the claps. He made everything that was part of his training into a performance. He had the heart of a fighter, but part of his heart was also that of a showman. I vividly recall a very young Muhammad Ali coming to that gym just so he could watch Sugar Ray. Of course, he was known as Cassius Clay then.

Grupp's Gym was also where Jimmy Williams came to know Robinson's train-er, Bill "Pop" Miller. Jimmy has fond memories of Miller. He said,

Some people called Pop arrogant and fussy, but I thought he was wonderful. They said he was born in the Virgin Islands and he admitted he was born on an island, but refused to name his place of birth. He was a short man, but had a big, loud voice and always wore a beret. I was told that he began fighting professionally in Philadelphia. He fought for four years before he enlisted in the Army during World War I. He would tell me stories about how black fighters were mistreated back in the late 1800's and early 1900's. He remembered the time when they didn't allow mixed bouts in New York and when black fighters had to be portrayed as untamed cannibals if they wanted to fight in Madison Square Garden. He also mentioned the rugged training camps he was part of. He told me about one where the roof leaked so bad that he woke up one morning to find every article of his clothing soaked with water. He worked with many big names. They included Panama Al Brown, Beau Jack, Eugene Burton, Tiger Flowers, Coley Wallace, Johnny Saxton and of course, Sugar Ray Robinson. He never took credit for making any fighter. I remember him saying, 'Fighters need more than the ability to take it. They need the ability to fight, and they need ambition. A youngster who has ambition to become something in the ring will succeed if he is given a little constructive advice. All I could ever do is offer advice. No one can make a fighter.' Pop Miller's dream was to see a fight club in Harlem that would be supported by blacks. Unfortunately, that never happened. When television arrived, it killed off all the small fight clubs.

Jimmy Williams' boxing career ended because of football. In recounting what happened, he said,

On a trip back to Florida, the football coach at Lake County High School smuggled me into a game against Hungerford High. I twisted my knee, and that was the end of my boxing career. I never thought I would make a living out of boxing, but I became a teacher and the sport has been very good to me. It proved to be financially rewarding as well as fulfilling. I have been truly blessed in that regard.

Jimmy spoke fondly of his years in the Big Apple when he said,

New York was a conglomeration of cultures when I was living there. There were Italians, Irish, Jews, blacks, Puerto Ricans and others, and each had their own neighborhood. All of the ethnics and nationalities stuck together. I survived in it and lived in it because I understood all of it. I was in Harlem during the 1950's, when it was home to 700,000 blacks. Jazz filled the air and the great civil rights movement had gained momentum. It seemed like there was a kid on every street corner hungry to be somebody. My generation had Jackie Robinson and Jessie Owens. We were a great generation of people trying to prove themselves, and Harlem was the capitol of the world to us.

During his time in Harlem, Williams rubbed shoulders with entertainers who became icons of America's pop culture. They included Sammy Davis, Jr., Miles Davis, Charlie "Yardbird" Parker, Duke Ellington and Sidney Poitier. Jimmy brought up another famous person he had met when he mentioned,

I also knew Ellsworth 'Bumpy' Johnson. He is still remembered as 'Black America's Robin Hood.' Bumpy not only stole from the rich to help the poor, he also kept the Mafia from taking over Harlem's huge numbers racket. I saw it all unfold. Every Christmas, he would buy turkeys for all the old people. He gave money away. He was like a Santa Claus. He was an untouchable. Even when he was sent to Alcatraz, he ran things from prison. A guy like Bumpy comes back from the blows he takes.

Jimmy Williams is a deep thinker, and it was during his years in Harlem that he developed his intellectual side. He said,

I was there during a time when young blacks were trying to find themselves. I read many books on philosophy. I was fortunate to be able to interact with Paul Robeson and Canada Lee, men who excelled in sports, theater and film. I also visited museums and art galleries to educate myself.

In addition, Williams learned that tough guys could also behave as gentlemen. He said,

I came from a good family. I used to pray to God, 'Please don't make me hard like all the guys I know here in Leesburg.' In the south where I was born, men carried their pride on the outside. It was all macho. In New York City, on the other hand, it was on the inside. A guy would put on a three piece suit and look sharp. He would act like a nice gentleman who would help old ladies across the street, but he was also a rough bastard who would take you outside and kick your head in just for fun.

After his years in Harlem, Jimmy always carried his pride on the inside. His experiences there led him to conclusions about what it takes to become a fighter. Jimmy went over these qualities when he said,

If a guy doesn't have heart, he won't make it as a boxer. A lot of guys look good in a gym, but if they get hit hard, they start to grab and hold onto their opponent out of desperation, which is not really fighting back. A boxer has the responsibility of being able to deal with being hit. You aren't married unless you accept the responsibilities that come with marriage. You are not a soldier unless you accept death. You are not a fighter unless you are prepared to get hit. It goes with the territory.

Jimmy finally accepted boxing as a calling, a ministry and a commitment. He realized that the best thing he could ever do in his life would be to share with the young all the lessons he learned from the Bible, his other readings and the great people he had met. During our visits, he confided,

I was a loner until I suddenly realized that the future lies in our kids. All the things I had learned will not do any good unless I share them. I always liked being around kids. I was interested in getting into their minds. I have found that most teachers don't want to get into the kids' world, but I'm willing to do that. I realized that the kids were human beings, and part of my calling was to be willing to listen to their troubles and treat them with compassion. Even today, they know I am for real.

If somebody hates me, I don't hate them back. I don't have time for that. My philosophy is, 'I am who I say I am and you are who you say you are.' If I tell you I'm a dancer, I'll dance in front of you right now. If I say I box, I'll show it to you. If I ask who you are, I don't expect you to tell me who you are. I expect you to show me who you are. That's how you relate to people. Don't tell them who you are, show them who you are.

JIMMY WILLIAMS' EDUCATIONAL PHILOSOPHY

The black man who was in his late forties and the white boy who was still not a teenager spent countless hours together. James often ate dinner at Jimmy's house and frequently stayed overnight. The teacher and his wife Rebecca were like family to the Salerno's, and they would often come to Sal and Joanne's home for Sunday dinner. James' parents saw improvement in James' conduct and were hopeful that he would learn responsibility and maturity from the boxing guru.

Williams formulated an approach that succeeded in not only teaching James how to box, but also helped the boy develop courage in the ring. Under Jimmy's tutelage, the youngster became a fearless fighter, unafraid of any man he faced. All of this resulted from the marvelous philosophy of fighting and of life that he learned from the master teacher. The keys to Jimmy's approach were consistency, fairness, patience and perspective.

In recalling those years, Jimmy Williams said,

Contrary to what you may think, James was not born with natural fighting instincts. I don't believe any person is. The greatest thing I could offer James was the fact that I was a black man and I could teach him a black style of boxing. It's very difficult for a white man to do that. I had been a professional dancer and had learned to not just develop, but to nurture my sense of rhythm so that it became both esthetic and efficient. I had also come up with a way of teaching a certain degree of rhythm to just about anybody, including heavy footed white boys. I began to do this with James and the other white kids by teaching them how to jump rope. I would have music playing, so that they would learn how to jump in time to the music and develop a rhythmic groove.

When I first worked with James he needed to develop his coordination, and jumping rope is an excellent way to do this. The rope work teaches coordination because it involves all four extremities. They key was to incorporate music. Many great fighters were excellent at jumping rope. The list includes Roberto Duran and Muhammad Ali, but probably the most theatrical was the great Sugar Ray Robinson. He could have used his rope jumping routine as a nightclub act.

I believe that boxing is nothing but dancing and knowing how to move. It is also very similar to playing the drums because drummers must use their hands and feet at the same time in order to produce the rhythm needed for the performance. A boxer must master the art of jabbing with one hand while moving their feet laterally.

I taught rhythm to the white kids by playing black music and having them learn how to dance to it. One of the dances they learned was Rufus Thomas' Funky Chicken, and they became surprisingly good at it. I always had confidence in my teaching ability, and I believe I could teach anyone if they would listen.

It was important to have music playing while James and the others were practicing their boxing skills, but it was just as important to show them what they had to do rather than just tell them what needed to be done. There is a lot of truth in the old saying 'Seeing is believing.' I enjoyed an advantage over most trainers by being blessed with the ability to demonstrate boxing skills at a high level, and I kept myself in good enough shape to do it for decades. I would say that my teaching methods are mainly visual. I would constantly be saying to the kids, 'Watch me!'

Jimmy Williams' visual methods of instruction were just what James Salerno, a boy who probably had ADHD, needed. Williams also said,

Humans have to be taught everything. When a person comes out of their mother's womb, they must be taught how to walk and how to talk. We are born ignorant. We are not like birds or animals. They know most of what they need to know from instinct. If a kid is willing to learn, there is a beautiful opportunity present. At that point, it all becomes making the instruction as visual as possible. It is important to remember that if you are around young children, you must be very careful about what you do in front of them. They will imitate whatever they see. The earlier that you start working with a kid, the quicker they will pick things up. I would begin working with kids when they were between the ages of seven and ten. At that stage, I marveled at how quickly they progressed and would be amazed at how well they were mastering the mechanics. When they were thirteen or fourteen, though, they started getting interested in girls and that was when I started to lose them. It's similar to working with concrete. When you first pour it, it's soft and easy to work with. As time goes on, it becomes so hard that it takes a crowbar to break it up. That's how a young person's mind works. It becomes more rigid as they get older. By the time a kid is fourteen years old, their mind is made up. This was why it was very important for me to start working with the boys when they were young and didn't have girls on their minds. When they were ten, eleven and twelve, it was unbelievably pleasant to work with them in the gym.

Kids are most receptive when they are young. This is why young children do very well at learning languages. When they get older, they want to question the teacher.

After a certain age, you can't teach them anymore because they think they know it all. This is a big mistake on their part because once you think you know it all, your intelligence level goes down. You have cut yourself off from the universe of knowledge. The more an intelligent person knows, the more they realize they don't know. A person must remain humble. If they become arrogant, they are headed down a path toward ignorance. We should never stop learning. The minute that a person becomes unable or unwilling to learn anymore, their end is in sight. Dealing with young people and young minds keeps a person young.

In addition to teaching boxing skills, Jimmy Williams did a superb job of helping his young fighters to develop the courage needed to succeed in the ring. He clearly explained how he did this when he said,

Boxing is ninety percent mental. The weakest part of a man is his body. His body is only a tool for his mind. It is the mind's vehicle. There is no limit to the human mind. It can still be very effective even if it happens to be within a frail body, but without a mind, a body is useless. I taught James and the others that their bodies were illusions. The real person is all contained in the mind. Our minds have imagination, and our imaginations are so powerful that they can take us anywhere in the world without leaving our chairs. A vivid imagination can enable a person's mind to feel as though they had accomplished legendary feats. On the other hand, an imagination can also become a very dark thing that poisons a person's mind and ruins their life. I would tell the fighters, 'Your opponent's body is an illusion. You are not going to win by trying to destroy his body. You are going to win by outthinking him.' I would also tell them, 'There is no reason to fear anyone you face in the ring. It doesn't matter if you are fighting Muhammad Ali in his prime. Anyone you face has just two hands and he can only hit you with one hand at a time. If he tries to hit you with both at the same time, it will be easy to duck his punches and he'll probably miss. Remember; you are not fighting your opponent, you are fighting what he is trying to do to you.'

The best example is driving your car. The only thing you can control when you are behind the wheel is your vehicle. You cannot control the other vehicles on the road, anyone on bicycles or pedestrians. When two boxers are in the ring, neither of them can control the other. The secret to winning is for a fighter to control themselves. By doing this, they can avoid taking a big hit. A boxer must keep in mind that the smallest extremities any person has are their hands. In addition, boxers can punch with effect only by using one hand at a time. They are not allowed to kick with their feet. They cannot physically assault you with their eyes or their hate. If your opponent hates you, that really has nothing to do with you. It's their problem. The only thing you have to worry about is if they hit you, and this is another reason why there is no need to run away from an opponent. All that should concern you as a boxer is maintaining control over your body and remaining calm in the heat of battle. By doing this, you can avoid taking a big hit or being knocked out.

When your opponent fails to connect with a solid punch, it will wear on their mind and they will become frustrated. This can be seen in bullfighting as well as boxing. A matador is able to kill a rampaging bull that weighs hundreds of pounds singlehanded because the bull puts all his energy in one direction. The cape is an illusion. The bull wants to hit something that is no threat to him and he is expending so much energy and emotion that he can't stop himself. The bull doesn't have the mental capacity to understand that he is charging at a cape and not a matador. If he understood that it was just a piece of cloth, he wouldn't be charging at it. The same principle can hold true for boxers. Ali used the term 'float like a butterfly and sting like a bee.' What he meant by that is your opponent cannot win if they cannot hit you. The psychology behind boxing is similar to what happens when two parties argue. If one person is arguing aggressively and the other is passively resistant, the fiery one often becomes frustrated. Frustration can lead to anger and if a person becomes angry, they use up a lot of energy and can put a lot of tension and stress on themselves. They could also become prone to making mistakes because of the pressure they are placing upon themselves. Boxers who put pressure upon themselves will self destruct because they will be draining themselves of their energy. The secret to victory is to get the opponent to lose their enthusiasm. Enthusiasm fuels the body the way gasoline fuels a car.

Boxing is a frame of mind game. A fighter's success depends upon their frame of mind when they go into the ring. James Salerno understood this at a very young age. He displayed intelligence and great common sense when he was boxing. He would frustrate grown men who were veteran pros to such a degree that they couldn't hit him. He would wear on them mentally and make them look foolish. They were macho guys who had fallen into the trap of becoming arrogant, and they were ripe for being plucked. James was a tall kid, but he was very skinny. He had height and a long reach. What was even more important was that he knew how to use his height and reach effectively. They underestimated him because they didn't know he had a lot of heart and understood my philosophy. I taught James from the perspective of the technician, while the older men had not been taught that way. It was a big mistake for them to get mad at James because you can't box at your best if you become angry.

The best way I can describe James' courage in the ring is to say that he was taught to never be afraid to find out what will happen. This fear of what might happen is what I call the 'illusion of the unknown.' From the very beginning, I told him,

'You can't get out of this world alive. Nobody does that. Until The Master decides that your final day has come, you will live through whatever happens. You must remain calm during the storm because you should know that you will live through it.' I remember when I was a kid back in Leesburg and did something wrong. My sister telephoned my mother at work and snitched on me. My mother told her, 'Tell him I'm gonna beat him when I get home.' When I heard about what was coming my way, it ruined my whole day because I spent hours worrying about the horrible beating I was expecting. By the time my mother got home, though, she was so tired that all she could do was give me a couple of swats that didn't hurt at all and tell me not to do it again. There is an old saying; 'A coward dies ten thousand deaths, while a man dies once.' I had died ten thousand deaths waiting for my mother to get home and give me my beating. The way to be courageous in the ring is to be able to achieve a frame of mind in which you are willing to go through whatever happens, knowing that you will live through it. FDR said, 'The only thing we have to fear is fear itself,' and he was right. You cannot cross a bridge until you get to it. This is why it is so important to teach young boxers about the mind as part of their training.

A BOXER'S LEFT HAND CAN BE USED AS A MACHETE

While we were discussing James Salerno's development as a great boxing talent, Jimmy Williams said,

The left hook is perhaps the most difficult punch for a boxer to learn. It requires mastering several complex body movements which must be perfectly coordinated for the punch to land with full force. All of my fighters were right handed, and I would say to them, 'Watch me. Take a six inch step directly toward your opponent with your left foot. Do this by sliding the foot forward without lifting your leg. Next, pivot on your left toe, turning your left hip and left shoulder to the right. Now, whip your bent left arm toward your right shoulder and at the same time, shift your weight over to your right leg. The power in the left hook comes from the whip like motion of your entire body.' As I was giving my verbal instructions, I would also demonstrate each part of the technique.

During our conversation, Jimmy wasn't simply telling me about boxing techniques, he was up on his feet and demonstrating them in a very animated way as he spoke. Even at his advanced age, his movements were graceful and fluid.

He continued his presentation by saying,

Once James had mastered the left hook, he developed a great right hand. He would hold his left hand low. By doing this, he was inviting his opponent to throw a right hand at him, but this was creating an illusion for the man he was fighting. Presuming that we're talking about right handed fighters, once a boxer throws a right hand, they are leaving themselves open to get hit. This is because the right hand comes at the other fighter in a straight line, and anything that comes in straight can be slipped or rolled under. If a fighter throws a right hand, they become vulnerable to being hit in the liver or on the chin. I taught all the kids I worked with that the left hand is unrestricted, while the right hand is mainly used to protect the chin against a left hook, which is the most dangerous blow because it comes from the blind side. Anytime a fighter throws a right hand, they are leaving themselves open for a dangerous left hook. There is a way to counter that, and I helped the boys I worked to learn how to protect themselves by teaching them the technique of stepping inside when their opponent threw a left hook. I consider the left hand to be the fighter's machete. In addition to jabbing, I taught my boxers to throw double hooks and uppercuts with their left hands.

I normally didn't want my boxers to hold their left hands down low. I would tell them, 'Take your hand out of the bucket!' James, though, was a different situation. He insisted on keeping his left hand low because that's what Muhammad Ali did. So, I taught him to step over to one side or the other and then kill them with a left hook.

I taught James and the other boys I was working with, such as Larry Barfield, a great deal more than the fundamentals of boxing. As I mentioned before, they also learned about rhythm and how to use it. They learned how to get their timing down.

Williams was very good at teaching rhythm because in addition to performing as a drummer, he had at various times been hired to give lessons in drumming. His knowledge about teaching various beats was a big part of his approach to teaching boxing. Jimmy provide insight into how he did this when he said,

I would assign a number to each type of punch, such as one for a left jab, two for a right hook and three for a left hook. I would ask my boxers to throw the correct punches as I called out a sequence of numbers, such as 'One, two, three' or 'One, three, two.' I would always have music playing while I was conducting these drills.

I would insert the word 'and' between each number in order to bring in the element of rhythm. You see, just as playing a drum is about rhythm, so is boxing. If I were to say, 'One and two and three,' the word 'and' is power, while each number is reaction. This is because the word 'and' allows a hesitation which gives the fighter a chance to get their body set before they throw a punch. A large part of the black style of boxing is to emphasize rhythm, timing and getting into a groove.

In addition to the instruction he received from Jimmy Williams, James Salerno gained a great deal by studying other fighters and by spending hours sparring in the Orlando Sports Stadium's gym. He often took on successful professional fighters. In recalling this, Jimmy Williams said,

I took him to see many fights, and he studied the fighters closely. We would discuss what he had seen afterwards. He also intensively studied films of fighters who had similar characteristics to him. One of these fighters was light heavyweight champion Bob Foster. Foster was tall, like James. There were other similarities. They both carried their hands low and they were both left hook artists.

James also did a great deal of sparring. I believe in 'sparring up.' By that I mean it is good for a fighters' development to spar with someone who is older or more advanced, provided the sparring is done in the right spirit and no one tries to hurt

each other. A sparring session in many ways should be another form of a classroom. This is why I went along with James' sparring with pros when he was only fourteen or fifteen. I could always stop the session if a fighter became too much for him, but I never had to do that. He sparred with Mike Quarry and Mad Dog Ross, both of whom were putting together winning streaks at the time.

Mike Quarry disliked James. I think it was because he was jealous of the boy's advantage in height and reach, together with the fact the boy had mastered the use of those advantages at such a young age. Quarry would become upset over the fact that James was the better boxer and Mike couldn't hit him. He became so enraged at him one time that he tried to hurt the kid by rushing James hard to shove him up against the ropes and try to overpower him. The boy stepped aside, which made Quarry run right by him, and that just made the hardened pro even angrier. I immediately stopped the sparring session when that happened because it no longer served a useful purpose. That was the last time Mike Quarry ever sparred with James.

Mad Dog Ross was another professional who tried to brutalize James. I ended their sparring session quickly by telling Ross, 'You are a man fighting a boy. I'll let you move around with him, but take off your power. I don't want you throwing any power shots at him. The only thing you should be concerned with is matching his skill and technique.'

James participated in sports other than boxing. He loved to fish, and would go to the small lakes around Orlando. I always kept fishing poles and other angling gear for fighters who came down to Florida to train. They all seemed to like to go fishing. It was probably a way for them to get away from the pressures and worries about their upcoming fights and other concerns in their lives.

I remember the first time I took James out of town to box in an amateur show. After arriving in the town where the fights were being held and the matches were set, I said to him, 'James, you're fighting the main event tonight.' That didn't sit well with him, and I could tell that he was worried. I then said to him, 'James, I think you misunderstood what I was saying. I'm sorry that I didn't explain things better. What I meant to say is that it just so happens that you're gonna have the last fight of the night. There really is no main event.' That seemed to relax him. He was never worried about any amateur fight after that. Whether it was a main event or not made no difference to him.

Just as he seemed to do with every adult in his life, James tried to see how much he could get away with in his relationship with Jimmy Williams. He didn't get too far with the wily trainer. In recalling what happened, Jimmy said,

One time when he was about twelve years old, James came into the gym behind the Sports Stadium carrying his equipment bag. Immediately after he came through the door, he said to me, 'Coach, I had a terrible headache last night, and I hurt my leg right here.' He pointed to a place on his left calf that he claimed was giving him pain. I said, 'Okay, James, go back home. You have to understand that when you come into this gym, you are entering the house of pain. I'm here to make you suffer. I'm not here to give you compassion. Go home.' He replied, 'Uh… I'll try to do it anyway, Coach.'

'No, no, no,' I said. 'I'm being open with you. I need to make you suffer. I can't be compassionate with you.'

James had a pleading look in his eyes as he said, 'Please, Coach, let me just try it.'

I answered, 'Okay, but don't expect any sympathy.' I walked away from him and then a few minutes later, I looked over and saw his reflection in one of the large mirrors that were mounted on a wall. He was working on a heavy bag, and he was working hard. That was the last time he ever tried to slack off. Boxing had become such a big part of his life that the worst punishment you could give him was to not allow him in the gym.

I often told him, 'Don't play games with me. If you are really sick or injured, I have to know about it. If you tell me something's wrong with you and there really isn't, how will I know if you're telling the truth. You have to be honest with me because I don't want to push you to the limit. If you aren't feeling well, you've got to be real with me because I don't want to drive a tired horse into the ground. I'm not a slave driver, but I want you to be in shape and be ready to box.'

In addition to demanding honesty, Jimmy was determined that his fighters would become true sportsmen. He said,

I insisted that the boys show up dressed properly for any amateur bouts they were fighting, whether home or away. I told them that their appearance reflected the pride they had in themselves. They had to be wearing collared shirts, dress slacks and shined shoes. Each kid I worked with had to act like a gentleman, no matter whether they won, lost or fought to a draw, or they would no longer be part of the boxing club. I demanded that they shake their opponent's hand after a fight. I told them that knowing how to handle a loss is just as important as winning. I would say to them, 'The greatest winners are the ones who keep their poise in defeat. I am going to teach you how to lose because we are all going to lose at some point in our lives. Some of you may lose a pet, some may lose a job and some may lose a loved one. As life goes on, you may suffer even greater losses. Just remember that every-body loses sometime. The important thing is to know how to deal with it when it happens to you.'

There are some trainers who teach their boxers to get mad at their opponents. I didn't teach my fighters that because a boxer cannot perform at their best if they are angry. I would tell the kids, 'Boxing is the only sport that allows two participants to hit each other and not have to worry about going to jail. Boxers must control themselves and not wear their feelings on their sleeves.' I also tried to teach them not to hate because I knew that if the kids grew up with hate inside them, they would carry it with them for the rest of their lives. I was trying to build men by teaching them when to fight and when not to fight.

I would have all the boys bring their report cards to me. The two Monks brothers, Donald and Michael, got A's all the time. James got F's and D's. I tried to get him to apply himself, but unfortunately, his grades never improved.

As part of their training, I had James and all the rest of them sweep the gym, do cleaning and work on the yard which surrounded the building. This helped instill discipline and made them understand that there was a price to be paid for the priv-ilege of being part of a team. I kept them so busy in the gym that they didn't realize how tired they were until they got home and all they wanted to do was go to sleep. They were too tired to get into trouble. I was using their energy for something con-structive; otherwise they would have used it for something destructive. The greatest compliment I ever received was when a mother from an upper middle class white neighborhood said, 'Thank you for raising my kid.'

DON'T APPLAUD, THROW MONEY

In describing the normal routine at the Orlando Sports Stadium's amateur boxing club, Jimmy Williams said,

I would be at the gym all day. The pros would out from noon until two o'clock in the afternoon. The kids would come to the gym from school. The pros would train five days a week, but the young amateurs would not only be there on weekdays, but also on Saturdays. James was hungrier for a championship than anyone there. He would put in as much time as he could. He often spent seven days a week in that gym. When he was fourteen, he began sleeping over in the two houses that were behind the gym. Even at that young age, he was used to coming and going as he pleased.

All of the hard work Jimmy's amateurs did during their training was put on public display during the Sports Stadium's "pro am" fight nights. These events usually consisted of half a dozen or so amateur bouts, followed by two or three pro fights. The amateur fighters ranged in age from nine to almost thirty. This all took place prior to the establishment of the Florida State Boxing Commission, so pro am cards are a thing of the past.

The crowds who attended the shows were predominantly male and they weren't shy about making their feelings known. They would show up in such aggressive moods and were drinking so much beer that they often fought among themselves. Perhaps it was their way of feeling they were part of the action, but it was sometimes dangerous just to be sitting in stands. Bob Barfield's cousin Sylvia was married to the late Sandy Tait, who worked as a timekeeper for many amateur and professional boxing matches throughout Florida. She and her husband had some amazing experiences. Sylvia said,

Sandy was involved with boxing for most of his life. He and his brother Malcolm fought as heavyweights and grew up in Miami. They trained at the famous Fifth Street Gym, which was operated by the Dundee brothers. This was back when an Army Air Force veteran named Charles Buchinsky was also regularly working out there. When Sandy asked him what weight he was planning to fight at, Buchinsky replied, 'I'm not a boxer, I'm a thespian.' Charles Buchinsky moved on to New York, landed TV and movie roles and went on to become a famous actor whose screen name was Charles Bronson. Bronson is best remembered for his roles in such films as The Magnificent Seven, The Great Escape, The Dirty Dozen and Death Wish.

When Sandy began working as a timekeeper, he had a problem finding a bell that could be heard in the noisiest of arenas. He finally made his own bell. It was loud enough to wake up the dead. He carried it with him to all the fights he worked.

Sandy and I went to boxing shows at the Orlando Sports Stadium whether he was working as timekeeper or not. It was always an adventure. Instead of pro am shows, they should have called them 'pro am spectator' shows. One time, Sandy was the timekeeper and I was seated at ringside when two fights broke out among spectators seated behind me. The fight in the ring was a good one, but I was also keeping my eye on the two battles behind me. I was very busy that night.

Amateur fighters like James Salerno and Larry Barfield would put on such great performances that the pro bouts seemed almost comical in comparison. One time, a white hippy guy with really long hair fought as a pro. He was wearing a headband when the fight started, but he soon lost that. His hair was so long that it covered his face. Somebody hollered, 'HIT HIM IN THE HAIR!' That broke me up. I also found it hilarious when a white guy was fighting a black pro and somebody in the crowd hollered, 'GIVE HIM A WHITE EYE!' I'll never forget the night when one of the professionals was knocked down so hard that he split the seat of his trunks. He was crawling around on all fours with his butt hanging out. There were many times when the fans got bored with a pro fight and would start shouting, 'BRING BACK THE AMATEURS.'

If the fans enjoyed an amateur fight, they would throw money at the boxers; quarters, dollar bills or a couple of quarters wrapped in a dollar bill. There were times when two teenagers who had put on a spirited performance divvied up over fifty dollars. That was a nice piece of change when a McDonald's hamburger was thirty three cents and their French fries cost thirty cents. If the spectators felt shortchanged because of fighters' poor performances, they would throw other things besides money. That could have been dangerous. Sylvia Tait said,

From the moment Pete Ashlock first opened the Orlando Sports Stadium, Sandy and I were attending the fights. We were there one night when somebody threw a full can of beer at a fighter. Luckily, they missed. From that point on, beer was dispensed in large paper cups with a Pepsi logo on them. The fans didn't hesitate to heave half full cups of beer into the ring while they were booing fighters. Even kids fighting amateur bouts would sometimes end up soaked in beer.

There were times when things got completely out of hand. The worst experience we ever had took place on a night I happened not to be there. A man and his son

attacked Sandy while he was walking to his car and beat him up in the parking lot. They thought he was a referee. My husband suffered a black eye and some bruises. The next day, poor Sandy had to speak at the Baptist church we attended. We had to use makeup to hide his black eye and bruises. Some of the fighters heard about it and from that point on, they saw to it that Sandy was always escorted from the arena to his car.

The rough and rowdy fight fans and the intense atmosphere kindled enthusiasm among the amateurs who were being groomed at the Orlando Sports Stadium's amateur boxing club. It was a rigorous but effective proving ground for young talent. Jimmy Williams stated,

My young fighters had heart. They loved to fight so much that I would have to stop them from fighting each other. I remember the first time I took the boxing club on a road trip. After we all got in the car, I said, 'Anybody who loses is walking home.' I didn't really mean it, but the kids picked up on it. It became something they always said to each other whenever we left for a road trip.

Jimmy and his young fighters traveled often in search of the top opponents. Those trips proved to be priceless experiences for the both the teacher and his students.

TAKING THE YOUNGSTERS ON THE ROAD IN SEARCH OF WORTHY OPPONENTS

In a way, Jimmy Williams did too good a job. The boys in the Orlando Sports Stadium's amateur boxing club won so often that they ran out of people to fight. In order to match his pre-teen and teenage amateurs with worthy opponents, the kids had to be driven to other cities. After dominating the amateurs in Tampa, they traveled even greater distances for new fighters to take on. It didn't take long for them to whip everyone in Florida, so they headed for Georgia and then Alabama. In recounting this to me, Jimmy Williams said,

It became very hard to find opponents for my kids. I would have to drive them as far away as Fort Rucker, Alabama, Savannah, Georgia and Augusta, Georgia. Whenever we arrived at the amateur show, things would always follow the same pattern. I would meet with the other coaches to decide on the matchups and they would try to tell me, 'Mr. Williams, we don't have any fights for you.' They would always bring up the fact that my kids had only fought fifteen to twenty times each, while theirs had eighty or ninety bouts under the belts. I would reply, 'We have to fight. We came all the way from Orlando. These kids have come three hundred miles and they have to fight. Please match them. I'll be responsible.' They would finally agree to it, but always did so reluctantly.

Before the matches would begin, I would be in the dressing room with the kids, and would tell them, 'The fighters you're going up against have had many more bouts than you. So, what are we gonna do, run away because they throw the papers with their boxing records into the ring? We're not fighting pieces of paper. We're not fighting their records. It's one man fighting another man in one fight on one night. Just remember, you are not prizefighters. You are 'pride fighters.' Prizefighters fight only for money. Pride fighters are different. They go into the ring because they have heart and a will to win, plus a desire to see who is best.'

The parents of the young boxers had faith in Jimmy because they could see that the master teacher had created an environment that was secure, stable and encouraging. They knew he was bringing something reassuring into their lives. Jimmy said,

I believe God was with us, and this was why it always worked out well. My pride fighters would return home without any scars on their faces. They won practically every bout. None of them were ever knocked out. We never had car trouble or any

other problems on the road. Their mothers trusted me. When their sons went to them and said, 'Coach Jimmy is taking us to Alabama,' all the moms did was see that they had clean clothes and tell them to mind me. I could take the children anywhere I wanted because I had the trust of the parents. I was aware that I had been given a great responsibility, and I did all that I knew to protect them. That was why I worked them so hard and made sure that they were ready to be pride fighters, not prizefighters. I was taking mothers' babies and trying to help them become men.

Sal Salerno once offered to give me extra money in addition to what I was being paid. I told him, 'I can't take your money. Working with your son and the other boys was the reason I was put on this earth.'

It is my calling and it is a labor of love, but it has never been easy, especially back then. In addition to driving them to their fights, I would wrap all of their hands, and I worked the corners for each of them. It would be midnight by the time the amateur boxing shows were over and we were ready to leave. We would sometimes have to drive hundreds of miles back to Orlando. I would be so tired that I would give anything for forty winks, but I had no money for a place to stay. I would usually stop at a McDonald's to get them hamburgers and soft drinks. I would also pick up a plastic bag full of ice at a convenience store. Within a mile after leaving the convenience store, I would look in the rear view mirror and never fail to see all of the little white faces and black faces with their eyes closed in a deep sleep. They were dead to the world, and each of them usually had an arm around a first place trophy. Thankfully, there was always one who would volunteer to ride in front with me. He would be my co-pilot, and his job was to keep me awake. Whoever agreed to do it knew what was involved. He'd say, 'Coach, I'll sit up with you. I'll stay awake all night if I have to.' I knew that might not be enough to keep me from becoming hypnotized by the white lines and telephone poles we would be passing by, so I would take some ice cubes out of the plastic bag and hold them in one hand to keep me awake and alert. As the miles rolled by, I would offer up a prayer and say, 'Lord, I've got no one else to drive. Please help me get this precious cargo back to their mommas.' God blessed me each and every time. I truly believe that I never had a wreck because He was watching over me.

I've lived long enough to know that when you do things for kids, our innocents, you are rewarded. The Lord has blessed me and continues to bless me. I'm almost ninety. I'm still here and my mind is still sharp. I also have the memories of those grand and glorious road trips. To me, that's worth more than cash, diamonds or gold.

PART THREE
JAMES' DAYS
AS AN AMATEUR

JAMES AND THE OTHER MISCHIEF MAKERS
IN HIS NEIGHBORHOOD

The Winter Park neighborhood where James and Larry Barfield grew up was a very special place where talented adults and children lived. In addition to boys like James and Larry who possessed athletic ability, there were those who excelled in music, modeling and other forms of entertainment. The entire Barfield family was remarkable in this regard. Everyone in the family, including Larry, appeared in print ads and TV commercials. Larry's sister, Terri, won a major pageant when she was seven. Her prize was a brand new Toyota Corolla. Bob Barfield sang with local theater productions and still has a fine singing voice. Bob's brother was also quite a singer, and their musical talent was passed along to Larry and his brother Tracy.

There were also several people in the neighborhood who were devoted to snakes. Even James' uncle, Joe Salerno, had a python for a pet. It wasn't surprising that James also acquired a love of reptiles.

He was attracted to a wooded area just down the street from where he lived. At the age of ten, James began spending a great deal of time there. He would take a pillow case with him, turn over rocks and look for snakes. If he found any, he would pick them up, tuck them away in his makeshift sack and take his captives home to keep as pets. It didn't bother him in the least that the snakes would be wiggling and wobbling in their cloth confines. When he was twelve, he found an Eastern Hog Nose snake. He named it Stanley and it became his favorite reptile of all.

It was not a dangerous snake. The Eastern Hog Nose is a non-venomous reptile with elongated, grooved teeth located in the back of the upper jaw. It is slightly less than two feet long, and is a colorful snake that is characterized by its upturned snout. The snout helps it dig into sandy soil by using a sweeping, side to side motion. They are known to be timid creatures that will hide from predators by burrowing down into leaves and sand.

The snake did not defend itself by biting. It only attacked its prey, which were usually frogs and toads. It's possible that James might have been in danger of being bitten if he smelled like one of those creatures, but after Stanley discovered his keeper was no threat, the snake became quite loving toward the boy. It liked to be held by James, and it displayed a lot of personality. Salerno kept the slithery creature in an escape proof tank. When frogs or toads weren't available, he would feed it eggs, insects or mice.

James was fascinated by his pet, and he spent a great deal of time observing it. He learned that if the snake felt threatened, it would put on a show by flattening its neck, raising its head off the ground like a cobra, hissing and pretending to strike at the threat. If that didn't work, Stanley would roll onto to its back and play dead. It was an Academy Award performance. While it was in that position, the snake would emit a foul odor and sometimes fecal matter. It would also let its tongue hang out of its mouth. Once in a while, the tongue would be accompanied by droplets of blood. Even when it was in its death pose, Stanley was paying close attention to its surroundings. It didn't take long for James to figure out that his pet would "resurrect" sooner if he were looking away from the it, rather than looking straight at the creature.

Sal Salerno brought up an interesting angle to James' pet snake when he said,

Just think about it. A snake has no arms. It keeps its eyes open, so it can focus on its prey. When it makes its move, it strikes instantaneously. James spent a great deal of time observing Stanley. I truly believe that he incorporated what he learned from the snake into his boxing technique.

James was not the only snake lover on his street. The four Campbell boys who lived next door also kept reptiles. They didn't have any Eastern Hog Noses, so they raised mice to feed their snakes. The boys enjoyed having their reptiles coil around their bodies. On cold winter nights, the creatures would enter the Campbell's home for warmth. This was perfectly all right with Ernie Campbell and his sons. Judy Campbell hated having reptiles slither through her well kept house, but she was outvoted and there was nothing she could do about it.

In addition to snake lovers, the kids in the neighborhood where thrill seekers. They soon learned that James was the most adventurous of them all. He was willing to take any dare. In discussing this with me, Judy Campbell said,

Nothing frightened James. He did things that scared the daylights out of me, and he had my children doing them too. He was a ringleader. I don't know if you could call him a bad influence, but James was James.

James and Larry Barfield loved to dive from the very peak of the Salerno's roof into the backyard swimming pool; the equivalent of a two story drop. This was very dangerous. If the boys had missed the water, they would have landed on solid concrete. Sal had total confidence in the boys' diving ability, and he even shot some film of them doing it. The fun came to an end when Judy Campbell "busted" them by reporting it to Joanne Salerno. James' mother told him in no uncertain terms that he was to stop it. He obeyed her because he knew that he had gone a bit too far, and she meant business.

For a brief time, James had some fun with a BB gun he had obtained from another kid in the neighborhood. Salerno and Larry Barfield lay in wait for the men making the regular trash pickups to ambush them and shoot them in their butts. The trash haulers reported it to Bob Barfield, and he quickly brought it to an end.

Next to Stanley, James' most prized possession was his moped. Most of the kids in the neighborhood had their own motor vehicles by the time they were teenagers. Joanne gave James the moped when he was twelve years old to use for going to school and to his training sessions at the gym behind the Orlando Sports Stadium. The stadium was about four miles from the Salerno's home.

The boys in the neighborhood were always outside competing in various games. James and the Barfield boys would box with each other, but Judy Campbell didn't want any of her sons boxing. Wrestling was fine, and so was football. James and Larry often took on the Campbell boys in these two sports. If no one else was around to roughhouse with, Larry would take on James, even though there was a two year age difference. In recalling those times, Larry said, "I could never whip James' butt. It frustrated me, and I became jealous of him. There were times I really became very angry about it."

Angry kids sometimes do extreme things, sometimes even destroying their friends' most treasured items. One time, Larry became very upset at James, and he tried to shove James' moped down a sewer. When he saw what his pal was doing, he ran to Larry's mom, hollering, "MRS. BARFIELD, MRS. BARFIELD, LARRY IS LOSING HIS MIND!" Luckily, the moped didn't quite fit through the sewer opening and the vehicle was none the worse for wear.

The meanest thing Larry did to James was to release Stanley, Salerno's beloved pet. When the boy saw that his Eastern Hog Nose was missing, the first person he went to was Larry. His best friend immediately owned up to it. James never found his prize pet. It didn't end the friendship between the two boys, but Salerno never forgot the slight and would bring up the topic every now and then. Over twenty years later, he would occasionally say to Larry, "I still can't believe you let that damn snake out."

As the James approached his mid teens, he desired more powerful transportation. Sal upgraded him from the moped to motorcycles. James' first motorcycle was a Kawasaki Enduro KZ 100. He later moved up to a Kawasaki KZ 750 Custom. When he was not quite fifteen, he had a really bad spill on his cycle. The bike slid out from under him when he lost traction going around a turn in the Goldenrod subdivision. He flew off and went in one direction, while his motorcycle bounced along the other way down the road. James was fortunate to get his leg out of danger at just the last instant. The machine was a total loss, but the teenager escaped with only scratches and abrasions. Afterward, he said to his father. "Dad, I felt like a cowboy whose horse went down and nearly rolled on top of him."

When Sal Salerno spoke about James' first car, he said,

I didn't give him an endless supply of money, but his mother and I bought big ticket items for him. She bought him a mint condition red 1971 Mustang and had a maroon crushed velour interior put in it that cost almost as much as the car. I also bought him a trailer and landscaping equipment so that he could make money doing lawn work for people in our neighborhood. He became very good at it and eventually had his own landscaping business after his boxing career was over. We did these things for him in order to push him in the right direction.

Judy Campbell said,

When James had just turned fifteen, I happened to be outside doing yard work. Sal pulled up in a gorgeous red Mustang convertible. Sonny handed the keys to James. When I realized he was giving James the car, I went crazy. I said to Sonny, 'You've got to be out of your mind!'

Outside of boxing, James' only concern was whatever seemed the most fun at that particular time. He strictly lived in the moment. He thought he was ready for anything, but had no idea how ill prepared he was for everyday life. Ready or not, he was on course to experiencing the fight game at its best and its worst.

PETE ASHLOCK BUILT THE BOXING FACTORY WHERE JAMES HONED HIS FIGHTING SKILLS

Jimmy Williams trained James Salerno, Larry Barfield and other amateur fighters at a gym which was part of the Orlando Sports Stadium, a facility built by Pete Ashlock in 1967 which resembled a big barn. It was located ten miles east of Orlando along the Econolahatchee Trail. The surrounding wooded area was close to a swamp inhabited by alligators.

It cost $740,000 to build. Architects suggested using 468 tons of steel, but Ashlock made do with only 168 tons. The structure would be considered primitive compared to today's arenas that resemble palaces. It lacked air conditioning, and it had a bare concrete floor and bleachers made of wood planks. Some, but not all, of the stalls in the bathrooms had plywood doors and the rest had no doors at all. Though it lacked amenities, it became a popular venue attracting large crowds.

The man who built it had a colorful background. His real first name and middle initial was Grover C., but he preferred being called Pete. He had begun his working life as a rodeo star and he won championship belt buckles as a saddle bronc rider and a steer wrestler. Throughout his life, he maintained membership in the Rodeo Cowboys Association and proudly carried his membership card number 712. He became known as "the man in the ten gallon hat." For Pete Ashlock, his choice of headwear was a symbol of his most outstanding quality... determination.

Ashlock came up the hard way. Born and raised in Decatur, Texas, he dropped out of school with only a sixth grade education. Pete once remarked, "I had to ride horseback fourteen miles to get there. Do you have any idea how many side roads there are in fourteen miles?"

He grew to be 6' 1", 180 pounds and tough as nails. Ashlock served in the United States Marine Corps during World War II.

After he hung up his spurs and retired from rodeo competition in 1951, his motto became "Go east, young man," and he headed for Orlando in the Sunshine State. Ashlock once remarked, "My financial success is purely accidental. All I did was to recognize Florida as a frontier and drop a few bucks into it." His first project consisted of buying a bulldozer and clearing land. While watching other entrepreneurs erect buildings on the land he was clearing, Pete decided there was money to be made in putting up buildings. He also got into paving. In 1958, Ashlock was awarded government contracts to prepare sites for military bases in Oklahoma and Texas. Pete suffered a setback when the prime contractor went bust just before the ex-rodeo cowboy was to be paid. Ashlock was owed $600,000, which was the equivalent of millions back in the 1950's. He reacted by gritting his teeth, biting down on his ever present cigar and doggedly pursuing payment of what he was owed. Years later, he summed up what happened by saying, "To collect from dear old Uncle Sam took me nine years, eleven months and seventeen days."

The disappointment he experienced while working under a government contract did not sour him on pursuing other entrepreneurial activities. Pete went into the crane business. He had rented a number of them for his building projects, and he decided to invest in some and rent them out. His timing was superb. He got in on the ground floor of the Cape Kennedy building boom and then the construction of Walt Disney World. He recalled that period by saying, "Whenever I heard of work, I'd spend anywhere from $30,000 to $180,000 on another crane." In August, 1973, Pete's 27 cranes were making him $6,000 per month. Ashlock added, "Funny thing was that in the beginning I never wanted more than a couple of cranes." By the early 1970's, his real estate holdings were growing constantly. He even invested in a 10,000 acre cattle ranch in Colombia.

Pete Ashlock was driven to succeed. He thought of himself as a real life Marlboro Man and lived accordingly. He always wanted to do things his way and would often become impatient. When his daughter was born while he and his wife were visiting in Dallas, Pete bought an airplane for $38,000 and flew it himself to get the family back to Orlando. When asked why he did it, he replied, "I wanted to get home." His wife said many times, "There isn't another like him." There was another story of him going into one of Orlando's finer restaurants and ordering onion slices. After sending them back twice, he was still not satisfied with what he had been brought. He then got up from his table, walked across the street, bought an onion, came back sliced it into huge pieces, ate it and finished the rest of his meal.

Orlando was a small town when he arrived on the scene. The local sports attractions were pretty much limited to high school athletics and a Tangerine Bowl football game played each December. Ashlock decided to fill the void by building an 11,000 seat indoor arena that would offer boxing, wrestling and rodeos. He was surprised when his idea met with resistance from the local politicians. He had to fight an uphill battle to build his stadium, but he eventually prevailed.

Once the building was erected, he was hindered by Orange County's refusal to pave the dirt road leading to it. Ashlock persisted and negotiated a deal whereby he supplied the materials and the county supplied the labor. Orange County grudgingly went along with it, but then had the last word by raising the property taxes. In addition to his problems with the politicians, the Orlando business community seemed to have it in for Ashlock. None of the regular ticket outlets would do business with Pete. Ticket buyers could purchase their ducats at only two bars; the Clock Tavern and the Point After Lounge.

Some said Ashlock's stadium looked like a giant aluminum tool shed. Larry Barfield fondly recalled the facility and said,

It was a cool place to go. Even though it only had wooden bleachers that were easy to pick up splinters from and a few sections of folding chairs, it was an exciting place to be. Amateur fights were held Tuesday nights, even though the kids who were fighting had to be at school the next day. When I fought in amateur shows, there were times when I would show up at school with a black eye or bruises. They had wrestling every other Sunday night. Dusty Rhodes, who was was the Hulk Hogan of that time, appeared there, as well as other big names. The boxing and wrestling shows drew good crowds before there was cable television.

It was affordable entertainment for those wanting to get out of the house for an evening. Boxing tickets were priced at five dollars for general admission and eight bucks for ringside. The ringside seats consisted of twenty rows of folding chairs placed around the ring. The prices might seem cheap, but eight grand a year was a decent salary back then. Beer was sold in big paper Pepsi cups, and this was done even during amateur boxing cards. Vendors were also pushing peanuts, popcorn and hot dogs. Since the building had no air conditioning, the concession stands were all the open air type because of the hot months in Florida. There was a constant presence of unhealthy foul odors and smoke from cigars and cigarettes.

In order for his boxing promotions to maintain their appeal, Pete Ashlock knew that he had to maintain a steady flow of talent. He brought in Jimmy Williams to start the Orlando Sports Stadium's amateur program, which would serve as incubator for new fighting talent. Before coming to work for the promoter, Williams had a good paying union job as a fork lift operator for Inland Container in Orlando. Jimmy was one of only two blacks employed by the firm at that time.

His life changed dramatically when he received a phone call from Ashlock in 1973. Pete offered him more money to train both amateur and professional fighters. Williams had job security, but he was getting tired of his hours being constantly switched from daytime to evenings to the graveyard shift. Jimmy accepted Ashlock's offer and would end up being the only black employee at the Sports Stadium.

Pete had invested in a gym located at the back of the sports stadium because there wasn't a suitable facility for training fighters in all of Orlando. He also built a couple of three bedroom homes behind the gym to house fighters. It was a true boxing factory. Jimmy Williams said,

In addition to the amateurs I was training, Pete Ashlock would bring in fighters from Texas, Alabama and even as far away as California. At any given time, there would be fifteen pros and twenty five amateurs training in the gym. He provided the professionals with living quarters that were right on the stadium property, and he would also feed them.

One of my duties was to bring in the groceries. I would also drive our fighters into Orlando a couple of times a week so they could pick up personal items. If the boxers asked for loans or advances against their purses, Pete Ashlock would dole money out to them and mark down how much they were given. He made sure he got it all back after they fought and the gate was divvied up. The usual arrangement was for him to keep one third of their purse. They were also charged for their housing and food.

In 1976, Ashlock hired Dominick Polo and placed him in complete charge of the gym and the fighters who trained there. Jimmy Williams was no longer in charge and Polo became his immediate supervisor. Dominick was a heavyset former heavyweight with a round face who wore his hair long enough to completely cover his ears, which was a style that was fashionable back in the 1970's. He was described in Sports Illustrated as "a man who envisions himself as a mixture of Napoleon and Caesar." He took pleasure in telling anyone willing to listen to him, "My record is 263 plus wins and only 19 losses." The record he claimed would have placed him among the all time legends of prizefighting, but no one ever challenged the veracity of that statement.

He was in his thirties when he began running the stadium's boxing operations, and was a man of many talents. In addition to his boxing expertise, Dominick could play the piano beautifully without the aid of sheet music. He was reputed to have worked as a social worker for four years. His job description was that of a trainer, but he was not at all like Jimmy Williams. Jimmy was lean, lithe and kept himself in shape, while Dom was heavyset. Williams taught classical boxing, while Polo taught brawling. Jimmy was a mentor and father figure, while Dom was a taskmaster and very controlling.

Dominick Polo ran a tight ship. He would allow spectators into the Sports Stadium gym to watch the fighters work out, but they could not go beyond a roped off area, talk to the fighters, smoke, drink beer or hard liquor or talk in a loud voice. The boxers were ordered not to spit on the floor, practice any karate chops, karate kicks or other martial arts techniques, lean on the ropes or put their hands or feet on the walls. Polo was a bug on neatness and image. He once said, "When a boxer is referred to as a club fighter, he sounds like a loser who fights in some basement every five months. My fighters do not look like those tomato cans. I insist that they polish their shoes and make sure their robes aren't wrinkled. The very least that they can do is look good when they enter the ring."

In describing the regimen which the fighters followed, Jimmy Williams said,

There was a three mile long stretch of dirt road next to the housing for the fighters. Dom Polo would get up early in the morning and drive his car along that running path. He would trail the pro fighters racing through the misty darkness to make sure they were doing their daily running. Each morning, they would run to the end of the road and back, for a total of six miles. They would do that each and every morning. When Polo wasn't trailing the fighters, he sometimes spent a lot of time waxing his car.

Jimmy Williams also spent time behind the wheel. In his search for boys to become part of the Orlando Sports Stadium's amateur team, Jimmy would drive throughout the greater Orlando area in his white Fiat sports car. The color of his car matched that part of Florida, which was predominantly Caucasian then. Williams was so determined to mine pugilistic talent that he was willing to venture into Ku Klux Klan hotbeds. A couple of those places were close to the Orlando Sports Stadium. One town was called Christmas and the other was named Bithlo. The standing joke about Christmas was that it never snowed there, but the place was always white. For decades, the residents of Bithlo were punch lines for jokes about poverty, ignorance and lack of dental hygiene, but it was a fertile ground for tough kids who were quick with their fists. Even today, it is populated by rednecks. In recalling those trips, Jimmy Williams said,

I was very popular out there because I was training the sons of Klan members and providing them with a way of making some money. I don't know of any other black man who was ever welcomed in that community.

I also recruited several black pro fighters from Tampa, St. Petersburg and as far as Jacksonville to fight on pro cards at the Sports Stadium. Many of the fights were on TV. All in all, I would have to say that I have a lot of positive memories of those days. We had some great times and great fights out there at the Orlando Sports Stadium.

In his later years, Pete Ashlock, the former rodeo champion and promoter of sports events and rock concerts, was a commercial fisherman. He passed away in 1988. Pete was the heart and soul of central Florida boxing for nearly twenty years. His contributions were recognized in 2011 when he was inducted into the Florida Boxing Hall of Fame.

THE ROCKINGEST PLACE IN CENTRAL FLORIDA

In addition to being a sports showcase, Pete Ashlock's arena once hosted a political convention when George Wallace campaigned for president there. It also became a concert venue that was well regarded within the Deep South. At the time the stadium was built, there were no other places to hold rock concerts in either Orlando or central Florida. Tickets were priced at five to ten dollars each, which was the cost of a vinyl album back then.

On April 23, 1976, the Sports Stadium played host to the Rolling Thunder Revue Tour which was headed by Bob Dylan. Six months later, the King of Rock and Roll appeared in the facility. On February 15, 1977, Elvis Presley performed at an 8:30 P.M. show. It was one of his last public appearances. He died August 16, 1977. Other famous rock and roll acts that performed at the Sports Stadium include The Beach Boys, Three Dog Night, Ruth Copeland, Black Sabbath, Amboy Dukes, Southern Comfort, Cactus Power, Jefferson Starship, Rod Stewart and Faces, Grand Funk Railroad, Tin House, Edgar Winter and Deep Purple.

Led Zeppelin also appeared in the Sports Stadium. Their only concert there was billed as "An Evening with Led Zeppelin." The price for tickets purchased in advance was six dollars. They were the only act that appeared that night and played for two and a half hours.

The Orlando Sports Stadium deserves a place in the history of rock and roll, but even the most nostalgic of those who attended concerts there will admit that it was small and rather disgusting. Those who chose to sit rather then stand throughout the performance would find themselves a few feet above a roller rink shaped floor occupying two by four boards that could easily deliver hefty splinters. The only other choice was to sit in front of the stage on a sticky concrete surface coated with spilled drinks. There were always battles waged for space immediately in front of the stage. The victors were rewarded with music pouring out of stacked amps and speakers at such high decibels that their hearing was diminished for hours and their ears rang for days. There was no air conditioning and everyone was allowed to smoke or chew whatever they wanted. Marijuana was puffed openly and there was talk of LSD being used on the premises. The atmosphere was similar to San Francisco's legendary Fillmore Auditorium.

An unfortunate situation took place when John Sebastian appeared for a Friday night concert at the Sports Stadium in September, 1971. A large number of people without tickets gathered outside the front entrance. A group of them created a disturbance to distract the security guards present, while other groups rushed the gates. The manager became frightened and called the local sheriff's department. This resulted in two deaths. A sheriff's sergeant rushing to the scene was heading east on Colonial and ran a light at State Road 436. He collided with a vehicle occupied by two girls and both were killed. When sheriff's deputies arrived at the stadium, they were met with resistance and eight of them were injured. A decision was made to tear gas everyone in the arena.

Sebastian, former member of the Lovin' Spoonful, was performing with his acoustic guitar when the chaos ensued. He tried to calm everyone inside, but the noise from the commotion taking place at the entrance drowned out the volume of his microphone. Those inside remained seated until they finally had to head for the exits when the tear gas came wafting in. The ones sitting on the floor had to assist a man in a wheelchair. There was no way he could make it back to the entrance. Several men lifted him, chair and all, from the floor to the stage so he could leave through an exit behind the stage.

News of the event reached the local rock station WLOF remarkably fast, considering there were no cell phones then. The disc jockey on the air at the time asked people who were there to come to the station or give them a call. Some of those who were at the scene went so far as to drive to the station and give firsthand accounts of what they had experienced.

In the aftermath, twenty nine youngsters were arrested, only one of whom was a female. Twenty two of them sat in jail without bond. No report ever surfaced `of what happened to the sheriff's sergeant who ran the red light. It became a legal quagmire because the stadium was outside the jurisdiction of the city of Orlando.

After that debacle, there were no concerts at the Sports Stadium for a while. "Festival seating" was somehow blamed as the cause and when the concerts resumed, it was no longer used.

Even with its warts, the Orlando Sports Stadium is fondly remembered by those old enough to have attended the concerts and been part of the counter culture experience. Pete Ashlock's Sports Stadium really rocked back then.

It is strange that a place where so many big names performed has largely been forgotten. The building was closed by the Orange County Building Department because of code violations and was demolished in November, 1995. The land on which it stood is now occupied by the Econ River Estates housing development.

EVERYONE WANTS THE DIAMOND IN THE ROUGH ONCE IT BECOMES A POLISHED JEWEL

In discussing James Salerno's development as a fighter, Jimmy Williams said,

When he first came to me, he was very emotional. He had problems with everybody in his life. I saw him cry like a baby many times over small things. He was upset because he had a crush on a girl named Maggie Thomas, but she wasn't all that interested in him. There were things he and his father disagreed about. James, however, would do everything that I told him to do. He bought into my program and would show up at my front door at 8:00A.M., and sometimes even earlier. At that time of the morning, he had already done his morning run, had his special breakfast of raw eggs and milk and was ready to train. As the years went by, there were times when he would have an argument with his father and he would stay with my wife and me. He always had his own transportation; first motorcycles and then cars.

James fought his first amateur bout on November 27, 1973, when he was twelve years old. When he was thirteen, he beat twenty one year old Robert Spencer. He made short work of it. The referee stopped the fight in the second round and declared a technical knockout for Salerno.

During that same year, Jimmy Williams introduced James to a karate expert named Dennis "Rocky" Black. Rocky took Salerno to a karate show in Ft. Lauderdale. Sal Salerno had never liked karate, kick boxing or other martial arts because he thought they were too dangerous. It was only because of Jimmy Williams that Sal allowed his son to attend the show. After they arrived, Black learned that one of the kick boxers was unable to compete. He was curious about how well James would do in kick boxing, so he volunteered the boy's services and served as his corner man. Just before the bout began, Salerno asked Rocky, "What should I do?" Black replied, "The important thing to remember is that you must throw eight kicks before you can throw a punch." James didn't have any problem with that. At the start of each bout he fought that day, he threw the required number of kicks as quickly as he could and then knocked his opponent out. Even though he had gone to the karate show without any intention of competing, he went home with a large trophy. When he showed it to Sal, he said, "Dad, please don't be mad at me for kick boxing without your permission." The father told the son not to worry. He was proud of what he had done.

In addition to the physical and mental training he gave James, the black teacher also played a key role in the development of the youngster's spirituality. When I spoke with James' sister Gina, she said,

Jimmy Williams encouraged James to read the Bible, and he gave him a small pocket sized version. My brother really picked up on that. He intensely studied the Bible. He knew the Scriptures, he became very spiritual and he knew all about Satan and Jesus. As time went on, he knew the Bible like the back of his hand. I remember him often quoting Scriptures. He was the first one who told me, 'Don't worry about your life. Jesus told us don't worry about tomorrow. Tomorrow has enough trouble of its own.' There's no doubt in my mind that Jimmy Williams helped James to develop a very spiritual quality within him.

The Salerno's next door neighbors, Ernie and Judy Campbell were big fight fans. In recalling his first days as an amateur boxer, Judy Campbell stated,

When he was thirteen, James weighed about 130 pounds and was about 5' 9". He wasn't muscular, but he had become an amazing boxer. He had lateral movement, a fantastic jab and could evade people. He was always moving. If a boxer wanted to hit him, they had to find him, and that was not easy. He was so good at his craft that it was shocking. He had an amazing amount of knowledge for someone so young.

Jimmy Williams added,

James became a true student of boxing. To give you an example, Mike Quarry was part of Ashlock's stable, and Quarry was knocked out by Bob Foster. Foster was a light heavyweight from Albuquerque, New Mexico and a left hook artist. Foster was similar to James in that he was tall and had a great left hand. He also shimmied when he boxed. James watched every film of Foster he could get his hands on. James liked the way Ali shimmied when he boxed and he wanted to do all he could to develop his own shimmy.

In 1975, Muhammad Ali came to the Orlando Sports Stadium to participate in a boxing exhibition as part of a fundraiser to benefit black performing artists. James Salerno fought in an amateur bout that was part of the under card. Ali was wowed by the performance put on by the thirteen year old, and he wanted to meet the boy.

The champ walked into the kid's dressing room just as the wraps were being removed from his hands. When James saw his boxing idol, he immediately began doing his impression of the great fighter. Muhammad Ali was captivated by the kid. He told James, "You can't be white and fight like that."

A bystander captured the priceless moment with a Polaroid. Ali signed his name on the photo and also wrote, "To James Salerno, a future world champion." He handed the autographed item to the kid and said, "Let's go for a ride in my limo and we'll get something to eat. We have a lot to talk about." The champ and the boxing prodigy dined together at Orlando's renowned House of Beef, and their visit lasted over two and a half hours.

Sal Salerno had walked into his son's dressing room shortly after James had left with Ali. He was flabbergasted when he found out what had happened. It had a profound effect upon the father's perception of how talented a boxer his son had become. He had never thought of his kid as a prodigy before, but he now realized the boy was very special. James had transformed from a child who had so much trouble in school and was picked into a fighter with unusual talent. The ugly duckling had become a graceful swan. The big question was "What path will James' life take?"

JAMES AND HIS PARTY PAL, JOHN HAYDEN

By the time he was fourteen, James was beginning to walk a path headed in a direction contrary to the one Jimmy Williams hoped he would follow. As he strayed from the straight and narrow, he was accompanied by a friend who was the same age named John Hayden.

James met John when they were in the seventh grade at the same middle school in Maitland, Florida, which is on the border between Orlando and Winter Park. John is half Japanese and was a foster child at the time. His home life was not all it should have been. Sal and Joanne Salerno told me that they never met his foster parents and John often slept over at the Salerno's. He and James became the best of friends and continued their friendship until their late teens.

Both of the boys were being trained by Jimmy Williams, and the wise teacher of the sweet science had the complete respect of the two kids as well as his other students. They hung on his every word and carried out every order he gave them. Under Williams' guidance, Salerno developed rapidly and John became a fine boxer in his own right. He earned the nickname "Hurricane."

There were serious problems brewing, though. After receiving so much attention from Muhammad Ali, James began to think that he could act like a grown man. He had forgotten that he was still just barely in his teens. He and John Hayden found themselves in a world filled with temptations, and unfortunately they succumbed. In the end, the long dark path he began to follow would ultimately end in tragedy.

In recalling what James was like at the age of fourteen, Judy Campbell said,

James dressed stylishly. He looked at what the other boxers were wearing. He would talk about their suits and their jackets. He always paid attention to other boxers' lifestyles. If he wanted anything in the way of clothes, he just went to the store and bought it. His parents gave him an allowance of forty dollars a week, and that wasn't all the money he was getting. Sonny and Joanne had no idea that he was being slipped twenty dollars every time he would spar with a professional at the gym in the back of the Orlando Sports Stadium. James told me about that himself. He didn't keep many secrets. He always liked to tell people things which he thought would make him sound important.

By the time Salerno was fourteen, he, John Hayden and had met several top pros who were housed behind the Orlando Sports Stadium and learned a great deal about their personal habits. These fighters included Mike Quarry, Irish Gene Wells, Maurice "Termite" Watkins, Edgar "Mad Dog" Ross and Victor "Taco" Perez.

When the three boys first met Mike Quarry in 1975, the light heavyweight from California had compiled a record of 48 wins, five losses and three draws. Quarry had spent 1973 fighting mononucleosis, which had been undiagnosed for most of that year. Before the illness was detected, he had dropped decisions to three high ranking contenders whom he had previously beaten; Chris Finnegan, Tom Bogs and Andy Kendall. Quarry's only other losses had been to Bob Foster in their 1972 world title bout, which took place when Jerry was only twenty one, and a disputed decision in Johannesburg, South Africa to Pierre Fourie. That fight had taken place in 1974, and even the South African newspapers had labeled it as a robbery. After Pete Ashlock took charge of his career, Mike Quarry returned to peak physical condition and won six straight fights. In 1975, the future looked bright for the twenty three year old younger brother of heavyweight contender Jerry Quarry.

Irish Gene Wells was a thirty one year old middleweight when James and his two pals met him. His career was in the process of being rejuvenated by Ashlock. Only a year before, the fighter who was three fourths Irish and one quarter Creek Indian was hanging around his hometown of Mobile, Alabama, playing pool and doing some part time welding. Pete Ashlock signed Wells to a contract, moved him to Orlando and breathed life into his career. In a span of ten months, Irish Gene won twelve out of thirteen bouts. The only loss was to Tony Licata by a narrow split decision. At the time James was working out with the 160 pound Wells, Irish Gene was riding an eight bout winning streak and his recent victims included Manuel Elizondo and Marcel Clay. His overall record at that point was 34 wins, four losses and three draws, with 14 knockouts.

Termite Watkins was a lightweight sensation from Houston. He had won the National Golden Gloves lightweight title at the age of sixteen. His amateur record was 112 wins, ten losses and one draw. He turned pro when he was seventeen.

Mad Dog Ross was a junior middleweight who had lost only one fight and had just one draw in the three years prior to his meeting Salerno. He had compiled 26 knockouts in that period.

Taco Perez was of Mexican descent. He was born in Tampa. At one time, he had been a drafting engineer. He moved to Sanford, Florida after Pete Ashlock signed him. He became a very popular fighter in Orlando, and the fans referred to him as "The Taco Kid." He had won ten out of his last eleven fights when he met James.

At that time, Pete Ashlock Promotions controlled forty prizefighters in Orlando, Houston, Albuquerque, New Mexico and Corpus Christi, Texas, and Salerno, John Hayden and Larry Barfield were constantly around veteran pros. Ashlock himself was in charge of the Houston and Orlando facilities. He hired Paul Chavez to manage Albuquerque and Jack Irwin to direct Corpus Christi. The Albuquerque operation had been especially lucrative because of two bouts there which involved light heavyweight champion Bob Foster. Foster fought Pierre Fourie and Jorge Ahumada in the Duke City. In addition, Pete Ashlock formed a working agreement with Joe Gagliardi, who promoted boxing shows in the California cities of San Francisco, San Jose, Sacramento, Stockton, Oakland and Fresno. Pete Ashlock Promotions was a true coast to coast operation.

Unfortunately, being around the pro athletes led the three boys into bad habits. Larry Barfield said, "We looked up to guys like Mike Quarry. He was a successful pro athlete, and we also knew that he was smoking pot. If it was good enough for guys like him, it was good enough for us."

When they were around fifteen, James and John Hayden decided that they wanted to try pot. It was actually easier for James, John and Larry to buy pot than it was for them to obtain beer or wine. Many of their classmates at Lake Howell High were selling marijuana, although none of them were big time dealers. In recalling those times, John Hayden said, "They were in it just so they could make enough to smoke for free. We bought our first joints from a kid who lived up the street from the Salerno's. He was dealing pot out of his parents' home."

They smoked their first joints in James' bedroom. They didn't realize that, like anything else, there are rules and techniques involved in smoking pot properly. Unlike boxing, they didn't have an older person to provide instruction and precautionary advice on how potent various strains can be. Their first experience was far from perfect because they were unaware that the grass they had obtained was potent stuff that packed a wallop. John quickly smoked the entire joint, while James did the right thing by taking a few tokes until he felt a buzz and then quitting. Hayden had a bad reaction. He hallucinated and became very paranoid.

John became frightened and asked James to wake up Mrs. Salerno so she could take him to an emergency room. James wasn't about to do that. It would be asking for trouble. He put on an act for his best friend and made it appear that he had gone to his mother's bedroom, awakened her and told her that John wasn't feeling well. When he came back to his bedroom, he said to Hayden, "She asked if you were bleeding or anything. When I said you weren't, she told me that you should go back to sleep and we'll see how you are in the morning." Fortunately, John slept off the effects of the marijuana and never had a similar problem with it.

Salerno sometimes told his best friends bold face lies. James had a tendency to follow the path of least resistance. His only concern was having as much fun in the present moment and not allowing anything to interfere with that. He had no concern about future consequences. If it was more convenient to tell a lie, he would do it; even if it meant lying to his best friend.

Once Hayden got past his initial experience, he and James became regular pot smokers and "partying pals." They were especially fond of sensimilla marijuana, also known as "sensi," which is seedless pot. The two party pals established an odd code of conduct. They smoked pot regularly, but refused to drink. In recalling those times, John Hayden said,

We were into getting high and drinking Coca Colas. We were never into alcohol. That was never an issue with us, but we did not totally abstain from it. Once in a while, we might have some beer. It had nothing to do with physical conditioning. We didn't think that drinking would harm our chances in the ring. It was simply that drinking didn't appeal to us.

They were also at the age when their hormones were raging and sex entered the picture. James first became interested in girls when he was thirteen, but he was somewhat picky. He was so good looking that many girls were attracted to him. He never had any problems meeting women, but he found it virtually impossible to sustain a relationship. Judy Campbell said,

Usually if a girl became interested in James but wasn't interested in boxing, he wasn't interested in her. I remember a girl named Renee who lived across the street. She was about three years older than him. She was blonde and attractive in her own way. She had big boobs, she smoked and she also slept around. To put it politely, she was free with her affection. One day, I happened to be walking past her house. Her parents had a swimming pool, and there was a hedge bordering the property. I happened to look over the top of the hedge as I passed and caught a glimpse of her and a teenage boy going at it in the backyard. I could not believe my eyes. After that, I would not let any of my four sons to go anywhere there.

James had a fling with Renee, but it didn't last long because she probably couldn't get interested in boxing. The love of his life back then was Maggie Thomas. He had a major crush on her that began in the seventh grade. He would later immortalize her in one of his rap songs and sing of how he made a vow to her that he would win a world championship. He was able to go out on a few dates with her, and he also brought her home to meet his parents. In recalling the girl, Joanne Salerno said, "Beauty is in the eye of the beholder. All I remember about her was that she was similar to Renee in that she had big boobs."

James' sister Gina added,

I think he truly loved Maggie, but she broke his heart. I think she saw how irresponsible he was becoming and she found someone else. I was only ten when they broke up, but I remember him taking it very hard. I could hear him crying in his room. He would be playing the song Color My World by Chicago, and I could hear the sobs.

By the time James and John Hayden were fifteen, Salerno was sexually experienced, but his party pal was still a virgin. Out of loyalty to his friend, Salerno decided to remedy the situation. He took his pal down to Orlando's notorious Orange Blossom Trail. It was a place known for all kinds of hustles. James hired two hookers, one for him and one for his friend. He paid each whore fifty dollars. He also paid for a hotel room. Both of the prostitutes were black. In recalling the incident, John Hayden said,

I can't remember James ever dating any black women, but he had a good time that night. The woman he was with also enjoyed herself. She was howling. She was very young, and I'm not even sure she was an adult. Mine was much older.

The escapade set James back around $150. He was making money doing lawn work, plus he was getting cash from Dom Polo for sparring with professional fighters.

In addition to the pot and sex, James was honing his interest in music. He really liked the Spinners, the Supremes, Motown hits and black dance tunes. Sal and Joanne had accumulated a large collection of vinyl albums and singles. The teenager's life had become a world of sex, drugs and rock and roll.

James' self absorbed pursuit of pleasure became a bad influence on his best friend. He would often convince John to cut class. They would leave their high school, head to the Salerno house, cook up a dozen eggs and listen to music before heading to the gym.

In commenting on Salerno's failure to go to class, Judy Campbell stated,

James played so much hooky and missed so much school that I still can't figure out why they just didn't kick him out. Plus, he would talk his friends into playing hooky with him. Sonny and Joanne were so busy with their work schedules that they didn't know James wasn't going to school. I knew everything my kids did because I was totally involved.

John Hayden added,

At that point in his life, he just did not see how school fit into the equation. James was all about James and living in the moment. That was all he really cared about. If he didn't have any pot and he knew that a friend had some, he wouldn't hesitate to go to the friend and say, 'I know you don't have much, but could you spare just a joint?' He would connive the friend out of any little bit that he could possibly get just to make his mission a success. It was all about making sure that he got what he wanted. It wasn't that he would never pay it back, mind you. It was simply that James was about the present moment. His life seemed to be built around taking advantage of opportunities and getting what he desired right then and there. If he was hungry, he would do whatever it took to get something to eat. If he wanted pot, he would go all out to get pot. He had no problems with going to people, even total strangers, knocking on doors and getting what he needed. Other than boxing, it was very difficult for him to follow directions, conform to rules of conduct or even obey laws. He didn't think that any of that applied to him. They were just a bunch of dumb rules. He had his own code of behavior and made up his own rules. He would connive, use his persuasive powers and manipulate people, but he would never outright steal anything.

As a high school student, James got along much better with his classmates than his years in elementary school. He was good friends with quite a few of them, but some of them still regarded him as a little too hyperactive. He couldn't sit still for a minute, he always seemed to be in a hurry and he had a motor mouth. A few of his classmates even said he was a freak.

He heard their comments. The things they said and the looks they gave him hurt. He coped with it by using the mask he could put on while dealing with the public.

He won over many of the ones who were critical of him with his tremendous sense of humor. He was great at coming up with funny lines and delivering them were perfect timing. He enjoyed being a comedian and entertaining whoever happened to be around. He was quite a performer and seemed on track to a career as a famous standup comedian as well as a world champion boxer.

This is not to say that all of the students at Lake Welles High were impressed with James. Some of his male classmates were jealous of him. In recalling the situation, John Hayden said,

There were wrestlers that tried to pick fights with us because our amateur fights were being covered by the Orlando newspapers. We went out of our way to avoid fights with them because they outweighed us by thirty to forty pounds. A smaller person cannot sustain an effort against an opponent with a huge weight advantage. So, we just put up with their taunts and insults. Another factor was that James could never bring himself to beat someone up or using his fists to respond to a slight. He was too sensitive for that.

James and I partied so much during our sophomore year that we would sometimes get high before we went to school. I remember sitting in a pre algebra class and wanting to fall asleep when the class was almost over. I put my head down on my desk and closed my eyes, hoping that would clear my head. The teacher didn't do anything or say anything because I wasn't the only one sleeping with their head on their desks. We went to Lake Howell High School, which was a good school, but it was up to the student to want to learn. James and I just didn't try hard enough.

James was definitely capable of finishing high school and even going further, but I don't believe he could think about schoolwork. His mind was focused on too many different things outside of school for him to concentrate on his classes. I was partly like that myself. We were boxing fanatics. All we thought about was boxing. School wasn't any fun at all for us. I struggled through it, no thanks to James. I followed his lead and missed many classes. I lost credit in a couple of courses and ended up having to take them over. Unlike James, I finally managed to graduate, but I'm not at all proud of my years in high school.

PART FOUR
HIS YEARS AS A
PROFESSIONAL FIGHTER

LESSONS FROM THE HISTORY OF BOXING
THAT EVERY PROFESSIONAL FIGHTER
SHOULD BE AWARE OF

There is an enormous difference between the way boxing and the other major professional sports are regulated. The biggest issue concerns the sport's lack of a central authority similar to the commissioners the NFL, the NBA the NHL and Major League Baseball, who rule their sports on a worldwide basis. Those who are officiating professional bouts are not under anywhere near the same amount of oversight which officials of the other major sports are subject to. To put it in the simplest terms, there are only two ways a prizefighter can be certain that they have won a bout. One is to knock their opponent out, and the other is if they are awarded a TKO. Since the very beginning, decisions of boxing judges have been the source of heated controversy. Just about every fighter has been screwed out of a decision at one time or another.

James Salerno lost a number of decisions as a pro. In fact, most of his losses occurred that way. He was never actually knocked out. There were times when the way the judges scored his fights appeared suspicious, but this was nothing new in boxing and it still goes on. If he had taken a close look at the history of the sport, he might have seen what was headed his way. This chapter will present some boxing history in order to show the reader that controversy has been a constant companion of world boxing titles.

Many years ago, legendary sports broadcaster Bill Stern told a story on his radio show which was carried coast to coast. Stern said,

There is the tale of a man who in his day won acclaim as a bare knuckle champion, but that fact has been forgotten in the immeasurably greater fame he achieved in other fields. He came from Virginia, the son of a well to do family. As a boy, husky and strong, he was handy with his dukes, and he loved a tough scrap. However, he had to do most of his bare knuckle fighting in secret, for his family of cultured gentlemen and gentlewomen would have been horrified if he were discovered engaged in the brutal sport. But that boy from Virginia gained such a wide reputation in the fistic circles of his time, that when he was only sixteen years old, he was recognized as bare knuckle boxing champion of Virginia.

All that happened a long time ago. His fame as a fist fighter has been completely forgotten, but curiously enough, we will always remember him as another kind of

fighter, for he was the Father of Our Country and the first President of the United States… George Washington.

The reason George Washington's participation in boxing was considered a mark of shame was that most of America's first prizefighters were slaves. In fact, the first heavyweight champion of the United States was a black man named Tom Molineaux.

Molineaux was born into slavery in Virginia in 1784. He came from the same state as George Washington. He was taught how to box by his father, who was a slave boxer at a time in the South when it was the custom for plantation owners to pit their best fighting slaves for high stakes. Tom's twin brother was also trained to fight by their father, to the delight of the family's master.

In those days, the fights were conducted bare knuckle style. Bare knuckle prize fights put human bodies through a supreme test. They might be fought at six in the morning, at three in the afternoon or, if necessary, at midnight under the pale glow of burning candles which cast grotesque shadows on the surrounding countryside. Rounds lasted as long as an hour or as short as a few seconds because a round ended when one of the fighters went to the turf. A match ended only when one of the fighters could no longer continue.

An official stakeholder was appointed to collect, hold and later pay off all bets. Usually he was a large bruiser who could take care of himself if need be. More often than not, the stakeholder also supervised setting up the ring. Where feasible, bouts were fought in gullies and ravines so that a natural amphitheatre was formed that would allow a large crowd to have a clear view of the action. It was doubtful that any women ever attended these fights.

A ring was formed which was twenty four feet square. There was also an outer ring where two umpires, the timekeeper and major backers were allowed to stand. Two umpires were generally used and each fighter was allowed to choose one. There were also "wipers out" stationed at ten foot intervals within the outer ring. Their job was to keep any mob violence from disrupting the match. It was common for backers of a fighter who was losing to crash the ring and break up the fight before an official decision could be reached. This often led to serious head injuries and gashed stomachs from knives. Anyone attending the bouts were free to carry weapons.

Bare knuckle fighters were allowed only two seconds (seconds later became known as corner men) to tend to them between rounds. A fighter would use the knee of one as a stool while the other second gave him a bottle of water to drink from and a rub down. Minor surgery was often performed in the corner. If a fighter's eye developed massive swelling, a second might jab a pen knife into the growth and suck out the liquid with his lips. Another trick was to bite a fighter's ear if it began to swell in order to lessen the chance of a cauliflower ear.

Every fighter had his own emblem beautifully embroidered on a large silk scarf. He wore this scarf into the ring and just before the timekeeper yelled "Time!" to begin the match, the scarf was tied on one of the ring posts. When a fighter lost a match, he lost his colors as well.

All fights were to a finish. A boxer could lose in either of two ways; by quitting or by failing to "come to scratch." Scratch consisted of a chalk line drawn in the middle of the ring. When a fighter was floored, he was allowed thirty seconds rest and then eight more seconds to get into a standing position at the chalk line. Speed and fancy footwork meant nothing. Light jabs were never used. Only knockouts counted. Gouging and "purring" were considered fair play and as much a part of the sport as tying the colors to a ring post. Gouging meant putting an opponent's eye out with a finger or a knuckle. Purring was the delicate art of kicking a fallen fighter with hob nailed boots, which all fighters wore. The crowds were loud and boisterous, and betting went on throughout the bout.

Knockout punches were not common. It wasn't that the fighters had not mastered the knack of knocking an opponent out. Knockouts were rare because whenever a fighter went down, he was immediately dragged to his corner, where he would have thirty seconds to recover. Knockouts generally occurred late in a fight after one man had received a terrific beating and was so weakened by loss of blood that a light jab would put him away.

Pugilists were terrible looking sights after a match. Punching an opponent with a naked fist had a tendency to swell the flesh over and under the eyes in such a way that a man was often blinded before he was otherwise hurt. The boxer dishing it out also had worries. The continual cracking of his fist against bone caused his knuckles to swell and puff up so that succeeding blows caused the puncher sheer agony. As the fight continued, the swelling grew larger and eventually the hand softened to the consistency of a sponge. Fighters looked forward to the point in a bout when their hands grew numb and they were able to punch without feeling pain. In order to offset this problem as much as possible, they would train for matches by soaking their hands in brine for hours at a time. Bare knuckle fighters were known to have skin as tough as elephant hide.

They were a tough breed, and Tom Molineaux became the toughest of them all in America. He beat everyone in the south and made his well to do owner even wealthier. It was said that Tom's master won not only large sums of money but deeds to land and batches of slaves. The master had some good qualities and showed his gratitude by giving Tom Molineaux his freedom.

After leaving the plantation, Molineaux headed north. As a slave, he had never learned to read or write, so his best option for making a significant amount of money was as a prizefighter. He ran up a string of victories along New York City's waterfront. Boxing was not regarded as a lawful activity back then, so there were no recognized champions in the U.S. Still, there was no doubt that the short but stocky 185 pound former slave was the best fighter in in the States. He decided to go to England where the best fighters in the world could be found and take on Tom Cribb, who was one of Great Britain's greatest champions.

He had no money to travel with, so Tom worked his way across the Atlantic on a sailing vessel. He was met in Bristol by Bill Richmond, who was an older black man and had been a slave boxer. He had been brought to England by British officers following the American Revolution. Richmond took Molineaux under his wing and got him a fight against Jack Burrows on July 24, 1810. The American whipped Burrows in 65 minutes. He won another fight easily and acquired a nickname: "The Moor." Molineaux the Moor was finally given the chance he was waiting for when he was scheduled to face Tom Cribb on December 10, 1810. The bout was held at Shenington Hollow in Oxfordshire. The stakes were 200 guineas (equivalent to $470,000 today) and a belt symbolic of the championship of the world. Contrary to the traditional bare knuckle rules, only one official was used; a referee. Molineaux the Moor had no say in who was chosen to serve in that capacity.

Boxing historian Pierce Egan was in attendance and documented that Tom Molineaux stood five feet eight and a quarter inches tall and weighed 198 pounds for that match. Few people expected the fight to last long and many in the crowd had wagered that it would take Cribb no more than ten rounds to whip the ex-slave.

The black man proved to be a powerful and intelligent fighter. He and Cribb battered each other in the early rounds. After nearly twenty rounds had gone by, the two combatants became locked in a wrestler's hold, which was legal under the rules of that time. The referee stood by and did not try to separate the fighters. Even though the grappling was within the rules, the crowd became upset at the lack of action and rushed the ring. One of Molineaux' left fingers was broken in the melee, but the fight went on and the former slave continued to get the better of Tom Cribb.

At the end of the twenty third round, Cribb showed signs of exhaustion. After the allotted thirty second break following that round, the English champion couldn't come to the center of the ring, take his mark and continue to fight. He was given eight seconds to do so and summoned three times, but was still unable to take his mark. The referee should have awarded the decision to Molineaux at that point, but he listened to an indignant handler form Cribb's corner who accused Tom Molineaux of concealing lead weights in his fists. The arguing lasted several minutes. The referee overruled Cribb's backers, but the time spent bickering allowed Tom Cribb to recover enough to resume the battle. It also caused Molineaux to stand around stripped to the waist in the cold December air, and he suffered a chill. After the thirty fourth round, Molineaux said he couldn't continue, but Bill Richmond persuaded him to go on. The tide turned and Cribb won the bout in the fortieth round. The next day, Cribb had possession of both the money and the championship belt, but everyone who attended the fight admitted that Tom Molineaux had actually won.

A rematch was held the next year. It was staged on September 28, 1811 at Thistleton Gap in Rutland and watched by 15,000. Pierce Egan was there and stated that Molineaux weighed no more than 185 pounds and was in no condition to fight. The accounts written back then stated, "He had taken to rum." It was also reported that before he slipped through the ropes, the black fighter had devoured an entire chicken and a huge pie, then washed it down with a couple of quarts of stout. He had enough in his tank to come out hitting Tom Cribb with great power at the start, but he ran out of gas and was outfought. Cribb knocked Tom out in the eleventh round, breaking his jaw in the process. After the fight, Molineaux and Richmond, the two former slaves, parted company and never spoke to each other again.

Molineaux's boxing career ended four years later in 1815. He served a stint in debtor's prison and became increasingly defendant on alcohol. Three years later, he died in Galway, Ireland from liver failure. He was penniless and had been reduced to sleeping in an unheated hut assigned to a regimental band. Tom Molineaux was only thirty four years old at the time of his death.

Over a hundred years later, Molineaux was avenged to a degree when his great, great nephew John Henry Lewis won the world light heavyweight championship. He held the title from 1935 to 1939. He also successfully defended it against in London against a British fighter named Len Harvey. Lewis compiled an outstanding record of 103 wins, nine losses and six draws and a remarkable 60 knockouts. He was inducted into the International Boxing Hall of Fame.

One of the most outrageous decisions in the history of the sweet science occurred on March 26, 1909 at the National Athletic Club in New York City when Stanley Ketchel took on Philadelphia Jack O'Brien. Ketchel, known as the "Michigan Assassin," survived a terrible beating in the early rounds before mounting a furious comeback. He knocked O'Brien down four times in the last two rounds of the fight. When the final bell rang after ten rounds, Philadelphia Jack was lying unconscious. His head was in a resin box in his corner. There was only official for the bout; referee Tim Hunt. Hunt ruled that O'Brien was saved by the bell. At the time, only knockouts counted in New York because awarding decisions was outlawed. Because of the New York law, the Ketchel vs. O'Brien match was declared a "no decision contest," even though the Michigan Assassin had actually knocked his opponent out.

Bill Stern recounted the tale of another strange boxing match on his sports show. It was a heavyweight fight between 6' 7" 278 pound Primo Carnera and 5' 11 ½" 200 pound Paolino Uzcudun that was held in Cataluna, Spain on November 30, 1930. The contest became embroiled in politics. Stern said,

It was on a Sunday afternoon that 140,000 fanatical spectators jammed the huge outdoor arena where the bout was scheduled to take place. It was the biggest crowd ever known to see a boxing match. The fight was scheduled to begin at two thirty. The appointed time came and went. Not a soul had appeared in the ring. The huge crowd began to stir with impatience. The atmosphere began to be charged with ominous foreboding. Thousands of military police and soldiers were present, armed to the teeth.

Unknown to the great crowd, a drama of unusual significance was taking place in the fighters' dressing rooms. The president of the Spanish Boxing Federation had handed Carnera a brand new pair of boxing gloves for the contest. Carnera took one look at them and refused to put them on. He insisted that he would use only American made gloves. There was a long and bitter argument.

Half an hour passed, then an hour. Still the giant refused to give in. Finally, the president of the boxing federation lost all patience. Shouting angrily that Carnera's

refusal to wear Spanish gloves was an insult to the whole nation and its people, he rushed to the door and barked a sharp command. Into the dressing burst several Spanish soldiers, their rifles cocked and ready. Another command and the rifles were lowered ominously, aiming straight at the big broad chest of the Italian colossus.

Senor Carnera, said the president of the Spanish Boxing Federation calmly, you will use our boxing gloves or I will order those soldiers to shoot.

Needless to say, Carnera immediately acquiesced. He drew on the gloves and left the dressing room without another word. Once inside the ring, another bitter argument took place. Primo refused to go ahead with the fight because both the referee and the two judges were Spanish. A compromise was effected. New appointments were made. There would be one Spanish judge, one Italian judge and an English referee.

At last the fight started. Paolino proceeded to slam the clumsy Carnera from pillar to post, winning every round of the contest. At the final bell, the Italian judge and the English referee hastily handed in their sealed verdicts and immediately rushed out of the arena to catch a plane. When the announcer opened the sealed ballots, he almost collapsed with shock. Both men had given the decision to the badly beaten Carnera! There was nothing for him to do but make the announcement. Then the storm broke!

The fanatical fight mob went wild. Men stood and cursed. Women wept and screamed. Bottles flew through the stands. Another minute passed and knives began to flash in the bright sun. Rifle fire spluttered. Pistols barked. Fans fired into the ranks of police. Police and soldiers fired back at the mob. The huge Primo Carnera quickly dove into the security offered by the space beneath the ring.

Above his head, the battle raged on. It endured for nearly an hour. Then suddenly, a stillness fell on the great arena. Primo Carnera waited another minute then cautiously crawled out of his hiding place. He looked around him in wonder. The place was deserted. All who could had left, but here and there on the ground and in the rows of seats lay still bodies of men and women who had been shot. There were almost fifty dead and injured left behind in this strangest aftermath of any prize fight ever known in sports history.

Perhaps the strangest of all heavyweight championship fights was the Joe Louis vs. Jersey Joe Walcott title bout of December 5, 1947. Bill Stern discussed an interesting back story to the fight on his radio show. He stated,

When Joe Louis was at his peak as a champion, he had a great deal of trouble keeping sparring partners. One day while preparing for the second Schmeling fight, a husky unknown came seeking a job with the great champion. He was hired at twenty five bucks a day.

The stranger did not prove to be the usual catcher. Joe Louis just couldn't seem to put him on the floor. Not only that, when there was a furious mix up in the middle of the ring, it was Joe Louis who caught a hard blow from the husky stranger and was dumped unceremoniously.

The next day, the sparring partner was out of a job. He was hastily paid off and told to beat it. He left, vowing that somehow, somewhere, he would show the great Joe Louis and the rest of the world that he was a lot better than a sparring partner.

The years went by and the sparring partner who had been fired from Joe Louis' camp tried to win fame in his own right. He wasn't very successful. For years, he fought for handouts in shabby, two bit clubs. Four times he quit the ring in disgust. He was swindled, pushed around, ridiculed. He starved and hungered. His name is Jersey Joe Walcott.

Walcott had an up and down career. His real name was Arnold Cream. He had begun boxing professionally in 1930 at the age of sixteen. He had won some, but by 1940, he had been knocked out three times. He was the father of six children and in 1944, had been so hard pressed that he was on the New Jersey welfare rolls. Joe Louis, on the other hand, had won the heavyweight title in 1937 and successfully defended it twenty three times. Championship bouts were contested at fifteen rounds then. During that span of fights, the Brown Bomber had needed to go the full fifteen round distance only twice. In his last fight before facing Jersey Joe, Louis had knocked out Tami Mauriello in the very first round with a blow that came after a crashing left hook to Mauriello's jaw.

Joe Louis seemed supremely confident. When asked the day before the fight about how he thought it would go, the Brown Bomber replied, "I plan to still be champion, and the fight won't go fifteen rounds." The betting odds were as high as 15 to 1 against Jersey Joe Walcott.

At the opening bell, both fighters started slowly, probing with their left jabs. Then, Louis backed Walcott into a corner and started swinging with both hands. Suddenly, Walcott walked away to his right and crossed over with a short overhand right that dropped Louis to his knees. Up at the count of two, the Brown Bomber charged at Jersey Joe and was staggered by another walk away right hand. Louis fought back savagely, but could not land an effective punch.

The next two rounds were nip and tuck, with Louis pursuing and Walcott counterpunching. Both rounds were close and could have gone either way. Round four opened with Louis still coming forward behind his left jab. Walcott was dancing side to side, using what broadcasters described as a "cakewalk step." Suddenly, Jersey Joe walked away, planted his left foot and nailed Louis with a vicious right to the jaw. The champion went down again. Louis was badly hurt this time, and he stayed down for a count of eight. When the fight resumed, Walcott swung wildly, but the Brown Bomber, who was still shaking the cobwebs out of his head, managed to keep out of trouble for the rest of the round. The round ended with Louis, now fully recovered, chasing Walcott.

Round five began with Louis retreating, but Walcott declined to lead. Louis decided to come forward and Walcott, getting cocky, clowned and slapped Louis backhanded with his right. Referee Ruby Goldstein warned Walcott for his blatant illegal maneuver and the round ended. In rounds six and seven, the pattern remained the same. Louis was the aggressor, but Walcott scored the points.

As Louis came out for the eighth round, his face was swollen on the left side. Walcott was clowning and feinting when he suddenly got a right hand squarely in on Louis' left eye. The eye started to close. Jersey Joe scored with two more rights to the left side of the champion's face as the eighth round ended.

The ninth round found Walcott jumping off his stool and pumping in two more rights to the left side of Joe Louis' face. Louis, in desperation, threw a left hook which cut Walcott over his left eye. Walcott was now in danger, and he began fighting back furiously, chopping Louis with short right hands. Louis suddenly jumped in with a right uppercut and he landed a right cross which hurt Walcott. Louis backed Jersey Joe into the ropes and banged away at him with both hands as the round ended. Everyone in Madison Square Garden seemed to be on their feet.

Walcott came out for the tenth round and resumed his retreat. The tenth round was uneventful except for a long right by Walcott which landed high on Louis' head. In round eleven, Walcott regained his confidence and kept retreating behind his sharp left jab. Louis kept plodding in after his opponent, but could do no damage and caught a savage right for his trouble. The Brown Bomber spent the remainder of the round clearing his head.

Round twelve was more of the same, with Louis moving forward, but Jersey Joe doing all the damage. By the end of the round, Louis' left eye was almost completely closed. Round thirteen was all Walcott's, as he kept on his bicycle, landing his jab at will. Louis continued to plod forward, hoping for the big punch that might turn the tide in his favor. Near the bell, Walcott threw a long right hand, missed and fell down to the canvas. He got up laughing.

After the thirteenth round, Walcott's corner told him that if he stayed away from Louis for the last two rounds, the fight was his. Walcott shuffled one way and then another for the last two rounds of the fight.

It seemed like an eternity before ring announcer Harry Balogh collected the ballots and then grabbed the mike in mid ring. A dejected Joe Louis with a look of defeat on his face tried to climb through the ropes, but his handlers stopped him. Balogh read the scorecards. "Judge Frank Forbes scored the fight eight rounds for Louis, six for Walcott, one even." The crowd booed. "Referee Ruby Goldstein had it seven rounds for Walcott, six for Louis, two even." Cheers went up from the gallery. Then came the final tally. "Judge Marty Monroe had it nine rounds for Louis…" The rest was blotted out by the vociferous crowd expressing their disagreement with the two judges.

In his dressing room, Louis revealed to the reporters that he had hurt one of his hands in the fifth round and that he had been trying to crawl through the ropes because "I was mad at myself for fighting such a bad fight." Walcott was despondent. He was weeping as the reporters entered his dressing room. He said, "I thought I had won. Louis' punches never hurt me. My corner told me I was ahead and to coast in that last round."

The importance of Walcott's mentioning that his corner told him to coast for the final two rounds came to light several years later while Senator Estes Kefauver was conducting a congressional investigation of corruption in boxing. The testimony and exhibits presented during that inquiry revealed that Walcott's manager, Felix Bocchicchio, had a police record dating back to 1927. The charges included white slavery and suspicion of murder. He worked closely with Frank Carbo, a Mob figure who controlled professional boxing. Five years after the Louis versus Walcott bout, Jersey Joe defended his heavyweight crown against Rocky Marciano.

During the early stages of that fight, Bocchicchio, without Walcott's knowledge, had Jersey Joe's corner men smear a mixture of Vaseline and cayenne pepper on their fighter's body while he sat on his stool between rounds. The concoction blinded Marciano and nearly cost him the fight.

This leads to an interesting possibility. Since Bocchicchio had no reluctance to do underhanded things, is it possible that the manager had bet against his own fighter and told him to ease up so he would lose the decision? It wouldn't be the first or last time a manager betrayed his boxer.

There are lessons to be learned from all of this. "Never rely on boxing judges to see things your way." "Scorecards often bring unpleasant surprises." "The only sure thing is a knockout." The most important lesson is that professional boxing is more of a business than a sport. Since there has never been a central authority for prizefighting, underhanded activities became so common that they were accepted as normal. Until there is a "National Boxing League," nothing will change. Even legends of the ring such as Joe Louis, Rocky Marciano and Muhammad Ali were screwed over in one way or another and that will continue until there is some means of reining in the greedy people and bringing more honor to the fight game. Nobody told James Salerno about any of this. He had to learn it the hard way. It wasn't until late in his career that he finally figured it out.

JAMES TURNS PRO WHILE STILL
A HIGH SCHOOL SOPHOMORE

James Salerno's path to turning pro began with his winning the 156 pound open championship in the 1977 Florida Golden Cloves. His victory sent him to the national championships which were held in Hawaii that year. He lost in the nationals, and John Hayden maintained that easy accessibility to marijuana on the island paradise had something to do with James' failure to win the national crown. Anyway, it proved to be the kid's last amateur fight. Sal Salerno explained what happened next when he said,

Almost as soon as he returned from Hawaii, Dom Polo and Bruce Trampler, the matchmaker for the Orlando Sports Stadium, visited Joanne and me in our home. James' amateur record was 157 wins, 17 losses and 89 knockouts. They claimed there was no one left for him to fight as an amateur, so they said it was time for him to sign a pro contract. Joanne was adamantly opposed to it. I could understand why she thought that way. He was her first child and he could be seriously injured as a prizefighter. Dom Polo's argument was, 'He can go to the Olympics, but that's not the way you want to go. He could win a medal and some trophies, but we can start him out as a professional. The way he is going, we can get him fights with journeyman boxers all around the country.' Polo also brought up the point that Pete Ashlock had working agreements with promoters from coast to coast. They gave us the impression that within a couple of years, James could be making a huge amount of money.

Jimmy Williams stated,

I'm the type of guy who can spot a diamond in a rough. The problem is that when a diamond is found, everybody sees it and knows that it is valuable. They all have ideas about what to do with it. When a talented young fighter is discovered, everyone wants to tell them what to do. It then becomes a case of too many cooks spoiling the broth. A lot of the fathers of the boys I trained would get upset with me because I could teach them things that they couldn't teach their sons. They saw how well their boys were doing, but they forgot that they weren't born that way. They failed to recall what their sons were like when they still had two left feet and didn't know their right hands from their left hands.

When Sal told me he was going to allow James to turn pro, I said to him, 'He's your son, so I suppose you have the right to go ahead and destroy him if you want.

I wouldn't do it if I were you.' Parents often do not understand that kids are born through them, not of them. Just because you bring a child into the world, you do not own that child. That is God's child. The child has a mind of their own. The parent's job is to give their children roots and wings to prepare them for the time when they are old enough to make major decisions about their future. The problem with James was that he was allowed to choose to do something at the age of fifteen that had a profound effect on his life. He made a major decision that he wasn't equipped to make and his father went along with it.

Sal had had misgivings and held up on signing anything. When he explained what happened to me, he said, "All along, I had a feeling in the pit of my stomach that down the road, it would all turn sour."

He questioned Dom Polo about the negative aspects of his son turning pro at such a young age, but Polo seemed to have an answer for everything. When Sal learned that his son would not be allowed to fight on television until he was eighteen, Polo assured him, "It won't make any difference. He'll have built up a winning record by then which will drive his price up." Polo's basic theory of managing fighters was to "fight your way up the world rankings, and then they'll have to come to you."

This was faulty reasoning on Polo's part. There was little likelihood of what Dom suggested actually happening. James Salerno would ultimately find it impossible to get a fight that rewarded him with a big pay day. Promoter Don King provided insight on this aspect of the fight game in March, 1979, when he testified during a congressional hearing on the creation of a federal boxing board. King stated,

Boxing is a business predicated on lies. You are dealing with people that very rarely tell the truth. They do not lie just to lie. Their prevarication is in a search for survival.

You have thousands of fighters that are seeking one coveted award. Every enterprising manager must go to the man who is the champion, or one that can get him an opportunity to fight for this award. Instead of saying that his fighter can beat the guy who has the title, he has got to say, 'My fighter is a good kid. This is a pay day for us. Let him go ahead and fight your man. You're going to beat him.' The guy with the title has got to think that he has the advantage in order to take the match.

Unlike all of the major sports which use devices such as playoffs to assure the public that they will see the best opponents compete for the top honors, those who control professional boxing seem do all they can to avoid staging fights that the fans want to see. As it turned out, Polo and Ashlock did not have the clout to look after James Salerno to the extent that a powerful promoter such as Don King or Bob Arum could.

James' mother remained firm in her disapproval of her oldest becoming a professional at such a young age, and Sal didn't like going against Joanne, the love of his life and mother of his children. Sal still hadn't entered into any firm agreement as the end of May, 1977 approached. Ashlock and Polo grew impatient, so they took matters into their own hands.

Even without a written agreement, they scheduled a pro bout for James to take place on May 24, 1977. He was still only fifteen years old and a sophomore at Lake Howell High School. The kid was 6'4" and weighed 171 pounds. When they told the boy about it, he was delirious with joy. For him to be stepping into the ring and launching his pro career was his dream coming true. He could hardly wait to tell his dad about it, and he figured his father would square things with his mother.

When Sal heard the news, he wasn't sure of what to do, so he made the mistake of doing nothing. He made his choice without any words and strictly with his actions. He drove his son to the Sports Stadium on the evening of the fight. Joanne Salerno refused to accompany them because she had made it clear that it was against her wishes.

It is important for a fighter to warm up enough to break a good sweat before their bout. James was clad in his boxing gear and was shadow boxing to make himself perspire. Sal was watching his son warm up when Pete Ashlock and Dom Polo entered the dressing room. There was unfinished business to be settled. They went up to Sal and said, "He doesn't go in the ring unless you sign this paper." The father realized he had gone past the point of no return, so he signed a contract where all the spaces had been left blank, to be filled in later. Sal never received a copy of it.

James' sister, Gina, said,

The way they got my dad to sign the contract almost amounted to blackmail. My mother never liked it. From the very start, she never wanted James to do it. He was her first baby, and it just broke her heart.

James was now a pro, but it was not easy to obtain bouts for the boxing prodigy. What would an established pro have to gain by fighting a fifteen year old? If they lost, they would look foolish. If they won, they might be regarded as a bully. In the beginning, Polo and Trampler were forced to pit the teenage pro against fighters from weight classes other than the kid's.

James' first professional fight was against Henry "Tiger" Hall. The fight was scheduled for a four rounds. It was part of a card that consisted of four professional fights and two pro kick boxing bouts. Hall was a twenty/six/year/old black fighter from Sarasota, Florida who was classified as a middleweight, while James was a light heavyweight. Tiger came into the fight with a record of 2 wins and 10 losses. Hall would end up fighting from 1975 through 1981 and compiling a pro record of 5 wins and 35 losses. He was knocked out 20 times. His most famous opponent was Florida Boxing Hall of Famer Elisha Obed. He fought Obed in April, 1978 and was knocked out in the seventh round. He also fought another Florida Boxing Hall of Fame inductee named Scott "Golden Boy" Clark. Clark was a welterweight who was managed by Ashlock and Polo, just like Salerno. In fact, Polo arranged for Hall to be the Golden Boy's first opponent and later did the same thing for James.

Regardless of Hall's record, it was still a case of a teenage boy going up against a grown man hardened by twelve previous bouts. When asked about Salerno by a sports writer, Dom Polo replied, "We don't intend on babying him. We're putting him in with seasoned pros. He's got all the moves, and I think he'll do just fine."

James set the tempo early by putting Tiger Hall on the canvas in the first round. It was a shock to the Sarasota pro because it was the first time anyone had ever done that to him. Hall quickly realized that his only hope was to muscle inside where the still growing Salerno was the weakest. James foiled that plan by meeting each of Hall's lunges with crisp, sharp combinations. Salerno knocked out Hall's mouthpiece twice and put him on the canvas again in the fourth round. Throughout the entire fight, the veteran pro could not effectively penetrate through the long reach of the high school sophomore. The kid made superb use of his height and reach, and he won the fight by a unanimous decision. After the decision was announced, Dom Polo crowed, "That's my Seattle Slew. He'll be a contender in two years. He looked and moved like a pro and hit Hall with every shot in the book. He really surprised me. I didn't think he could do so much that quick. Mark my words. He'll be a contender in two years."

James was interviewed in his dressing room and proved to be a quote machine, even at his young age. He said to the sports writers, "I wasn't nervous, but I knew he didn't want no fifteen year old kid to beat him. He was really in better shape than me. I knew I couldn't outmuscle him. It was much different than amateur fights. I never hit a guy with so many hard punches before. My knuckles are sore. I wanted to knock him out, but I found out it was not going to be as easy as I thought it would be. Those were the longest four rounds of my life."

Salerno's share of his purse was $175 for the twelve minutes of action he provided the fans. Back then, Ashlock normally paid $100 a round, which meant that James' purse for his four-round baptism into the fight game was $400. Of course, there were deductions made for various expenses. That is also part of professional boxing. When a sports writer asked him what he was going to do with the money, James said, "I'll buy a KD175 trail bike. I can't get a license to drive a car yet. I can't get a beer and I can't get into R-rated movies, but I can still go after the girls."

Jimmy Williams worked in James' corner that night, but wasn't happy with anything that had taken place. He stated,

I knew that once I had built the foundation for James' boxing, everybody would want to take control of him and guide him in a different way. They succeeded in gaining control, and I saw them destroy him. Polo and the others got the boy's head turned by telling him how great he was and that he no longer needed me. They got him to believe that he was born with the skills and philosophy I had taught him. I just shook my head at what they did to that kid. It never fails. When you start to build a house, nobody wants to help you build it. Once it starts raining, though, everybody wants to come in. All of a sudden the kid started telling me what to do. At that point, I knew I had lost him. They took him from me, and he became a tragedy waiting to happen.

THE WINS PILE UP, BUT THE FAMILY
PROBLEMS BECOME WORSE

James Salerno's second pro fight took place on June 14, 1977. He knocked out Mike Rivers in the first round at the Orlando Sports Stadium. Salerno was originally scheduled to take on Eddie Walker of Eustis, Florida, but Rivers was brought in as a last minute replacement. It turned out to be Mike Rivers' first and only fight. This would not be the last time that James would bring an early end to a professional fighter's career.

Two weeks later, on June 28, 1977, James fought Frank Bass, a cruiserweight from Pensacola. Once again, the bout was staged as part of a pro am card at the Orlando Sports Stadium. Bass came into the fight with a 1 and 1 record. Salerno won when the Pensacola fighter was disqualified in the second round.

Dom Polo had no hesitation about scheduling James to fight the very next day, June 29, 1977. James knocked out Billy O'Dell in the first round of a bout, held in Gainesville. For the second time, James ended a pro's career before it got started, since it proved to be O'Dell's only professional fight. Salerno had fought four times and he was still only fifteen years of age. His unbeaten record resulted in his being ranked fifteenth in the nation as a light heavyweight by Ring Magazine.

James celebrated his sixteenth birthday on July 12, 1977 by going the distance in a six round bout at the Orlando Sports Stadium and winning a decision on points. His opponent was Leon Futch, a middleweight from Augusta, Georgia. Leon came into the fight with a 1 and 10 record and his final pro mark was 1 and 12, but he was reputed to be a better fighter than his record indicated.

A little over two weeks later, on July 27, 1977, James fought Billy Rich at the Front Row Theatre in Highland Heights, Ohio. Rich was a middleweight from Camden, New Jersey. They met in a four round bout which went the distance. Salerno won a decision on points, and his victory brought a quick end to Rich's professional aspirations. Billy Rich's final pro record was 1 and 3.

On September 15, 1977, James took on a heavyweight named Charles Cyril Clark at the National Guard Arena in Daytona Beach. Clark had the nickname "Soul Singer Babe." The bout was scheduled for six rounds. It went the distance and James won by a unanimous decision. It was Clark's next to last fight, and he finished his pro career with a record of 6 wins and 16 losses.

Twelve days later, on September 27, 1977, James scored a third round knockout over Willie Chaney at the Orlando Sports Stadium. Chaney's final pro record was 4 and 15.

As James' career progressed, some critics stated that he lacked a power punch. Jimmy Williams' response to that was,

Muhammad Ali had no power punch, but he got a lot of knockouts. Power punchers are not going to knock you out with one punch. Ali knocked men out by throwing combinations. He did what I call 'romancing' his opponents. He would make them miss and when they got tired, he would knock them out. Ali was not the type of fighter who would step out of his corner and knock his opponent out with a single blow. He would float like a butterfly and sting like a bee. His secret was in being evasive. Making a guy miss you causes just as much damage as hitting him. If you box your opponent for two or three rounds and make him miss, he'll get discouraged. He burns up energy, and then you knock him out. That's the way that I taught James to fight, and he became a master at it.

The more success James enjoyed in the ring, the more difficult it became for his parents to deal with him. He would ignore their orders, and sometimes talk back to them. He often argued with his father, but never raised his voice. Thankfully, there were never any instances of screaming or violence.

After James quit high school during his sophomore year, Joanne insisted that he enroll at Seminole Community College to get a GED. Enrolling was one thing, but getting him to attend class was another. When James' mother received the inevitable phone call informing her that her son had not been at school for weeks, she realized his days of formal education were over. .

Sal and Joanne's relationship with their oldest son became a roller coaster. They would endure exasperating moments and then James would say to a TV reporter or a sports writer, "I want to thank my parents for everything. I couldn't do anything without them." When they heard that, their hearts would melt and they would experience a moment of happiness that would carry them through until the next upsetting incident. They found themselves having to deal with a man child who knew how to push their buttons.

Even though he was expecting to be treated as an adult with his own income, he had no idea of how to handle money. His aunt, Jeanie Salerno, said,

When it came to money, if James had it, he would spend it and then borrow some more from somebody else. If you needed money, he'd give you ninety percent of what he had. He was the most giving person you would ever know in your whole life.

Joanne Salerno talked about how generous her son was when she said,

When the holidays rolled around, he would go out and mow lawns. He would then take the money he made, buy turkeys, take them down to a black section and give them to poor people living in little shacks. He would also use his earnings to buy dolls and other toys, take them to Church Street and give them to black kids who wouldn't otherwise have any Christmas presents, bless his heart.

Joanne added,

He never had a checking account or credit card during his entire life. If he had ever had them, he probably would have either lost them or would have been overdrawn all the time. He would leave a lot of his cash at home. If he knew he was going out with friends, he would go to his Aunt Jeanie and ask her to hold his money for him until he got back. When it came right down to it, he was like a two year old in many ways.

The boy had been accepted by the men involved in a brutal, violent profession as one of their own. His tragic flaw was that he lacked the maturity of judgment needed to become a person who could be relied upon to do the right thing. He had opted for the college of hard knocks, but it was not an accredited institution of higher learning that could teach him what he needed to succeed in life.

BOYS WILL BE BOYS IN MIAMI BEACH

James was a success in the ring, but his home life had become a disaster. Sal provided more specifics about the situation when he stated,

Unfortunately, the publicity and attention had gone to James' head. My wife and I had to raise Gina and Matthew, and we could no longer put up with our oldest son's behavior. Even though he was underage, he wanted to come and go as he pleased. Since he was a professional athlete, he felt he could do anything he wanted. I really don't think he cared about how much he was paid to fight at that point. We never saw any of the money he was being paid, and he used our home strictly as a headquarters.

It could not go on like that, so Sal went to see Pete Ashlock to discuss the situation. They talked about James permanently moving into one of the houses behind the stadium, but the father didn't think that would improve the teenager's conduct. Dom Polo was in control of James' boxing career at that point. Jimmy Williams had very little say about what the boy would do, and that was how Polo wanted it. Sal believed that James would respect, listen to and obey Angelo Dundee, since Dundee was Muhammad Ali's trainer. Pete Ashlock had a working agreement with the Chris and Angelo Dundee, so after some discussion, Ashlock made a deal with the two brothers in Miami Beach to take over James' contract.

The Salerno's drove to Miami, met with the brothers and discussed their son's future. Angelo was most impressed with Joanne. He told her, "You're going to be rewarded in Heaven for what you've gone through."

Jimmy Williams said:

Angelo was the trainer and his older brother Chris was the promoter. Chris ran the Fifth Street Gym, and he was constantly there. He was the money guy and the head of the operation. Angelo would be busy training their fighters, being away at training camps or being on the road for fights. Angelo's most outstanding talents were as a cut man and a psychologist. He had a knack for coming up with just the right thing to say to a fighter at a crucial point in a bout.

The plan was for James to move to Miami Beach right away and then be joined by John Hayden after he graduated from high school in late fall. By then, James would be settled in. Sal and Joanne believed that John Hayden was a level headed young man and would be a good influence on their son. The Dundee's would arrange housing for the two teenagers. They would be charged rent, but the Chris and Angelo would find work for the boys which would hopefully provide for their food and shelter, keep them occupied while they weren't training and also teach them some responsibility.

It was a plan that was doomed to failure because the town offered far too many temptations. Legendary middleweight champion Jake La Motta not only fought in Miami Beach, but also lived in that city and once operated a nightclub there. He knew the place well. In his autobiography Raging Bull, La Motta stated,

There is one thing you've got to understand about Miami Beach. You don't go there for culture. You go there for a good time, which means broads and booze to start with. Then some betting of one kind or another, and from there on, you're on your own. Now, the city fathers of the Beach, elected or not, understand this perfectly. The problem they face is that if things get too rough, the local yokels who pay the taxes start raising hell and something has to be done. A little scandal and sin they don't mind because that's what brings the tourists down. Take my word for it, whether you arrive in Miami Beach and it is running wide open or whether a reform wave is rolling high, you can get anything from babes to dope, if you know where to look. You don't have to look too hard, either.

La Motta, who was known as the Bronx Bull, had written of a time that existed twenty years before James and John were living on the Beach, but nothing had really changed. The babes and dope were just as plentiful, if not more so.

During his first day at the Fifth Street Gym, James became friends with Lee Canalito and Vinnie Curto, who were two other members of the Dundee brothers' stable. At 6' 5", Canalito was just as tall as James, but he was a heavyweight. He was quite a bit older than Salerno; there was an age difference of eight years. Lee had originally been a football player. He was an all-state lineman at Sterling High School in Houston in 1972. After graduation, he enrolled at the University of Houston. He played two seasons at defensive tackle for the Cougars under legendary coach Bill Yeoman. Canalito's football career was derailed by a knee injury.

Lee then took up boxing and became practically an overnight sensation. He won the heavyweight title in the Houston Golden Gloves and turned professional after fighting only seven amateur bouts. By the time James met him, Canalito was 7 and 0, with six KO's to his credit. He had fought four and six round bouts in Louisville, Las Vegas and Savannah, Georgia. Lee was billed as the "Italian Stallion" and was being groomed as a Great White Hope who would soon lay claim to the world heavyweight crown.

Lee Canalito said,

James Salerno had a very outgoing personality and was very good at his Muhammad Ali impressions. He was a helluva guy and a helluva a fighter. I used to spar with James. Angelo Dundee would say, 'Lee, I want you to work with James because he's very fast.' Even though I was a heavyweight and he was a light heavyweight, we worked very well together. He was very quick. He had great footwork. He would glide left and glide right. He would throw multiple jabs and then hook off the jab. He was a rare talent. Angelo was always talking about him. Angelo said, 'The kid has all kinds of talent.' I recall that Lou Gross used to work with him too.

James, Vinnie Curto and I always used to have breakfast together at Wolfie's delicatessen. Sometimes we would have lunch there after a workout and sit and talk. We would make comments about how each of us looked that day. We would bring each other down to earth with comments like, 'You looked like hell today.' We were keeping each other humble. All three of us were known by the servers for ordering burnt toast and coffee with peanut butter on the side. That was what we ate on mornings when we had weigh ins. It sounds like a strange meal, but it was actually very good. A fighter can throw punches like Muhammad Ali after having some burnt toast and coffee with a little peanut butter.

I'll never forget the time a customer didn't want to pay his bill because he didn't like the food or the service. He got into an argument with the manager and became so upset that he pulled out a .22 pistol. Vinnie Curto happened to be sitting at the counter and he leaped into action. He dove at the armed man, shoved his gun hand out of the way and then knocked the guy out with a right hand shot and a left hook. The police were called and they hauled the guy away. It was a very risky thing for Vinnie to do, but the three of us laughed about it for two years.

When that incident occurred, Canalito and Salerno were unaware of a deep, dark secret that Vinnie carried within him about his parents. In 2013, Vinnie Curto was interviewed by Robert Ecksel of Boxing.Com. Curto told Ecksel that he had been sexually abused by his alcoholic father from the time he was a little kid. The father would become a monster when he was drunk. Vinnie had been told that his father had served in the United States Marine Corps during World War II and was discharged on disability after suffering a fractured skull. As time went on, Curto eventually learned the truth. His dad was not injured while performing assigned duties. His skull was fractured because of his sexual preference. That was the way gay men were dealt with by Marines back then. Vinnie's mother was a lesbian, and his parents had married in order to hide their sex lives. Curto stated, "My grandfather would have put a bullet in his son's head if he had found out that he was a homosexual."

If being molested by his father wasn't a big enough burden to carry, Vinnie Curto's parents also turned out to have a complete lack of honor. Vinnie stated,

When I turned pro and I was fighting, I was making some money. It wasn't a fortune, but it was a decent amount. My father forced me to live like an animal because he took all of it. He used to come down to Miami Beach every time I fought and grab the check. He'd tell me, 'I'm investing the money for you.' I was living in a one room shack that was the cheapest place I could find. Angelo Dundee and Dr. Ferdie Pacheco couldn't understand why I lived in such a horrible place. They'd ask, 'What the hell's wrong with you?' I couldn't tell them that my father was taking all my money.

He bought a lot of properties, but I never saw any of it. My parents cheated me out of everything my father bought with my money. They also cheated me out of property that my grandfather left me by forging my name to legal documents, selling it and keeping the money. I didn't learn about it until after my father died. When I found out, I told my mother, 'I'm gonna expose you and Dad and have you arrested.' She said, 'Go ahead. I'm too old to go to jail.' She believed she was above the law. She died two months later. She left me two hundred dollars. I'm surprised she left me anything.

Curto, the courageous 5' 7" middleweight from Boston, had an outstanding boxing career. In spite of all the adversity in his life, he still compiled a record of 62 wins, ten losses and three draws. At one point, Sylvester Stallone was his manager. His last fight was on September 20, 1996. He won a twelve round decision over Jimmy Haynes in Lincoln, Nebraska that earned Curto the WBF super cruiserweight title. Vinnie retired as a champion. Not many fighters can say that.

Curto fervently believes in the positive things about the sport he devoted so much of his life to. Vinnie said,

Boxing was nothing but a helper for me. Boxing was my best friend. It saved my life and it's going to save millions of others. Make no mistake about it, boxing is an all around good guy. Even if you don't become champion, it gives you discipline.

It makes you believe in yourself when nobody else does. Time and truth, no matter how far apart, always come together; and everyone who steps into a ring faces a moment of truth.

Lee Canalito also did some remarkable things. Like Curto, Sylvester Stallone managed Canalito's fighting career for awhile. Lee compiled a pro boxing record of 21 and 0, with 18 knockouts. He retired unbeaten, which few fighters can say. He enjoyed an acting career and had a featured role in the Sylvester Stallone movie Paradise Alley.

Things happened quickly once James was in Miami Beach. Shortly after his arrival, on Friday night, March 16, 1979, he fought on a card at the Savannah Civic Center in Savannah, Georgia. He faced veteran pro Henry "Slick" Mitchell. Mitchell came into the bout with a record of 25 wins, 42 losses and a draw. James carried only 168 pounds on his 6' 5" frame and knew he couldn't out muscle the much older man. He stayed away from Slick, boxed some and went after his opponent in the corners. Mitchell hoped to slow down the slender youngster's onslaught by spending the whole fight hanging on the ropes, covering up and then throwing wild, vicious uppercuts and body punches. His ploy worked only to a slight degree. Slick connected with some of his body punches, but James was too quick for the journeyman boxer and evaded the majority of them. Salerno's jabs and inside work wore away at his opponent, and Slick went down in the sixth, seventh rounds and eighth rounds. Since a three knockdown rule was in effect, referee Jacky Cranford stopped the fight and Salerno was awarded a technical knockout. When he was interviewed after the bout, James said to the sports writers, "Slick forced me to change my style. I usually like my opponent to come at me, and I hit them as I back away, but he forced me to go inside. I'm going to be a heavyweight when I'm through. Lee Canalito says I'll be bigger than he is. Stallone wasn't the real Italian Stallion. That's who I'm going to be."

Three months later, James received international publicity, thanks to the efforts of his father. In June, 1979, Sal was able to get video he had shot of James' Golden Gloves triumph into the hands of a man who lived in Orlando, had seen James fight several times and was with NBC Sports. The kid was seventeen at the time and had twenty pro fights under his belt. The story of a boxing prodigy becoming a teenage pro interested the decision makers at 30 Rock, and they scheduled an appearance on Good Morning America. The show was normally hosted by Sandy Hill in those years, but it worked out that James would be interviewed by Hugh Downs. NBC paid James and his father's airfare and booked them into a room at the Central Park Ritz-Carlton Hotel. He was set to appear live the day before a heavyweight title fight in Madison Square Garden between Larry Holmes and Mike Weaver.

A breaking news story about the tragic death of an NBC foreign correspondent prevented the interview from taking place. The network still wanted to put James on because they knew his story would have wide appeal, so they moved Salerno's appearance forward to the day of the fight.

It was big news in Orlando because it was the first time a homegrown athlete had received so much exposure. Larry Barfield was sixteen years old at the time and he was allowed to miss school so he could stay home and watch the interview. In recalling that day, Larry said, "For a local high school age kid who had fought twenty pro bouts to be on national TV was one of the biggest things to happen in town. It got everyone's attention. His interview was seen by people all over the world. Because of it, James received duffel bags full of fan mail from women in several different countries. "

During the live interview, Hugh Downs mentioned that James was not allowed to appear in televised bouts he was eighteen. James responded by saying, "I'll be eighteen in a few weeks, but until then, the American public is being denied opportunities to see the best white fighter of all." Downs then asked his guest if he was going to be the next Great White Hope, James replied, "I don't want to be a White Hope. I want to be a fact."

Near the end of the interview, James talked about how important it was to "have the right people behind you." It was a prophetic statement. Over the course of his professional career, none of Salerno's managers and promoters would be able to arrange a big pay day for him. In that respect, James never had the right people behind him.

It so happened that many writers were in town to cover the heavyweight title fight in Madison Square Garden. They caught the conversation James had with Hugh Downs and were captivated by the tall white teenage pro from Florida with the rock star looks. They loved the kid's brash attitude. As a result of the TV appearance, James and his father were invited to attend the fight and sit with the working press.

James had suddenly become a hot topic. Just before the championship bout got underway, Don King took the microphone and asked prominent boxers in attendance to step up into the ring and be honored by the fans. The Salerno's were surprised when King asked James to join the others in the ring and take a bow. The legendary promoter called James "my great white hope."

The Dundee brothers liked the publicity, but James' sudden high profile also created a difficulty when Don King quickly tried to take over James' contract. The Dundee's held firm, and Sal Salerno stuck with them. In hindsight, it might have been better for James to have been managed by King, since he has proven to be powerful enough to arrange big pay days for his fighters.

John Hayden joined the celebrity teenage pro in Miami Beach on December 1, 1979. By then, Joanne Salerno had loaned James her 1980 Cutlass Salon to use while he and John were living on the Beach. It had practically no miles on it and still had its new car smell. The two of them doubled up in the housing Chris Dundee had arranged, which was an efficiency apartment in the faded Henry Hotel on Washington Avenue. Chris gave them a break on the rent, but would stop by each month to pick up money from James. Their room was more like a cubicle than an apartment. It had a battered dresser, a refrigerator and a Bunsen burner to use in place of a stove. It had only one king size bed with a single bedspread, which the two friends shared.

The hotel was across the street from Howie's Bar and was a couple of doors down from Irish Mike's Show Bar. Next to Irish Mike's was the Paris Theater, where five bucks was the price of admission for two skin flicks. It was hardly a neighborhood for unsupervised teenage boys to live.

When John Hayden first arrived in town, he went to work at a Howard Johnson's as a dish washer. James, meanwhile, was employed in a security job at the Fontainbleu Hotel, the most historically and architecturally significant hotel in Miami Beach. James would use the Cutlass to drop John off and pick him up from work.

One night, James had to break up a party at the hotel because a guest had complained about the noise. When he went to the room which the revelers were occupying, he discovered that they had sensimilla reefer. Sensimilla was James and John's favorite strain of pot. The partiers also had cocaine. James took advantage of the situation and shook them down for some of their drugs. He didn't let on that he wasn't going to report them anyway. After they gave James some pot, he appeased the guest who had complained and then went about his business. After work, he shared the goodies with John and they partied.

Not long after that, Chris Dundee arranged for John and James to work as dishwashers at Joe's Stone Crab Restaurant. It was a high end restaurant that attracted celebrities such as Lucille Ball and Muhammad Ali. James and John were paid $7.49 per hour, which was good pay for that type of job. They worked a seven-hour shift, but were paid for eight hours. They worked from 5:00 P.M. to 12:00 A.M. Before each shift, all of the dishwashers would sit down as a group and eat. The free meals were a way of discouraging the help from stealing food. It was a pretty good job, but it was seasonal. It only lasted during the fall and winter months.

Some of the other dishwashers were Hispanic street kids. One of them became jealous of James and John because they were training to be professional boxers. John Hayden later recalled,

The street kid became angry with me one night over some stupid stuff and threat-ened to gut me. For the next couple of nights, I had to watch my back. James was also in danger because the way we normally took when walking home was through an alley. We both had to be very careful because we were concerned that they guy would try to jump us and knife us. Fortunately, nothing happened and the His-panic cooled off.

Hayden also said,

James' wardrobe began to reflect his mood. If he felt like a tough guy, he would wear a tattered sweatshirt and a red headband. He'd also let peach fuzz sprout on his chin. If he felt stylish, he'd wear a white suit, black shirt and a Gatsby hat.

It wasn't surprising that women became interested in the tall teenager with the film star looks. James began dating a single mother named Lana who had one child. She was blonde, of Russian descent and very attractive, almost a Marilyn Monroe look alike.

Hayden said of her,

She was about three years older than James. He usually went over to her place to see her. She slept with James and was even bold enough to give him oral sex in a park by the water. Their affair didn't last long. Like all of his relationships with women, he lost interest once he had gotten all the sex he wanted and would move on.

John Hayden added,

After breaking up with the blonde Russian single mom, James began a strange re-lationship with Cecile Melleto. Her friends called her Ceil. She and her mother hung out on the corners near the bar and movie theater next to the hotel where we

lived. Both of them were selling their bodies to support their drug habits, as well as those of Ceil's brother. Ceil was short, but hardly petite. She wasn't fat, but she was really built, with strong looking legs and backside. To be more precise, she was around 5'2" and about 125 pounds. Her body was more desirable than her facial features. She had dark hair that was somewhere between brown and black. She might have been Italian, but James never found out for sure. She wasn't ugly by any means, but she wasn't drop dead gorgeous either. Ceil's mom was a little thinner, probably because of all her drug use. She was also about 5'2". The mother was at least twenty years older than Ceil and not at all attractive.

James not only began spending time with her, he also invited her to move into the room we were sharing, which didn't have much space to begin with. This resulted in strange sleeping arrangements, with three people now sharing the king sized bed. We both slept with her, but Ceil would only have sex with James. This went on for a while until, out of loyalty to a friend, James asked Ceil to do him a big favor and screw me. She agreed to do so, but that was the first and only time. I was on my own after that.

A few months later, we upgraded to a two room unit in a nearby hotel, but it wasn't that much of an improvement. At least it had twin beds, a refrigerator and an actual stove, but the bathroom lacked a window. Since there was an additional bed, James asked Ceil's mom to join the three of us. He and Ceil would have sex in one bed while the mother and me occupied the other. I tried to have sex with the mother, but she wouldn't give it up. I guess even drug addicted whores have standards.

In recalling this period of her oldest son's life, Joanne Salerno said,

He was always telling us that his television sets were being taken from him. We sent three TV's down there. His grandmother Nancy, his father and I all chipped in to give him $150 for his eighteenth birthday. The next thing we heard, somebody swiped it from his wallet, so we sent him another $150.

Years later, the truth came out. James had gotten into a habit of selling things and then telling stories so that he could obtain money to replace them. Nothing had been stolen from him. When he needed cash, he would do just about anything to get it, including manipulating his parents and grandmother. Ceil had introduced him to a lifestyle he enjoyed, but he needed cash to support that lifestyle.

Joanne Salerno added, "We didn't approve of what he was doing. He wasn't brought up like that. Somewhere along the way, I felt that I lost my little boy."

Ceil was hardly the sort of girl you would take home to mother, but James still brought her to Winter Park to meet his mother and father. The visit took place in 1979 while James was in training for a fight. Joanne later recalled,

Ceil slept with James in his bedroom. I happened to walk into the room and found two big bottles of liquor. I started raising hell with the both of them. I said, 'He's supposed to be training, and this is what he's doing?' Ceil was bad news, just like all the people he was hanging around then. He always seemed to pick the losers.

The worst part about James' relationship was that from all indications, Ceil was the one who introduced James to cocaine. It was like introducing him to the grim reaper. Both Ceil's mom and her brother died of overdoses on the same day, and the drug would eventually be the cause of James Salerno's tragic demise.

YOU CAN'T WIN 'EM ALL.

James' twenty fourth professional fight matched him with Leon McDonald. It was staged in the Miami Beach Auditorium. McDonald was nine years older than Salerno and had led a much harder life. The fight took place only seven months after he had been released from the Florida state prison at Raiford. He had served ten years in a prison reserved for those accused of felonies who ask for a trial rather than accept a plea bargain and are convicted. McDonald had been found guilty of rape and sentenced to ninety years. He was only eighteen years old at the time and claimed innocence, but he had been through other scrapes with the law. The jurors just didn't believe him, and the rape conviction appeared to close the books on his life. Leon later said to sports writers, "They told me I was doomed. They said I'd never get out."

Boxing turned out to be his salvation. He was four years into his sentence when he began boxing at Raiford and became very good at it. During the February prior to his release, Leon won the Florida Caribbean Light Heavyweight Golden Cloves title in the open division. He had a 17-0 amateur record, but he was not permitted to attend the national Golden Gloves tournament in Indianapolis. When questioned by boxing writers, Leon explained what happened by saying, "They were afraid I'd escape. Plus, I had a parole hearing coming up." He missed the nationals, but he gained much more when the parole hearing went well and he won his freedom.

Once he was outside the walls, Leon immediately joined Georgie Small's boxing stable in Ft. Lauderdale. The Nightlife Club of Ft. Lauderdale, a social club of Broward County businessmen, took Leon under its wing. They sponsored him and gave him his nickname. He was given a maintenance job at the club and also performed volunteer work at the Broward Juvenile Hall. On the day before he faced Salerno, McDonald said, "I'm twenty seven and got maybe four years of boxing left. I don't think I'm that far away from a shot at the light heavyweight title."

He also claimed that two Miami Beach boxing commissioners felt the fight was a mismatch. After all, James had 23 straight wins and 18 knockouts. McDonald's record was only 6 and 1, and he had been knocked out in the fight just before his bout with James. Leon added, "No one should underestimate me. I know no one loves losers. I have been a loser. I never want to be a loser again."

The ex-convict trained at Tiger's Gym thirty miles up the highway from Miami Beach at Ft. Lauderdale. Leon wound down after two weeks of training by going through a vigorous pre fight workout early in the afternoon of the fight. McDonald told the sports writers who stopped by, "I sparred nine rounds a day for two weeks. Some of those rounds were with Michael 'Dynamite' Dokes. He's an unbeaten heavyweight. I've hit the heavy bag eight rounds a day. I've run day and night." He was leaving nothing to chance because his bout with Salerno was his biggest pro fight to date. While in prison, he was Leon McDonald, inmate number 027050. He was now boxing as Leon "Nightlife" McDonald.

James made a serious mistake by approaching the fight in the wrong frame of mind. He boasted late in the afternoon before the bout, "I'm getting mean and nasty for this fight." He went to the Fifth Street Gym for a brief workout, joked with some friends there and then left for his dishwashing job. One of his friends in the gym asked , "You're going straight from your job to the fight?" Salerno nodded yes and said, "I'm taking tomorrow night off. That's when I'll celebrate."

When Leon entered the ring late that night, James taunted him by saying: "You're a chump, McDonald. I'm gonna knock you out." As referee Bill Conners gave the fighters their instructions in the middle of the ring, James stared icily into McDonald's eyes. Leon did the same. Neither fighter wanted to be the first one to end the staring contest and return to their corner. Their faces drew to within inches of each other and then the twenty seven year old former prison inmate made the first move. He leaned even closer and kissed eighteen year old James Salerno. After planting the kiss, Leon Mc Donald said in a voice loud enough for onlookers to hear, "I love you too." For once in his life, the Mouth of the South was at a loss for words. He had no idea of how to top the stunt Nightlife pulled.

The fight developed into a brutal contest that featured a few thumb jabs and head butts. McDonald's first head butt occurred in the second round. The most spectacular blow occurred when Leon turned James' nose into a red gusher early in the fourth round. Moments later, the ex con followed with a right cross that kissed Salerno's chin and sent him bouncing off the canvas. He recovered and fought gamely after that. McDonald began to tire in the sixth round while Salerno was wearing a blood red moustache beneath his nose. Later in that round, James lost a point for a head butt. By then, his white trunks had turned brown from blood and sweat. Patches of blood coated McDonald's hair by the seventh round, and his right eye had begun to close by the eighth round. His manager Georgie Small turned into a pot bellied cheerleader between the rounds, screaming at Leon, "You're not tired! Go on and fight!"

The bout went the full ten rounds and when the war in the ring was over, the fate of the two combatants was placed in the hands of two judges and Florida Boxing Hall of Fame Bill Conners. Conners and judge Cy Gottfried voted for Leon, but judge Bernie Soto gave a slight edge to Salerno When it was announced that Leon "Nightlife" McDonald was awarded a split decision, the crowd of 2,000 in attendance were not pleased. They felt McDonald had won the bout outright. McDonald was happy to get a win any way he could and he was jubilant after the decision was announced. He bowed to the crowd and then trotted off to the dressing room.

Salerno was stunned at the way the night had gone for him. For the first time in his professional career, James left the ring a loser. He began a lonely walk back to his dressing room. Some fans taunted him and he became overly sensitive to their insults. He turned around and walked back into the empty ring. He picked up the microphone and announced to those who remained, "I want a rematch! I want a rematch with Nightlife Mc-Donald right now!" It was not something a veteran prizefighter would do. He was acting like a kid, and the crowd booed him again. He finally left the ring and headed to the dressing room.

A sports writer was waiting for him as he stepped into his dressing quarters. When the writer asked him what happened, James said it was too demanding to work and train to fight at the same time, but he needed the job to pay his rent. James also stated, "Yesterday, Chris Dundee paid up the rent I owed to a South Beach hotel. My share of the purse is $500, and it will all go to pay Chris back."

When the sports writer left, James sat there alone. His nose was sore. His cheeks, his chest and his back were scratched and battered. His pride was bruised. He was a frustrated and confused eighteen-year-old. His unbeaten streak was over and there would be no celebrating.

One door down in another dressing room, Leon McDonald savored the victory with his right hand stuck in an ice bucket. He had an ice pack on his head. A group of friends had gathered around him. Leon said, "My hand, my eye and my teeth all hurt, but inside it feels oh so good."

Leon was interrupted by a visit from James. Salerno groped for words, then he said, "We both wanted that fight. The mind games and the punches proved you had heart, brother. You were the better man." Immediately after saying that, he turned quickly and left.

After James had gone, Leon McDonald said, "He underestimated me tonight, but he's going to be some fighter. He has guts. The fight was good for me and it was probably good for him. We both learned something about ourselves." He put his hand back in the ice and closed his eyes. A trace of a smile cracked his lips as he thought of the good life. He was actually getting a taste of it.

Years later, James looked back on that fight and stated,

I lost the bout by one point. I had beaten everyone I had fought and thought I could beat anyone. I had a big head and didn't train hard. I was out in the streets, hanging out with a bad crowd, and staying up all night. Mc Donald was an ex-con, just out of prison and tough. He knocked me down, and that was the first time I had ever been knocked down. He also injured my nose. I got up and gave him a helluva fight.

Sal Salerno was there to witness his son's first professional loss. In recalling the bout, he said,

As the fight progressed, I asked myself, 'What in the world is James doing?' He was half a step slow and it looked as though he was trying to get hit on purpose. I had no idea at the time that he was using drugs. After I learned about his substance abuse problem, I understood what happened during the McDonald fight. The drugs were slowing him down and affecting his mind and his reflexes. I had to do something drastic to save my son from drugs.

It was a time of crisis for the Salerno family in more ways than one. Joanne had filed for divorce. As years went by, Sal and Joanne reconciled, and they are still back together.

Sal met with Angelo Dundee, and they came up with a plan. They arranged for both James and John Hayden to enlist in the United States Marine Corps. Dundee said there was a good chance they could become part of the Marine Corps boxing team. It would hopefully keep James away from drugs. It was also give him time to physically mature and possibly add enough bulk to fight as a heavyweight. Heavyweight fights usually bring bigger pay days. Salerno and Hayden entered the Corps in March, 1980.

JAMES' TIME WITH THE
UNITED STATES MARINE CORPS

A couple of months into the project, I received a welcome assist when James' mother found his unfinished memoir among items that had been stored away for decades. His handwritten manuscript began at the point when he and John Hayden had completed boot camp at Parris Island and were returning to their base after a ten day leave. They barely made it back in time to avoid being AWOL and almost didn't make it at all. James was driving the 1980 Trans Am that Sal had given to use. He wrote,

I was driving over the speed limit. I lost control and went into a spin. The Trans Am slid across the median into oncoming traffic that was headed in the direction opposite to where we were going. It was lucky for us that all the cars on that side of the highway swerved to avoid us. It scared the shit out of John and me. After that experience, we made it to Parris Island without further incident.

John was assigned to stay at Parris Island. His duties were to assist in fitting uniforms for recruits. I was sent to Camp Lejeune in North Carolina. It was the home of the United States Marine Corps varsity boxing team, but that was not what the Marine Corps had planned for me. My final destination was a hot, sweaty warehouse. We were ordered to load three hundred pound barrels onto trucks all day long. While I was working, I was telling the other Marines, 'I'm gonna be on the boxing team.' Many of my co-workers just laughed at me.

I finally got a chance to speak with J.C. Davis, who was the head coach of the team, in his office. I knew I would only have a couple of minutes, so I began to tell him a very short version of my life story. He cut me off after a minute or so by leaning back in his chair and waving his right hand. Coach Davis said, "I don't have to hear all that. Be in the gym tomorrow. You're going to spar with MacDonald.' Jim MacDonald was the All Marine Champion at 165 and one half pounds.

There was a lot riding on that sparring session, as far as I was concerned. I had to beat MacDonald or go back to the warehouse and all the three hundred pound barrels. Jim and I sparred for three rounds, and I impressed J.C. Davis enough that he called me into his office and said, 'Look, I got two more weeks and then I retire. My trainer, Gunnery Sergeant Waldo, is moving up to my position. I'm going to have orders cut for you to replace him as trainer.' It sounded too good to be true.

It didn't happen right away. A few weeks went by before I received written orders which stated, 'To Private James Salerno: Report to Base Special Services to serve as trainer for the United States Marine Corps varsity boxing team.' I was so happy that I kissed the paper the orders were typed on. I had achieved the position which was the reason for my enlisting in the Corps.

Because he was exceptionally handsome and looked so good in his dress blues, James was also assigned to serve in the Honor Guard for Regimental Head-quarters, which was a coveted assignment. His position with the boxing team brought him even more benefits. He wrote in his memoir,

We were privileged. We ran in the morning, ate when we wanted to eat and trained each day at either noon or two o'clock in the afternoon. We didn't have to wear uniforms. Everybody at Camp Lejeune was jealous of the way the boxers were treated. The ones who were jealous didn't understand that we trained harder than anyone else on base and were in the best physical condition of all the Marines.

John Hayden tried out for the boxing team. Out of 67 men, he was one of seven chosen for the squad. John fought in the 160 pound division.

James wrote,

The competition to make the boxing team and remain on it made for better fighters. I was unique because I was only eighteen but had a 23 and 1 professional record. No one else on the team was in my class as a fighter, but all I did was train and spar. We had some good fighters, such as John Hayden, Kenny Stigler, Frankie Warren, Jim MacDonald, Terry Anderson and Guy Sonenberg."

Other than John Hayden, the only fighter I hung out with was Jim MacDonald. He always told me, 'The way you box, you're going to be a world champion.' Jim would also come up with clever money making schemes. One time, he bought a tin toy for two dollars. He put it in a bucket of water and kept the bucket in a closest until the toy became rusty. When there was enough rust on it to suit him, we went to an antique show in Jacksonville, North Carolina. We told the people there that the toy had been passed on to Jim by his great grandmother and that it had been made in the 1870's. A man who claimed to be an expert on antiques offered forty dollars for it. We took the money and laughed all the way as we drive back to the base in Sal's Trans Am with extra spending money in our pockets.

Serving in the Marine Corps prevented James from taking any prizefights until the middle of 1981. He wrote,

After the Marines finally allowed me to fight, my first bout was a rematch with Leon McDonald on July 10, 1981. It was scheduled for twelve rounds and was held in Miami. It was the first time I ever had to fight that many rounds. It was a mistake to take the fight. I had no one to train me and no one to spar with. Out of desperation, I tried to use some basketball players to spar with me.

After I got down there, I got bored. I was by myself. With no trainer to help keep me focused, I wound up contacting Cecile Melleto on the day before the fight. I asked her what she was doing, and she came right over to the hotel where I was staying. I had not had any sex since my enlisting in the Marine Corps, and I gave into lust. It's not that I think sex is bad, but the day before a fight is the not the time for it. I was not in the proper frame of mind on the night of the fight. In addition to the sex, I had not fought in eighteen months. Dominick Polo and Angelo Dundee worked in my corner, but they couldn't work magic in just one night. I went the full twelve rounds, but lost a unanimous decision.

Upon returning to Camp Lejeune, James was informed that he was being sent to Okinawa, Japan. This would have thrown a monkey wrench into his plans to continue his professional boxing career. He decided to leave the Marine Corps. He was very fortunate to arrange a meeting with the general who was in command of Camp Lejeune. James wrote,

I said to the general, 'The Marine Corps has had a positive influence on me, and I believe I have had a positive influence on the men who are on the boxing team.' He agreed with that. I then said, 'Unfortunately, I feel that my talents are going to waste. I also have a major concern because my mother is going through a divorce and is having a very hard time.' My mother's situation resulted in my being granted an honorable discharge, with all the benefits that are included.

A PERSONAL CRISIS NEARLY DESTOYS JAMES' LIFE

James returned to Orlando and found that Pete Ashlock's Orlando Sports Stadium was no longer in operation. Jimmy Williams was running the Church Street Gym, which was located in Orlando's black neighborhood. He was getting funding from CETA, and was doing a lot of good things for young men in that community. Williams was on the front lines, and it was a labor of love for him. Salerno began working out there daily. He wrote,

I was the only white person in the gym. This made me feel special. I became determined to have more groove or rhythm than any other fighter in the place. Jimmy had some good fighters training there. They included Chris Wells, Greg Young, Jerry Holly and Bruce Johnson. Johnson had just pulled a big upset by beating Tony Braxton in Tampa in a fight that was shown on NBC. He was THE star in Orlando at that time. It felt great to be back with Jimmy again.

The boxing was coming along, but James was headed for a personal crisis that nearly destroyed his life. It all began near the end of his hitch in the Marine Corps, when he happened to be at a tattoo parlor near the base. He had kept pictures of himself with a stunning blonde girl from back in Orlando on his dresser. He impulsively decided to get a tattoo in honor of her. James explained where that led when he wrote,

As I was looking around in the tattoo parlor, it dawned on me that I loved her. I should have taken some time to think before acting but being the idiot that I was, I had a tattoo placed right above my heart. It consisted of her name, and it had a little heart on it. I couldn't wait to show it to her when I got home from the Marine Corps.

Things did not work out as he had hoped. Salerno wrote.

I brought her over to my family's home and I took her into my bedroom. I took off my shirt while she was sitting on my bed and asked, 'What do you think?' She was in a total state of shock. All she said was, 'I can't believe you did that.' I didn't think about the reality of our relationship. She was only seventeen and was in her last year of high school. She was hardly ready to settle down. My tattoo had put a lot of pressure on her, and got both of us into a terrible situation. She was angry and she didn't want to talk about it. She just said, 'Take me home right now.'

I took her home and I figured she just needed some time to cool down. The next day, I went by her house. Her parents were always happy to see me. They told me that she was spending the night at her girlfriend's place. I drove over there, parked my car, got out and walked up to the front door. The girlfriend answered the door and all she said was, 'She doesn't want to see you.' It crushed me. I wanted to die. I thought, 'Here I am a professional boxer who has lost his last two fights. I left the Marine Corps because of my boxing career, and now that's going nowhere. There's no other way for me to make a living except boxing. Plus, I have a tattoo on my chest of a girl who I thought loved me, but now won't even talk to me. What do I have to live for?'

Salerno was so depressed that he drove to a nearby 7 Eleven and purchased a pack of razor blades that he intended to use for slashing his wrist. He wrote,

I went back to the front door of the girlfriend's place. Nobody would answer the door. I knew they were in there, so I hollered, 'If you don't come out, I'll kill myself.' I got no answer, so I took out a razor blade, looked at my wrist and said to myself, 'James, you don't really want to die, do you? Well, if you're going to cut yourself, don't make it too deep. If you cut deep, you might injure a tendon. If you survive, which you know you will, you want to be able to box again.' At that moment, I was in the combined states of love, depression, frustration and stupidity. I cut my wrist. The girl I was so sure I loved was looking out a window and saw me do it. It caused a big scene. Paramedics arrived and strapped me down. The police were also there. The girl and my entire family were freaked out. My mother took it extremely hard because she thought she could have prevented it. It was nobody's fault but mine. I was extremely selfish and caused great pain to the people who loved me. I learned a lesson: Always listen to your head before your heart, except when it comes to family.

JAMES SQUARES OFF WITH KILLER JOE

Two months after his suicide attempt, Salerno was back training at the Church Street Gym for a fight. He was scheduled to face Killer Joe Dolphin at the War Memorial Arena in Fort Lauderdale on February 16, 1982. James wrote,

The family of the girl I thought I was in love with had just moved from Orlando to a place near Miami. I left tickets for them at the box office and invited them to come to the fight. They all came, even the girl. When she showed up, I took it as a sign that she still loved me.

James was nervous before the fight but when the opening bell rang, the butter-flies went away and the punches came. Salerno wrote,

Killer Joe started out by sort of covering up and I let both my hands fly. This went on for three rounds and then he started to get frustrated because he was unable to hit me. He began trying to butt me with his head. The referee warned him about four times. Finally, the referee disqualified Killer Joe and awarded the fight to me.

The Salerno-Dolphin bout was refereed by Eddie Eckert, who had officiated fights involving Willie Pep, Cleveland Williams, Jimmy Ellis, Michael "Dyna-mite" Dokes, Alexis Arguello, Tim Witherspoon, Leon Spinks, Wilfredo Beni-tez, Vincente Rondon, Mike Quarry and Termite Watkins. Perhaps the biggest fight Eckert refereed was the bout between John "The Beast" Mugabi and Terry Norris at the USF Sun Dome in Tampa in March, 1990. Eddie was inducted into the Florida Boxing Hall of Fame.

Eckert stopped the fight at 1:46 of the fourth round because Killer Joe Dolphin had committed too many head butts and awarded the fight to Salerno. The referee said, "Dolphin was using his head so much that he should have put a glove on it."

While Eddie Eckert was explaining his action to the ring officials, Dolphin initi-ated a shoving match with James that turned into a wrestling match on the floor.

James wrote in his memoir,

It all happened very fast. For a moment, I didn't realize the fight had ended. In that brief moment, I cold cocked Killer Joe with a right hand. All hell broke loose. He tackled me and knocked me to the floor. He was on top of me and was starting to pummel me, while I began to ram the top of my head into his face, just like he had been doing to me during the fight.

125

Some fight fan tossed a full box of popcorn that scattered all over the ring. Police rushed into the ring to separate us. The finally did, but it took about ten minutes.

After order was finally restored, Killer Joe said, "The fight was a set up. I'll never fight in Fort Lauderdale again as long as Eckert is the referee." Ed Morgan, the City of Fort Lauderdale Boxing Commissioner, said, "That's great because I'm banning Killer Joe Dolphin from ever boxing in Fort Lauderdale again. He's not the type of fighter we want to have here."

Both fighters provided lively copy during interviews after the bout. Dolphin said, "That referee took three fights from me; one as a pro against Lee Royster and two as an amateur. He was always telling me, 'Don't do this and don't do that.' I don't like the guy and he don't like me."

James said to the writers, "They told Dolphin I was a head hunter, so I punched holes in his gas tank."

In his memoir, James stated,

The girl I was trying to impress was there cheering for me. I thought that the fight was only the start of what was going to be a great night.

The night ended badly, however, and it was all James' doing. He wrote,

She went out with me and like the pig I was, I insisted on going straight to a hotel room. I put heavy pressure on her for sexual gratification. I felt I was entitled to it. She gave in, and afterward we went back to her parents' house. I slept on their sofa that night even though I had spent money for the hotel room.

His love life was in trouble, but James' boxing career had been given a much needed lift with his win over Killer Joe Dolphin. Salerno wrote,

The next morning, the newspaper ran a big story saying how different Killer Joe and I were. They wrote that all you had to do was look at Killer Joe's left breast that had his nickname scrawled on it. He had gotten his tattoo in prison, and it was a badge of courage for knocking out bullies. They mentioned that my tattoo was a message of love for my girlfriend. They wrote, 'She is a golden haired beauty who goes to all his fights.' Everything was true except for the part about her going to all my fights. I read the paper at her family's house. Her parents and brothers thought the article was great, but she had nothing to say about it. Her father loved to cook, and he made me a big breakfast. After we ate, I thanked him and said goodbye. The girl I wanted so badly acted very cool towards me.

JAMES' OBSESSION GROWS WORSE

James fought J.R. Spears on April 7, 1982. Angelo Dundee had entered him in the ESPN Southern Light Heavyweight Championship Tournament that was held in Nashville, Tennessee. Salerno wrote about that fight, stating,

I trained real hard and got the poison out of my system. I had three weeks to get ready, and Jimmy Williams did a great job of preparing me. My old Marine buddy Jim MacDonald was living in Nashville, and we had a reunion after my arrival. He told me that he had gotten married and was going to turn professional soon. We reminisced about the Marine Corps.

Spears would be the first left hander Salerno ever faced. He was a deputy sheriff and competed on a boxing team organized by his employer. James wrote,

In the beginning of the fight, I found it a little confusing to box against a left hander. He was very awkward and came rushing at me. I avoided his rushes and kept my jab in his face. By the fifth round, he had been cut pretty bad around his right eye and the referee stopped the fight. I won by a TKO. Al Bernstein interviewed me after the fight and complimented me on my jab and movement.

Jimmy and I were happy during the plane trip home. As soon as I got to Orlando, I got in my car, went to my connection, bought some cocaine and then headed to the girl I wanted so badly. Just as I always did, I would justify my using cocaine by saying to myself, 'It's okay once in awhile.' The trouble was that 'once in awhile' was becoming far too frequent. When I arrived at her house, the entire family was glad to see me, including her. They had watched the fight on television. Things couldn't have been better, but I managed to screw it up.

Once again, it was a case of James requiring immediate gratification. He wrote,

I checked into a hotel and talked her into coming up to my room. We started doing lines of cocaine. All of a sudden, I was sweating like a pig and my eyes were as big as silver dollars. I had to have sex. She became frightened and didn't want to put out. I grabbed her, put my hand over her mouth and said, 'If you don't have sex with me, I'll kill you and kill myself.' I couldn't believe what I was hearing because the voice that was coming out of me sounded like a real psycho. She let me have sex with her, but I'll never forget the look of fear in her eyes. Afterwards, we cleaned up and then I took her home. Things were never the same between us after that. I had lost her trust and whatever love she had in her heart for me that night. I really loved her, but I was really mixed up. Most of all, I was immature. I can never undo the bad things I have done, and God only knows how I have paid dearly for them. I went back up to Orlando the next day feeling like a shell of myself. I realized that all of my misery was self inflicted, and I had caused misery to someone I supposedly loved. She was still in high school, and I had robbed her of her innocence.

James kept none of this a secret because he had a compulsion to tell his friends about everything that was going on in his life, even if it were something bad. To hear him tell it, everything was always going good. He would constantly put a comedic spin on things and make any problem into a big joke. This was, of course, a defense mechanism. He could never show any type of vulnerability to any of his friends.

Larry Barfield said, "James explained what happened when he threatened the girl in the hotel room by saying, 'I put my hand over her mouth and told her, 'I know you got in on you, so give it up.'"

James' next fight was against Anthony Phillips on May 7, 1982. The bout was fought at what was formerly the Orlando Sports Stadium, but had been renamed the Eddie Graham Sports Center. The boxing show was co-promoted by Wally Zozak, whose son Jeff had gone to school with James, and Kent Foyer, who was a well known Orlando promoter. Salerno wrote,

There had not been a boxing show in Orlando for years and it was hard to attract public interest. The promoters lost their shirts on the deal. Anthony Phillips was from Georgia. He was built like Mr. Universe and wasn't a bad boxer, but I was too fast for him and Jimmy Williams had me in tip top shape. I boxed from long range, picking my spots, and finally stopped him in the seventh round.

The only thing that was on my mind after the fight was going to Disney World to look for girl I was obsessed with. A special Grad Nite was being held at Disney for that year's Florida high school graduates, and she was among them. When I made it to the theme park, everything was just finishing up and hordes of teenagers were coming through the exits. It seemed like there were 600,000 of them. There were thirty gates to exit through and I had no idea where she was. The fight I won that night didn't give me a headache, but I got one as I frantically looked for her. After about ten minutes, I was dizzy, but then I suddenly saw her. She was happy to see me. I said, 'I won,' and we kissed. We had no time for anything else because she had to get on a bus with the other kids from her high school and go back to where she lived. I didn't consider the fact that my family and friends were waiting for me to go out and celebrate with them. On the spur of the moment, I jumped in my car and followed her bus all the way to where it was headed. The bus didn't set any speed records and the sun was coming up when it arrived at its destination. I hadn't slept for two days and I was a heel for abandoning my family and friends. I drove to her parents' home and knocked on the door. It was 7:00 A.M., but that didn't matter to me. Her father was half asleep when he came to the door. He said, 'James, what are you doing here?' I replied, 'Oh, I just won my fight and I came to visit.' He was always a very nice guy. He told me to go to sleep on their sofa until everyone was up. When he went back to bed, I didn't go to sleep because I couldn't wait to see the girl I wanted so badly. I knocked on her bedroom door. She opened it.

It was always a case of my needing to have whatever I wanted right now. I was really a self centered idiot, and that was putting it mildly. I finally bothered her enough that morning that she gave in and agreed to go out with me. When we went out, I headed straight to a Holiday Inn. I had one thing on my mind and even if she wasn't in the mood, I had an answer for that. I had brought along some cocaine and would try to get her in the mood with that. If that didn't work, I would take the coke. I was the devil himself and I didn't realize how bad I was getting, but she did. We ended up having sex in the hotel. We didn't get home until 5:00 A.M. the next day. Her father didn't say much to me. I could tell that he knew something was up. He still let me sleep on the family sofa, though, and when I woke up, he fixed me another big breakfast. After we ate, I said goodbye and drove back to Orlando. I caught hell for disappearing the way I had, but I was not treated nearly as harshly as I should have been.

A few weeks later, Salerno was back in the ring. James stated in his memoir,

Angelo Dundee set me up with a fight in Macon, Georgia on June 26, 1982, where I took on Bobby Lloyd. Lloyd fought a real strong bout for three rounds, but I danced, jabbed and made him miss. He ran out of gas after the three rounds and wouldn't come out of his corner for the fourth round, so I was awarded a TKO. The victory was nice, but the real highlight of the evening for me was a beautiful card girl named Kathy Wright. She took me to her place and lived up to her name by treating me right.

The twenty one year old fighter's emotional issues were still troubling him, but as far as his boxing was concerned, he was on the comeback trail. James fought Robert White at the Civic Arena in Pittsburgh, Pennsylvania on August 27, 1982. His opponent had just beaten a big puncher named Cornell Chavis and was rated number ten by the WBA. White had formerly been a running back for the University of Pittsburgh football team. Jimmy Williams said,

"At the weigh in, White and his handlers took one look at James and started laughing. They thought he was just an ordinary white kid who didn't know from nothing."

Salerno wrote,

Jimmy got me in great shape. I ran my ass off and all the work paid off. I knew White could punch, so I just kept moving and jabbing. White kept chasing me. At the start of the fourth round, my jab opened cuts on both of his eyes and I moved in for the kill. The next day's newspapers stated, 'James Salerno followed Robert White around the ring, just waiting for the right moment to jump his unsuspecting victim. When that moment came, Salerno applied a savage beating, both hands inflicting punishment with equal ease. The referee was forced to stop the bloody beating at the end of the fourth round.' I made Jimmy real proud of me.

In recalling that bout, Jimmy Williams said,

From the moment the fight began that night, all the black fight fans fell in love with James because he had all that rhythm, shimmy and shake and bake. He put on his moves and stopped Robert White with a TKO. The fans crowded around him and said, 'Man, you fight like a black fighter.' He replied, 'I'm able to do it because my trainer is black.' Many of the black fans swarmed us and followed us all the way into our dressing room. They wanted to put their arms around him and make him their friend. Robert White came into the dressing room and embraced James. White invited us into his neighborhood so we could go to his favorite nightclub. We accepted his invitation and while we were there, James got up on stage and started imitating Ali. He brought he house down and they all fell in love with him. It was amazing.

James had a great time in Pittsburgh, but he was still obsessed with the girl back in Florida. He wrote,

As soon as I got back to Orlando, I got in my car and headed for the girl I couldn't get out of my mind. I just didn't get it, and maybe I didn't want to understand that there was no longer anything between us. When I got to her house, it was a very awkward situation. Her family still liked me and treated me good, but she hid in the bathroom. I tried talking to her through the door, but that didn't go on very long. Things became a game of hide and seek when she tried to sneak out of the house. She tried to lose me, but I was right on her ass.

Looking back, I put her family in a hell of a situation. They liked me, but I couldn't get it through my head that she wanted nothing to do with me. It should have been no surprise after the way I had abused her and mistreated her. I now realize that losing someone's trust in you is worse than losing their love. She could never trust me again. After two days and no progress, I finally drove back home to Orlando. That was not the end of it, though. I made repeated calls to her, but she refused to talk to me and wouldn't even come to the phone. My mother became angry about the incredible phone bill I had run up, so I finally stopped.

AN UNEXPECTED REUNION WITH MAGGIE THOMAS

James wrote in his memoir,

One day, I walked into the house and heard the phone ring. I picked it up and heard, 'Hello. Is James there? This is Maggie Thomas.' I was in a state of shock. It was Maggie's voice, and I'm sure she could hear the joy in mine as I answered, 'I'm here.' She told me that one of her old girlfriends had mentioned that I was trying to get back in touch with her. She said that they had given her my number. She also told me that she had just gotten divorced and was living with her mom and little brother in Clearwater. I was so excited that the girl I had been dreaming of and chasing for ten years had called me. I quickly got her address and arranged to meet her at her mom's house.

This was after my mother had taken the stylish car I had been using away from me as a form of punishment. She was upset at the huge phone bill and all the miles I put on the car by making so many trips to see the girl I had to have. I was reduced to driving an old rusted white Ford truck. I called it my 'Rolls Canhardly.' After it rolls down one hill, it can hardly make it up the next. It would be embarrassing to drive to Maggie in that pickup, but it was either use that or walk. During the drive across the state to the city along the Gulf of Mexico, several questions raced through my mind. Would she still like me? How much has she changed? Did she become ugly? I continued to go over the questions as I pulled up to the Clearwater address, walked up to the front door and knocked. She opened the door and was just as beautiful as I remembered her. Any depression I still felt because of the other girl I had been chasing instantly vanished.

James and Maggie went to a club called the Brown Derby and had a few drinks. He asked her to come up to the hotel room he had taken. Salerno wrote,

She thought about it for a few seconds and agreed to do it. We went up to the room and talked. She asked me, 'What possessed you to look me up.' I replied, 'I've always loved you, even when I wasn't sure you loved me. There were times when I was convinced that you didn't even like me, but I still loved you even then.' I looked at her and could tell that she believed me and knew that I wasn't just feeding her a line. I took her in my arms and kissed her. Blood was rushing to all parts of my body. The thought of having sex with Maggie was something I had been wishing for. It had been on my mind for over ten years. I was hoping that it was about to happen, but she said, 'It's time for me to go home.'

I had finally gotten Maggie alone. I had to have her but unlike the way I treated the other girl, I respected Maggie's wishes. I cooled off and got my composure back. I took her home, kissed her goodnight and went back to the hotel alone. We had made a date to spend the next day at Clearwater Beach.

I couldn't wait for that day to begin and was up very early in the morning. We chose a spot on the sand and spread out our blanket. I had brought along a thick notepad which contained an unfinished book about my life. I had worked on it while I was in the Marine Corps, but I never finished it. There was a great deal about Maggie in what I had written, and they were all good things. I read it to her, and she was flattered. My reading was interrupted when the song Color My World by Chicago came over the portable radio we had brought along. It was the same song I would be playing at night while I was in bed. I was twelve years old then and would be crying myself to sleep over Maggie. I was lying on the beach blanket when I heard it this time, and I began to cry. Tears of joy were running down the sides of my face. I kept reading, but held the notebook over my face to keep Maggie from seeing my tears. I think she knew I was crying, though. Suddenly, she jumped up and said, 'Let's go swimming.' She ran into the water and I ran right behind her.

The water was cold and wasn't deep enough to do more than wading. This didn't prevent Maggie from wrapping her legs around my waist. Not a word was said between us. We looked deeply into each other's eyes as my fingers slid her bikini bottom over. We made love right there. We tried not to let anybody know, but there were no waves at Clearwater Beach to provide cover for us. We weren't fooling the old people on the shore, and they were smiling at us. I didn't mind a bit that the water was so cold. I was the happiest man on earth.

We went back to our blanket and dried off. I took her to the hotel, where we made love again. I was happily surprised that she enjoyed it as much as me. I floated back to Orlando that day in the rusty old Ford truck. I was on cloud nine. Unfortunately, it didn't last long. Right after that wonderful day in Clearwater, Maggie moved out of her mother's house. I could never get her new address.

I couldn't believe it at first, but the more I thought about it, I realized that she needed more security. She was on the rebound from a divorce. I was getting my boxing career going again. I had never received any big purses. All I could give her was promises. I had a nice scrapbook, but that doesn't buy groceries or pay rent. My mother always told me, 'When poverty walks in the door, love goes out the window.'

A BIG, BURLY BEAR OF A MAN
BECOMES JAMES' MANAGER

There were big changes in the wind for both James and Jimmy Williams. Salerno wrote,

Jimmy Williams received a good offer from a Tampa promoter named Phil Alessi. He told me that Alessi even bought him a house as part of the deal to come to Tampa and train his fighters. At the time, Alessi was putting on shows in Tampa that were being televised by NBC. He was getting a lot of help from Dr. Ferdie Pacheco, who was known as the Fight Doctor. Pacheco was born in Tampa. Mark 'Golden Boy' Frazie was Alessi Promotion's big star at the time Jimmy joined the organization. Alessi also had connections with two upcoming prospects. One was named Mike McCallum. He was a Jamaican light heavyweight. The other was Edwin Rosario. Jimmy carefully thought over Alessi's offer. He figured he had given Orlando enough of his time and he was ready to make a move. With the national TV exposure Alessi would be getting, the offer that had been made to him was too good to pass up. Jimmy took the job as head trainer for the Alessi Promotions boxing gym. Immediately after Jimmy signed with Alessi, I left Orlando and headed to Tampa. Jimmy was staying in an apartment until the deal on his house went through. I also stayed there and slept on his couch. I began training right away at the Alessi Promotions gym.

That didn't last long. Soon I was headed back to Orlando for a meeting with a wealthy man who wanted to buy a piece of my contract. It had all started when my father was doing business with Glenn Martin, who was the president of a big life insurance company. Martin bought big collections of stamps and rare coins through my father. He loved publicity and was on the covers of business and money magazines. He was a multi, multi millionaire just like Daddy Warbucks. My dad set up an appointment for me to meet with this wealthy, powerful man. Martin's building and office in Orlando were the most beautiful I had ever seen. I felt like my dad and I were peasants who were given an audience with a king. After we told his secretary who we were, she said, 'You may enter.' The king was expecting us. I was surprised at what Glenn Martin looked like. I had expected him to be a big fat guy with a cigar hanging out of his mouth. Instead, he was young looking and in shape. I mentioned how healthy looking he was and he told me that he had once been a physical education and track coach for an Orlando high school. He also said that he stayed in shape by running. I quickly looked around his office. It was right out of Lifestyles of the Rich and Famous. I was thinking, 'Damn, P.E.

teachers make damn good money,' but I quickly learned better as he gave me a brief history about how he had made his dough. He told me that he started selling insurance and recruited people to work for him on a commission only basis and boom, he became one of the richest men in Orlando. He also introduced me to his lawyer.

I started to sell myself to them, but my dad had already sold them on me. They got right into the deal they were offering, and I agreed to go along with it. They would supply me with my own apartment, pay all my living expenses and give me $300 a week. I was still driving that rusted out Ford pickup truck, so I said, 'I need a car, and not just any car. I need a candy apple red Corvette with glass mirrored t-tops.' They said, 'No problem.' In return for what I was given, Martin would receive sixteen and two thirds percent of my contract. Glenn Martin's chief financial advisor went with me to pick up the 'Vette. The car cost $15,600. I was so young and stupid that I forgot to make sure the title was in my name. I believed I was being taken care of, so any thoughts of how the title was made out never crossed my mind.

Martin's organization immediately contacted Betty, who was Angelo Dundee's secretary, and informed her that Angelo was still my manager, but that he now had a new partner. I was told that Angelo was not too happy about it, but he didn't say anything to me about it when I drove down to Miami Beach to show him my Corvette. I thought at the time, 'What can he say? What's done is done. Glenn Martin is just what I needed.' Chris Dundee, on the other hand, had a lot to say to me. He said, 'Cars ruin fighters. Once Elisha Obed got a car, he was finished. It's as though cars are curses.' I'm sure Angelo's thinking was along those same lines. It wasn't that the car itself was bad, but you could get in a lot more trouble with one. It turned out they were right, but no one could have convinced me of that at the time. I was having too much fun.

Jimmy Williams had accompanied James on that trip to Miami in the new Corvette. At one point, they were cruising on a stretch of highway along the Tamiami Trail without another car in sight. James said to Jimmy, "Watch this," and he put the gas pedal to the floor. As the speedometer needle surged past the one hundred mile per hour mark, Williams pleaded with Salerno to slow down, saying, "James, please! I can't stand it. If you want to do this when you're by yourself, I don't care. I'm begging you, slow down!" James backed off, but it wouldn't be the only time he would try to open up the 'Vette.

When Jimmy told me this story, he said, "James loved to drive fast. He was ticketed for speeding several times. He ignored the tickets and that eventually cause him a lot of trouble."

Salerno wrote,

Even with all the financial support I was getting, I could never make my money last. One day, I was hard up for cash, so I sold the t-tops to the Corvette for $200. I then told Glenn Martin's financial advisor that they had been stolen. They got me another set.

I still couldn't the girl I was obsessed with out of my mind. I would make three or four trips a week to where her family lived, trying to get her back. She wouldn't budge, and there was nothing doing.

Since I couldn't get anywhere with her, I headed over to Tampa and got back into serious training at the Alessi Promotions gym. One day, a muscle bound guy walked in with a man who turned out to be his brother. The guy with the muscles remind-ed me of the Brutus character in the Popeye cartoons, beard and all. He was watch-ing me closely while I was shadow boxing. As he was looking at me, he was also whispering to his brother and laughing. The next thing I know, the muscle man asked Jimmy if he could spar with me. Jimmy told him, 'James is a professional.' The big guy said, 'I don't care. I'd still like to spar with him.' Jimmy then asked me if it was all right for the guy to get into the ring with me. I said, 'Sure.' When the bell rang to begin the sparring session, the muscle guy acted like a football lineman in a fourth and inches situation. He charged at me, and I just moved out of the way. I dropped my hands and stuck my chin out, baiting him to try and hit me. He wound up and threw a punch from left field that I slipped under. Suddenly he started yelling in pain because he had thrown his arm out of its socket. In spite of the pain he was going through, he waited around until I finished my workout. When I was done, he came up to me and said, 'Hey why don't you come out for a steak at my place? It's on a lake. I've got my own gym. You'll love it.' He wrote down his address and handed it to me, and then he screamed off in his mint condi-tion 1967 Corvette Stingray.

I headed out to the man's place that night. It was way out on the outskirts of Tam-pa. I had to drive to a tiny town named Odessa. I thought to myself, 'This guy lives way out in the boondocks. I wonder if he lives in a barn.' I turned onto Michigan and continued for a mile, then there was a sharp turn to the right and I saw a stone wall that was surrounding a mansion. This was where the muscle man lived.

I pulled up, and he came out to meet me. He introduced himself, saying, 'Jeff Trager. Glad you came out.' He invited me into his residence, which was a cross between a house and a castle. He went on to say how he had built it himself with boulders and huge rocks he had brought in from Colorado. He also told me that he used to play pro football with the San Diego Chargers until injuries forced him to retire. He explained how he had taken the money he made and invested it in land and a car wash that was in a great location.

I asked him, 'Why in the world would you want to box?' He then began telling me all about a girlfriend he had who was a model. She had recently left him, and he wanted some way to take out his frustrations. After the two women who disappointed me, I could relate to that.

Jeff was thirty two years old. He told me he had been in the United States Marine Corps. I told him that was something we had in common. He told me that he believed that lifting weights and doing squats would give me more power. I agreed to meet with him the next morning.

I drove out to his mansion again, and I worked out with him. We ran for five miles and then we were in his weight room for an hour. Jeff worked out like an animal. He did a thousand sit ups. I couldn't do that many. After that, Jeff came to the Alessi Promotions gym for two weeks just to work out with me. He eventually got around to saying that I should move in with him. He said he would make sure that I ate well and became strong.

I couldn't figure him out. I kept thinking, 'What is this guy's angle?' I finally decided to move into his place. The deciding factor was that his castle was on a big lake, and I love to fish. Jeff stayed upstairs on the right. My room was downstairs, on the left. Before long, we were 'talking turkey,' as Jeff would say. One day, he asked, 'Do you think you can get out of the contract with Glenn Martin, and how much longer does your contract with Dundee have to go? Do you think I could buy you out of them?' All I could say was, 'I don't know.' He kept talking about taking over my boxing career. He finally convinced me that he would make a good combination trainer and manager. He didn't con me, and he brought up a very good point. He said, 'I'm an athlete myself. I work out with you. The only thing you are able to beat me at is running and of course, boxing. Most managers wear a suit and tie. I wear a suit and tie, but I also wear a jock strap.'

Jeff agreed to give me the money to pay back Glenn Martin for all he had put into me. We drove over to Orlando and met with Martin. I made a big scene and Martin let me buy my way out of my contract with him. I also gave him back his Corvette. My father thought I was crazy for doing that and as it turned out, he was right. It was another of the big mistakes I have made.

Jeff Trager was now my manager, along with Angelo Dundee. By this time, I found out that Jeff was originally from Chicago. It so happened that the next fight Angelo arranged for me was in the Windy City.

James was matched with cruiserweight Fred Brown. The bout was held at the Congress Americana Hotel. Salerno wrote,

Jeff trained me in the morning and Jimmy worked with me in the afternoon. Besides being my manager, Jeff was also my chef. I ate like a king every night.

Jeff knew absolutely nothing about boxing, but he would sometimes yell out suggestions for me while I was doing my training at the Alessi Promotions gym. This would get on Jimmy's nerves. I want you understand, though, that Jeff had great respect for Jimmy as a teacher and trainer.

Angelo Dundee came up to Chicago to work my corner, along with Jimmy and Jeff. I worked my jab overtime on Fred Brown, but he wouldn't go down. I had to settle for winning by a unanimous decision. The fight was carried on Sportsvision, a cable channel that was broadcast into five states. I made everybody happy that night. Angelo went back to Miami Beach with a smile on his face, and Jimmy was smiling as he headed back to Tampa. Jeff and I stayed in Chicago because he wanted to take me out to celebrate. The first stop we made was the home of two of his friends, who happened to be brothers. He warned me before we went in, 'Don't gamble with these guys. They never lose.' I couldn't believe what I saw when I walked in. There was a big crap table right in the middle of the living room. It was just like Vegas. They served up a few drinks and got us in the mood to try our luck. One of Jeff's friend's was down two thousand dollars and won it all back on his last roll. I dropped three hundred dollars, but I had fun doing it.

Jeff then took me to was a big party at the home of someone in the fight game. There were wild women everywhere. People were boozing it up and doing lines of coke in bathrooms. I ran into a nice looking girl and she said, 'Let's go upstairs.' We went into a bedroom, and I did cocaine with her. I became so paranoid and worried that someone would walk in on us that I moved the dresser in front of the door. This caused a problem when I needed to take a piss. I wound up pissing in a little trash can. I didn't realize that cocaine could make me feel that bad. When I first tried it, it gave me a lift. That night, it just made me miserable. Later that night, I was watching a football game on TV. I was so paranoid that when a team went into a huddle, I was convinced that they were talking about me and exposing my darkest secrets. After I finished with the nice looking girl, I went back to the party and drank some beer to calm down. Jeff was socializing with some girls. He had no idea what I had been up to. When we started out, he made it clear that there was to be no drugs in my life. He told me that he used to mess around a little when he was younger and stupid. He learned his lesson the hard way. He insisted that drugs were for losers. Well, based on what I had done at the party, I was a loser that night. We went from the party back to the hotel. We flew back to Tampa the next morning.

I went back into training. Angelo had set me up to fight in a tournament out in Los Angeles. It was sponsored by Stroh's Beer and Dr. Jerry Buss, who owned The Forum in Inglewood. In the first round, I was matched with a fighter named Jesse 'Shotgun' Island. If I had not been in peak condition, I would have been in serious trouble. He kept putting on the pressure, and I kept dancing. In the seventh round, I noticed he was tailgating his left jab. I timed a right hand punch just right. He fell back on the ropes and his knees became shaky. I took full advantage of the situation by jumping all over him with both hands until the referee stopped the fight. It was a very big win for me because it advanced me into a semifinal bout which would be held a few months later. Jimmy and Jeff were very happy, and so was Angelo. I was ranked number five in the world among light heavyweights by the World Boxing Association. Stories about me began to appear in boxing magazines. I even got a full page picture in Boxing Scene Magazine.

Things began to get out of hand when Jeff began trying anything to grab headlines. The most outrageous stunt occurred because of my desire to fight Michael Spinks for the world light heavyweight title. I thought I had the perfect style to beat him. Even the boxing magazines called me 'The White Muhammad Ali.' I didn't think I could beat Michael Spinks, I knew I could.

Jeff Trager paid $6,400 for a quarter page ad in the Philadelphia Sunday Inquirer in August, 1983. The ad read: "WANTED! MICHAEL SPINKS CHAMP OR CHICKEN! APPOLLO CREED GAVE ROCKY A CHANCE IN PHILADELPHIA – GIVE ME A CRACK AT THE TITLE *NOW!* ANY PLACE! ANY TIME! JAMES SALERNO THE "REAL ITALIAN STALLION" RANKED #10 W.B.A. PRO RECORD 30 WINS, 2 LOSSES, 20 K.O.'S TURNED PRO AT 15 YEARS OLD – NOW 22 YEARS OLD MANAGER ANGELO DUNDEE TRAINERS JIMMY WILLIAMS AND JEFF TRAGER

James explained why he was calling Mike Spinks out by saying,

I was just getting frustrated because I know I can beat Michael Spinks. I have just the kind of style it takes to beat him. I'm as tall as he is and more important, I'm

better defensively and much faster. The only advantage he has is a hard right hand. That doesn't matter to me because I'm not going to let him hit me with it. Besides, I can take a mule kick if I have to.

Angelo Dundee reacted to the publicity stunt by saying,

I didn't know anything about it. But come to think of it, I'm not shocked by it. James is a pretty smart kid. I've always said you can get a well rounded education in the fight business. Between all the travel and the kind of people you meet, you can learn a lot. James has learned to promote himself.

Make no mistake about it, James Salerno can fight. He's a boxer with good power, and he can take a punch. He has a good chin. He really is ready for a title fight, but it's hard to get him in with the champion or even top contenders. I'll fight anyone in the country with this kid.

I know everybody in the business and I've talked to all of them. They all give me the same old national anthem: 'We've got to see him fight first.' I even got a call a few weeks ago from the Spinks camp trying to find out if we are interested in going with the champ. But we haven't heard anything back from them yet and the kid is getting a little impatient.

James had more to offer on the subject. He said to the sports writers,

I'm getting a little frustrated being in Angelo Dundee's closet. I've been fighting since I was thirteen and I'm twenty two now. I feel like it is my turn. After watching all those Rocky movies, I said to myself: 'I'm the real thing. I'm the real Italian Stallion. I should be up there. The world is ready for a white champion.' The best part about it is that I'm a white fighter with soul. In fact, my soul has soul. The black fans love me because I move just like a black fighter, while Spinks doesn't.

Don Majewski was the chief matchmaker for Butch Lewis Promotions at the time and he said,

Salerno may be just what we are looking for, but then again, he might not be. Sure a white guy who could really fight would be a big draw, but nobody really knows Salerno. I give him credit for taking out the ad and trying to promote himself. I called Dundee about James Salerno a month ago to find out if he was ready. I was told that he was. The problem was that we had trouble trying to line up TV money. The issue is that there's not one fighter in the light heavyweight division that the public is clamoring for.

In his memoir, James wrote,

The quarter page ad got Michael Spinks' attention. He was visibly shaken when he was interviewed on television about it. The TV people also interviewed me. It began to look like I was going to get my chance at Michael. I was training hard because I believed my title shot was only a matter of time. I heard through the grapevine that since the Super Bowl was going to be held in Tampa in January, 1984, NBC wanted to televise a fight to compete with the pregame activities on ABC. I also heard Spinks was offered $400,000 to fight on NBC that day. The next thing I knew, Butch Lewis, who was Spinks' manager, wanted video cassettes of my last three fights. After Lewis got the tapes, he wanted more money. NBC offered him and Spinks $500,000. That wasn't enough. Lewis wanted more. The network went up to $650,000. Lewis said the money was all right, but he also wanted promotional rights to my next three fights if I took the championship from Michael Spinks. Alessi and NBC were co-promoters and they wouldn't go along with that part of the deal.

After my big chance to fight Spinks fell through, I developed a bad attitude. It seemed like everything I had been doing was for nothing. It was a big waste of time, a waste of money and most of all, a waste of my dream. I never got the chance to see my dream of a world championship become a reality because of greedy people. I loved the sport of boxing, but not the business part.

JAMES AND JEFF TRAGER PART COMPANY

Salerno wrote,

With my soured attitude, I started taking trips to the town down by Miami to see the same girl I was obsessed with, even though she wouldn't give me the time of day. I also started using Jeff, really taking advantage of him. I ran his phone bill up and tapped him for money in other ways. One day, Jeff told me to get off the phone. I shot back with a wise ass crack. That did it. It was the straw that broke the camel's back. He tackled me, and that scared the shit out of me. He could bench 420 pounds. He was on top of me and was cursing me. He was yelling about how ungrateful I was. He never actually hit me, and I held myself back while he let out all his rage at me. He finally let me up and then said, 'Move out! Right now!'

This put me in a bad situation. I was on the other side of the state from my home and practically out in the street. I called Angelo Dundee, and he sent me money for an apartment. I girl I knew told me about a building that had furnished apartments. She also said it wasn't far from the Alessi Promotions gym. I went to the building and it was like something out of the Twilight Zone. The name of the business was the Morrison Court Apartments. The apartment they showed me had a Murphy bed with a steel name plate which showed it had been manufactured in 1908. The only reason I thought twice about taking the apartment was that I was told of many renovations they were going to make. I believed them. Boy, was I a sucker. The place turned out to be so bad that the health inspectors would have insisted it be painted before they could condemn it. The manager had to be paying off the inspectors. I got up one night, went to the kitchen, turned on the light and saw rats running everywhere. The next morning, I went into the office to complain about the rats. An older, prudish, snobby woman was there. She said she was the assistant manager. When I told her about the rats, she insisted, 'We don't even have mice at Morrison Court Apartments.'

I bought a rat trap, set it and waited for one of the rats to be caught. That night as I was drifting off to sleep, I heard a loud CLACK. I ran into the kitchen and found that a real beauty of a rat had died in the trap. The next morning, I took my catch into the office. The dead rat was dangling by its neck from the trap. I said to the snobby assistant manager, 'You were right. You don't have mice at Morrison Court Apartments. You have big, stinking, lousy rats!' I flopped the dead rat on her desk and ran out the door, with her screams ringing in my ears. I wasn't too popular with the management after that episode, but I didn't care. Angelo kept paying my rent and sending me a check every week for food and necessities. I was training for my second fight in the Stroh's Beer tournament out in California.

I began to slacken up in my training and started taking things for granted. When I arrived in L.A., I found that they had me favored to win the tournament. I was fighting Mike Sedillo, a Mexican boxer from Chino, California. I was told he had just gotten out of jail. He was listed as the dark horse of the tournament. I had forgotten the lesson I had learned when I fought Leon McDonald. I didn't remember that convicts stay in shape and come to fight. In my fight with Sedillo, I was lethargic and slow in the very beginning. I didn't break a sweat warming up in my dressing room, and I paid for that mistake. He hit me with a wild left hook and knocked me down. I got up and boxed for the rest of the fight. They gave him a split decision and put him in the finals.

Jimmy would hardly speak to me. He couldn't believe that I had let this guy beat me. He said, "James, you don't realize what you let go through your hands." He just shook his head at me.

The plane ride back was horrible. Jimmy wasn't mad at me just because I lost. He was upset that I had not given one hundred percent. After I paid my bills, I only made about a thousand dollars. The fight also dropped me in the rankings from number five to number seven.

NEVER GET CAUGHT IN THE LEGAL SYSTEM

James' situation was made even worse because of his failure to take the legal system seriously. Salerno wrote,

After returning from Los Angeles, I got in trouble with the law. It all began when I saw a poster in the window of a convenience store near my apartment. The poster had a picture of a lost dog and offered a fifty dollar reward. I happened to have seen a dog that fit the description and had a pretty good idea where it would be. I bought a can of Alpo that I intended to use to try to lure it to me. I found him, but he took off running, and I started chasing after him. He ran past someone's front yard, where three juveniles were sitting on the front porch drinking beer. When the punk kids saw me, they started hollering, 'Leave that dog alone!' and came running across the street toward me. Two of them had sticks in their hands and one had a pistol stuck in his pants. I retreated back to the convenience store. One of them followed me there. When he caught up with me, he started screaming in my face. There just happened to be a Tampa police car at a traffic light in front of the store. I motioned for the cops to come over. They pulled up and tried to talk to the kid, but he was ranting and raving. They told me to sit in the back seat of their police car while they heard the kid's story. While I was waiting in their car, I saw the kid fighting with the police. He even punched one of the cops. They finally sprayed him with mace, subdued him, put him in cuffs and threw him in the back seat with me. As they started to pull away, I said, 'Wait a minute. Where are we going?' They said, 'Downtown to fill out a report. We need you.' I thought, 'All of this began with me trying to do a good deed and pick up some reward money.'

I only spent about ten minutes at the police station and they drove me to my door-step. They told me that all I had to do was show up for the court date and that it wouldn't cost me anything. I never showed up, though. They needed me to verify the cops' story. But I wasn't there to do it. The kid's mother then threatened to file police brutality charges.

About two weeks after the court date, I saw a fat man walking through the hallway of my apartment building. He asked me where apartment number twelve was. I pointed to where the door to that apartment was and said, 'What a minute! That's my apartment!' He asked, 'Are you James Salerno?' I told him I was and then he said, 'James, you're under arrest.' He put handcuffs on me and took me to jail. The charge was contempt of court for not showing up for the court date. I appeared before a female judge named Susan Bucklew.

Years later, Susan Bucklew was appointed to be a federal judge by Bill Clinton. James continued the story by writing,

She sentenced me to six months probation. I explained that I was moving back to Orlando and asked if they could transfer it. I was told that wouldn't be a problem. I heard nothing from them. Months later, I was riding with a friend in their car. They were pulled over for a traffic violation. The officer also asked my name and ran it through the computer. He came back to the car and said, 'I'm sorry, Mr. Salerno. There's a warrant for your arrest. You're going to have to come with us.' I was handcuffed and placed in the back seat of the police car. My buddy was laughing at me as they took me away.

I was charged with violation of my probation and thrown in a cell. After I had been there ten days, I was watching television with some other inmates when some guy changed the channel we were all watching. I turned the channel back and we saw the rest of the telecast. That really pissed the guy off. He followed me to my bunk and waited until I sat down and took my shoes off. He got into my face. I wasn't going to take that from him, so I stood up. Just as I did that, he tackled me and I slid across the smooth floor because I was in my stocking feet. We were wrestling on the floor. He tried to claw my eyes out with his overgrown fingernails and at the same time, he was biting my chest. As soon as he started going for my balls, I grabbed a handful of his hair, pulled his head to one side and practically bit his ear off. Needless to say, he let go. The guards finally arrived on the scene, and I was thrown into solitary confinement. It was pitch black in that room and ice cold. I wasn't supplied with a bed or even a blanket. The floor and the walls were cold concrete, and the only thing in the room was a toilet. I sat there in the cold and felt the scratches around my eyes with my fingers. A person could really lose their mind in a place like that. They made me stay there until an investigation about the fight was completed. That took about two days. It was ruled that I had been attacked and had defended myself. I finally got out of that jail after 23 days.

A BITTERSWEET TRIP TO LOS ANGELES

James wrote,

When I got back to my place, the phone was ringing. It was Angelo Dundee. He told me that I had to be in California the next day. He had me in a fight against J.B. Williamson as a last minute replacement. Williamson's original opponent was hurt while training and Angelo got me placed in that slot. I was in no condition to fight, but I was too embarrassed to tell Angelo that I had been in jail for the last 23 days. Angelo made me feel a little confident when he said, 'Williamson is a blown up middleweight and you should have no problem with him.' I hopped on a plane by myself the next day. I told my dad about the fight and he showed up in California in time to accompany me to the weigh in. When I took a look at J.B., I thought, 'Maybe I can knock him out in one round. That way, I won't have to worry about going the distance.' Angelo was there to work my corner, so I knew he thought I could beat Williamson. Otherwise, he wouldn't have made the long trip from Florida.

I had arrived on a Thursday and the fight was on Saturday. Angelo told me, 'We're going to Muhammad's house on Saturday morning.' Sure enough on Saturday morning, Angelo picked me up in a big Cadillac. We drove to a neighborhood off La Brea Avenue in Los Angeles that was full of multimillion dollar homes.

Sal Salerno said, "It was the first time James and Ali had seen each other since my son had been to his training camp in Deer Park, Pennsylvania, which is near Pittsburgh."

James continued the story by writing,

We arrived at a guard house. After we were allowed to pass through, we pulled up in front of Muhammad Ali's house. It was just what you would have expected from a man who had made nearly fifty million dollars in his life. We knocked on the door. Muhammad's father in law answered. He brought us to a room in the back of the house where Ali was playing with his two daughters. Angelo and Muhammad said a brief hello, then everyone disappeared, leaving Muhammad Ali and me alone. The phone suddenly rang and before the second ring, Ali had run across the room to answer it. I hadn't seen him move that fast in ten years. After he finished the call and returned to me, I said, 'If it wasn't for me watching you as a kid, I wouldn't have taken up boxing.' Then I started doing impersonations of Howard

Cosell interviewing him. I played both parts. I said, 'Muhammad, your legs are not what they were ten years ago.' 'Cosell, who is the same as they were ten years ago? I'm gonna ask Mrs. Cosell if you're the same as you were just two years ago.' I got Ali to smile, but I wasn't through yet. I said, 'Ali comes out to meet Foreman, but Foreman starts to retreat. If George backs up an inch further, he'll wind up in a ringside seat. Ali swings with a left, Ali swings with a right. What a beautiful swing and the punch lifts Foreman clean out of the ring. Foreman's still rising, but the referee is wearing a frown because he can't start counting until Foreman comes down. Now, George Foreman disappears from view. The crowd is getting frantic, but our radar stations have picked him up. He's somewhere over the Atlantic. And who would have thought when they came to the fight they would've witnessed the launching of a colored satellite.' I was starting to get him in a good mood, so I had to throw in, 'Frazier might come out smokin' and I won't be jokin'. I'll be pickin' and a pokin', pourin' water on the smokin'.'

He couldn't believe that I remembered all his poems. It occurred to me that the worst thing Ali suffered from at that time was boredom. That thought made me sad. Ali then motioned for me to follow him. He led me into his trophy room. It was filled with trophies, but equally impressive were all the magazine covers he had been on. He had them all in frames that encircled the entire room, and the room was huge. After a few minutes, Angelo showed up and said, 'We gotta be going.' When we were out in front of the house, I couldn't resist dancing in front of Muhammad. Soon, he and I were slap fighting, just like we used to. I caught him with some rights over his left. Whenever I was with him, I was on cloud nine because he is my boxing hero, the man I consider the greatest. As we were driving off, Muhammad was standing on the sidewalk. He was wearing an all black outfit and sneakers. I yelled out the window, 'Shuffle for me, Muhammad.' He did, and it made me happy to see him do that. Evidently, I made him happy. I knew I got him pumped by reciting all those poems.

I only wish my fight with J.B. Williamson turned out as well as my visit with Ali. I rushed out there swinging like a madman in the first round, while J.B. just moved and covered up. I won the first round, but I was breathing hard. The second round was more of the same and when I went to my corner after it was over, I was again breathing hard. Angelo told me to relax. I tried, but I wasn't in shape. When you're out of shape, it's impossible to relax. In the third round, Williamson went under a wild right hand that I threw and hit me with a picture perfect left hook that knocked me down and gave me a bad cut over my right eye. I got up and threw a left jab, but he came over the top of it with a right hand that connected. I went down, but jumped right up. I was shocked when Angelo threw in the towel. The fight was stopped and J.B. won by a TKO. After we went back to the dressing room,

I asked Angelo, 'Why did you throw in the towel?' He said, 'You were a dead man out there. I didn't want to see you get hurt.' I was mad, but he was probably right.

I was so mad that they didn't have to use any Novocaine when they put seven stitches over my eye. It was the first time I had ever been cut in a boxing match. It was also the first time my corner ever threw in the towel. What made it extra bad was that J.B. Williamson was no knockout artist. I was only the third guy he ever stopped in over twenty fights. The referee didn't stop it. Angelo ended it by throwing in the towel, but it went down in the books as a knockout against me. I don't want to take anything away from J.B. Williamson. He went on to winning a world championship six months later. He held the title until his first defense. He lost that fight and then went downhill after that.

Later that night, Angelo handed me one thousand dollars. I thought, 'I guess my purse was two thousand dollars and his share was a grand.' I came to find out that my purse was actually six thousand dollars, the most I was ever paid for a fight. It was true that I owed him money, but he only gave me one sixth of my purse. I didn't think too highly of him for awhile after that, but I guess he thought I was through and he wanted to get his money back. Things like that happen in the business of boxing.

My father flew out for that fight and flew back with me. It was a long flight. With my seven stitches and two black eyes, I looked like a raccoon that had been run over by a car.

JAMES HAS MORE TROUBLE WITH THE LAW, FINDS A NEW LOVE INTEREST AND ENJOYS A BRIEF BUT SUCCESSFUL CAREER IN TELEPHONE SALES

James continued to disrespect the law. He ignored parking tickets, moving violations and even the terms of his probation. This led to serious consequences. Salerno stated in his memoir,

I neglected a traffic ticket, and then later was pulled over for not appearing in court over parking tickets. They arrested me in Orlando and then flew me to Tampa in a state trooper plane because that's where I had been sentenced to the probation which I had violated by neglecting the tickets. They shackled my hands and feet. You would have thought I was Charles Manson from the looks of things.

James never realized that when a warrant was issued for probation violation, law enforcement officers were not going to take any chances. They had no way of knowing how dangerous the individual was. All they were told was that the violator had to be returned as quickly as possible to the jurisdiction where they were placed on probation.

James wrote,

I was held in a jail that was in a section of Tampa known as Six Mile Creek. I had to stay there until my trial date. I was too embarrassed to call anyone and ask them to bail me out. I wound up waiting thirty days for my court date. I made the best of it. Every day, I ran, did pushups and did sit ups. One day while I was doing sit ups outside in the yard, a big black West Indian stood in front of me. He got into some sort of karate stance. I got up and started dancing. All of a sudden, he dropped down into a low stance and tried to sweep my feet out from under me. I jumped up and let his leg go by. His momentum made him turn his back to me. I didn't waste any time. I took advantage of the situation by jumping on his back and getting him in a Marine Corps choke hold. I had him at my mercy until the guards broke us up. He looked at me and said, 'We ain't finished yet,' but he never bothered me again.

When Salerno's day in court finally arrived, his attention was focused on a tall, very attractive young woman who was performing duties that were part of the legal process. Her name was Karen Piche. She was educated, athletic and a class act. Karen was twenty four years old and had graduated from St. Leo University, a Catholic university thirty five miles outside of Tampa.

She was the first woman at that school to a letter in basketball for four years. She started every game during her years at St. Leo, which amounted to over 80 contests. She had career averages of 13.4 points and 12.6 rebounds per game. Her career free throw percentage was 75 percent. She was St. Leo's athlete of the month three times. She also earned two letters in volleyball and two in softball. In addition, she was on the dean's list three years and was vice president of the Delta Phi Delta sorority. Karen would be inducted into the St. Leo University Athletic Hall of Fame in 1994.

James wrote in his memoir,

Karen Piche worked for the Salvation Army as a courtroom representative. She told you what you were supposed to do when you were put on probation. She was nice and very pretty. I happened to have a boxing program that had my picture on the front cover. As she was trying to tell me what to do, I said, 'I know you've heard this a million times, but I'd like to make it a million and one… your beautiful.' Then I handed her the program. She gave me her work phone number.

I was released that same day. I had Mary Ellen Jones, who was the ex-girl friend of a friend, pick me up. I stayed with her until I could get something better or get back on my feet. Mary Ellen was no beauty queen, but she helped me when the chips were down and she didn't ask for any rent. I didn't want to be a total mooch, so I looked in the paper for a part time job. I wound up working in telephone sales.

The place was set up like a kindergarten classroom. Each desk had a phone. The supervisor was an old woman. She sat in front of our desks, just like a teacher in school. We were hired to sell products made by the blind. The products were such things as bathroom towels, pot holders and Teflon coated ironing board covers. All of the items were ridiculously overpriced.

We were told not to deviate from the script we were given to use while making our calls. I couldn't help being creative, so I made up my own sales pitch. I would say, 'Hello, sir, my name is James Salerno and I know that if you're like me, you probably hate getting calls from salespeople. But you can't just turn your back on the lesser endowed in our community, sir. I'm talking about the blind, and we have the products which these people made to sell. I know if you're like me you would now be thinking the potholders have got three thumbs or something because they were made by the blind. That's not true. The products are as well made as anything you'd find in a Montgomery Wards catalogue. You would be amazed as I was when I saw them. Plus if you buy something, you will have a warm feeling in your heart from knowing that the blind person's only talent has not gone unnoticed by you.' If the person I was calling was still on the phone after I went through part of the pitch, they would usually be in tears. They would end up ordering things for themselves and their relatives. The supervisor would give me the dirtiest looks for deviating from the script, but I also got the two dollar daily bonus for selling the most. It was the most mentally draining and lowest paying job I ever had, but it was also the most fulfilling. I think every salesman should work at a job just like that one as a form of boot camp. If you can sell potholders made by blind people over the phone for thirty five dollars, you could sell anything. The job lasted about a month. All the while, I was training at the Alessi Promotions gym in Tampa.

JAMES GETS A BIG FIGHT IN MIAMI,
BUT SUFFERS A SERIOUS INJURY

Things begin to look up for Salerno when he was offered a big fight in Miami. He wrote,

One day, Jimmy Williams told me that Angelo had called. He had set up a fight for me with Leslie Stewart in Miami at the Jai Alai Fronton. I had only ten days to prepare. I was already in pretty good shape, but I needed to be in great shape. Stewart was rated number seven by the WBA.

Meanwhile, I was still on probation. One day, I went in for my visit and I saw Karen Piche, the girl I had met in court. I told her that I needed her to come outside because I had something to show her. When I got her outside, the only thing I wanted to show her was her lips on mine. She wouldn't kiss me in the parking lot of her workplace, but I got her home phone. I was able to get her to come over to the apartment I shared with Mary Ellen. I told her about my big fight in Miami and asked her to come down for it. We began to see each other regularly. She would stay at Mary Ellen's, caressing my head while I drifted off to sleep.

Karen later stated to a sports writer,

I was a little leery about going out with him at first because I thought he was crazy, but there was something about him that I liked. For one of our first dates, we went on a canoeing and camping trip at the Alafia River State Park, which is near Tampa. We didn't even bring a tent. All we had were sleeping bags. It was kind of miserable because it was cold, and there were lots of mosquitoes. James was scared to death. He was throwing bottles at raccoons to make them get away from us. I knew that the raccoons along the river are practically domesticated, and I told him that. It didn't make any difference because every little noise would scare him. He was supposed to be protecting me, but I ended up protecting him.

James wrote in his memoir,

Finally, fight night arrived. I was back in my dressing room loosening up before going on when Jimmy Williams walked in and said, 'Guess who came down to see you?' Karen walked in right behind him. I couldn't believe that she not only came but also paid her way in. I couldn't talk to her long because I had important things to think about, like my fight with Stewart.

When the bell rang for the first round, Stewart came charging across the ring. I side stepped and let him go by. I jabbed the whole time. At the end of the round, I didn't even sit down. Jimmy and I were talking and joking between rounds. The second and third rounds were more of the same. Stewart was charging and missing and I was sticking and moving. In the fourth round, I got cocky enough to pull off the Salerno Shuffle. This really made Stewart mad, but to no avail. He couldn't catch me until the seventh round. That was when he threw a 'rake,' which is a cross between a jab and an uppercut. It caught me square on the nose. It shattered the tip and cut the bridge. Water filled my eyes. Stewart sensed that he could move in for the kill. He threw everything he could muster until the bell sounded to end the round. This time, I had to sit down so they could work on the cut over the bridge of my nose. Stewart had won the seventh round and blood was all over me. My eyes were still watery at the beginning of the eighth round and I was in full defense. By the middle of the round, my eyes cleared and I got my jab going. The people were going crazy. It was a predominantly Latin/Spanish crowd and they love a good fight. We were giving them what they wanted… blood. The bell rang and Stewart had won the eighth round. Jimmy and I had it figured. I easily won the first six rounds by out boxing him. He won the seventh and eighth big. Jimmy said, 'Reach down and give it all you got.' At the start of the ninth round, Stewart hit me with a right. Jimmy said afterwards, 'That's when the other dude came out in you.' From that point on, I let my offense be my defense. I nailed him with a right that busted his nose. I was taking the fight to him. By the close of the ninth round, we were both bleeding and the crowd was on its feet. Jimmy said I won the ninth round and I thought so, too. In the tenth and final round, I nailed Stewart with another big right hand. He started backpedaling, but I was right on his case. I hit him with another right hand and I watched the expression on his face change. Now all he was trying to do was survive the round. When the bell rang to end the fight, I just knew I had pulled it off. I waited for the decision to be announced and then was shocked to hear, 'We have a split decision. The winner is Leslie Stewart.' I couldn't believe it, but there was nothing Jimmy or I could do. Everybody thought I won. Some of them said, 'If you weren't bleeding so bad, you would have got the decision.' Stewart was bleeding bad too from the nose and mouth, but his blood didn't stand out like it did on me because I had a much lighter complexion. Another factor was that the fight was in Stewart's hometown, right where his manager wanted it to be. I believe that made a big difference. The cable channel televising the fight had me ahead in their scoring, but they were not judging the fight. They were only voicing their opinions about what happened.

Even though I lost, Jimmy and Karen were proud of me. We were all disappointed in the judges' decision. My nose really hurt, but the ring physician said it was okay. Karen and I went back to the hotel. The next morning, we all piled into Jimmy's

Mercedes Benz for the ride back to Tampa. I held an ice pack on my nose all the way, and Karen was there to comfort me. The drive home seemed like it took forever. When I had my nose x rayed, I asked the doctor, 'Is it broken?' He laughed and said, 'Only in about twelve places.' The tip of my nose was shattered. I had to have it operated on. They recommended Dr. Edward Kampsen, a top physician, for the surgery. I called Angelo Dundee and asked him, 'Who's gonna pay for this?' He said, 'Don't worry. I'll take care of it.' He also told the doctor, 'No problem. Fix it.' I realized the days of my having a perfect nose were over.

I went into the operating room and emerged three hours later in intense pain. My head felt like it was stuffed, and it was crammed with cotton. I left the hospital with my nose in a cast. I looked pitiful. Karen was with me. She officially adopted me. She brought me back to the apartment which she shared with her two girlfriends. All three of them had been sorority sisters at St. Leo. I was confined to Karen's room when I was in Tampa, and she also shuttled me back and forth for visits to Orlando. Karen nursed me and cared for me all through Christmas and the Holidays. Things went well, considering the circumstances. I wore the nose cast for two weeks. When it finally came time to remove it, it wasn't a pleasant experience. They pulled cords out of my nose which were attached to about fourteen inches of cotton that had been packed up into my nasal passages. When the doctor started to pull it all out, it felt like my brains were being pulled out through my nose. It was a month or so before I could start sparring.

At that point, I began to look back on what had happened in California when I fought J.B. Williamson and also when I fought Leslie Stewart. I thought about how Angelo Dundee had given me only $1,000 out of my $6,000 purse. I also thought about the fact that Angelo didn't show up for the Stewart fight, but still took $1,000 of my $3,000 purse. He got a grand for simply making a phone call. Three months had gone by since my operation and the hospital and doctor's bill still had not been paid. Angelo had told me that he was going to take care of the medical bills, but a collection agency was after me.

James Salerno had experienced difficulty getting his medical bills paid, even though they resulted from his being injured in a professional bout. This happens far too often in sports, and especially in boxing. It occurs so frequently in prizefighting that it has become taken for granted. The fans want to see the athletes sacrifice their bodies, but no one cares when those whom they used to root for wind up crippled, maimed, brain damaged or dead. It's all part of the dark side of sports.

JEFF TRAGER RE-ENTERS THE PICTURE AND JAMES REUNITES WITH JIM MACDONALD

James wrote,

Jeff Trager contacted me. He had watched the Stewart fight and agreed that I had gotten screwed by the judges. We talked about giving it another shot. He called Angelo about releasing me from my contract. Angelo said, 'He still owes me $6,400.' Jeff and I flew down to Miami and met with Angelo at his office in the Plaza Bank Building. We managed to pay him off. After we returned to Tampa, I started training. Jeff met with Alessi Promotions, and that resulted in my signing a promotional agreement with them. I was to have six fights during the first year of the agreement and I was guaranteed $10,500 for that year, regardless of how many times I fought. The amount of money I was guaranteed was peanuts, but Phil Alessi made a verbal promise to me that if I won three straight fights on the USA Cable Network, I would get a fight on NBC. I talked Jeff into signing that agreement. He wasn't all that crazy about Alessi Promotions, but he agreed to sign.

The first fight Alessi arranged for me was in Tampa and televised by the USA Cable Network. My opponent was a fighter out of West Virginia named Dale Wilburn. He was only the third white fighter I had faced in thirty bouts. I caught him with a right hand over his slow left jab in the first round. He went down and got up on wobbly legs. After that, I jumped all over him with both hands and had him on the ropes when the referee stepped in and stopped the fight. I needed the win, because it ended my three fight losing streak. All of Tampa's Salvation Army was there, and they were all friends of Karen. For many of them, it was the first time they had ever been to a boxing show. Even though my fight didn't even last a round, they enjoyed it. I enjoyed it even more than they did. For the first time that I could remember, I didn't go out and get crazy afterwards. By this time, Karen had moved into her own apartment, but it was still in the same complex as the one she had shared with her sorority sisters. I had moved in with her, so we went to our new apartment after the fight, where we savored the victory over a bottle of wine and a late dinner and then went to bed.

Not long after my win over Dale Wilburn, Angelo Dundee called me and said, 'A guy named Stan Allen is managing a fighter named Jim MacDonald. He called me and said he needs you to help get MacDonald ready for Michael Spinks.' Jim had just knocked out Willie Edwards in Texas. He was fighting Michael Spinks for the light heavyweight title that coming June. I couldn't believe it. Jim was the guy *who was always telling me that I couldn't miss being a champ. Now, my former Marine Corps buddy was fighting Spinks, the man I always wanted to face in the ring. When I talked to Stan Allen, he told me, 'I want you to help Jim because you have a build that is similar to Spinks. Both of you are tall with long reaches.' He offered to take care of all my expenses, plus pay me $500 a week. I couldn't turn it down because Jim was my best friend in the Corps. I also figured that if MacDonald could beat Spinks, maybe Jim would give me shot against him in a title defense.*

Jeff Trager went with me to that training camp. When we arrived in Nashville, I quickly learned that Jim wasn't the same wild guy I knew in the Marines. He was married, had two daughters and was a born again Christian. That was fine with me because he was all the better for it. The first thing I asked Jim was, 'Mac, I haven't seen or heard from you for almost three years, and now you're fighting Spinks for the world title. How did it happen?' He replied, 'I took the fight with Edwards as a fill in and pulled off a major upset. Willie Edwards was the North American Boxing Federation champ. Although our bout was not for the title, the fact remained that I knocked him cold.'

I watched a video cassette tape of the MacDonald vs. Lewis fight. Edwards was all over Jim for the first four rounds, then Mac uncorked a right hand that put Edwards flat on his back. As the referee counted eight, Edwards could barely lift his head off the canvas. It was a very impressive knockout indeed. The win locked in Jim's fight with Spinks.

MacDonald and I sparred and ran in the mountains surrounding Nashville for two weeks. Jeff Trager did road work, sit ups, pushups and sprints with us. Even though he was 34 years old, he could keep up with us. He motivated us because he could sprint faster than me and he could also outdo us in sit ups and pushups.

When it came time to leave for the fight in Vegas, I wore bib overalls and a coonskin hat, complete with a tail. I'll admit that I looked like the village idiot, but I cracked everybody up with that outfit. I was just trying to keep Mac in a good mood and help him relax, and it worked. He laughed every time he looked at me. It would be the second time I had been to Vegas for a fight. I had fought Alvaro Lopez there in 1979 as part of an undercard to a Sugar Ray Leonard vs. Pete Ranzany bout. Lopez was a local guy, and I won a ten round unanimous decision at Caesar's Palace. The next day's sports page stated, 'Arthur Murray and Fred Astaire would have been proud of James Salerno's footwork.'

While we were sparring, Jim suffered a slight nose injury and he had to lay off the sparring for a few days. During Jim's layoff, I happened to be in the gym while

Carlos De Leon was working out. He was the world cruiserweight champion at the time, but he didn't impress me. He was fat. By that, I mean you could see cellulite on his stomach. I asked Stan Allen if I could spar with De Leon. He gave me the okay, so I got into the ring with Carlos. Carlos De Leon's nickname was Sugar, but I was sugar free that day. He tried to intimidate me with some smooth moves, but I filled his face with leather and had him bleeding out the nose and mouth before I was done. I thought, 'This guy is the champ? If the guy he's going to fight has anything, Sugar is going to lose.' Sure enough, that's what happened. De Leon lost his title a few days later when he fought Alfonso Ratliff.

I flew Karen out to be with me a few days before the fight. Don King was promoting it, and he called it D-Day in Vegas. He had arranged to have a large number of Marines in uniform there to root for MacDonald. I was in Mac's dressing room before the fight. His cousins from his hometown in Michigan and I escorted him to the ring, along with his trainer and manager. There was also a Marine Corps band and a color guard. All the pressure had Mac a little tight. In the first round, Spinks was constantly moving side to side and sticking the jab. I could tell that Michael Spinks had watched the tape of Jim's knockout of Willie Edwards. Mac tried to line Spinks up for a right hand shot that Michael wanted no part of. In the fourth round, Mac finally connected with a right, but Spinks was moving backwards and that reduced the full force of the blow. Michael Spinks was still visibly shaken, though. The fourth round was definitely Jim's best of the fight. The fifth round saw Spinks connecting with his jab, and he did damage to Mac's nose. It was bleeding freely. Mac was having trouble breathing, and Spinks sensed that this was the time to pick up the pace. Michael Spinks fired a vicious uppercut that caught Jim coming in, and it dropped him. Mac got up, but his nose was visibly broken and he was bleeding profusely. He charged Spinks, and then the fifth round ended. You could see that Spinks had a little too much experience for Mac at that point, and it would only be a matter of time. MacDonald managed to get through the sixth round, but in the seventh, Spinks caught him with some good combinations. Mac was still willing to continue, but the ref stopped the fight to save Jim from further punishment. MacDonald made everybody who knew him proud of him. He gave all that he had and rose from the canvas when most men would have been unable to continue. Well, at least he got a good pay day, and he didn't lose face in the eyes of the boxing people.

JAMES TAKES ON THE TORPEDO

Salerno wrote,

I arrived back in Tampa in fantastic shape. It was a good thing because Brad Jacobs, who was the matchmaker for Alessi Promotions told me that I was going to fight Grover 'Torpedo' Robinson from Fremont, California. Robinson was rated number six by Ring Magazine. He had just beaten Mike Sedillo for the Stroh's Tournament title. I was in the best condition of my life, but when I saw Robinson at the weigh in, he had me a little scared. Grover was my height, but he had longer arms, and he had muscles. I couldn't believe he only weighed 175 pounds. Karen had gotten her co-workers to buy tickets for themselves and their friends. The Egypt Temple Shrine was packed. The fight was carried on the USA Cable Network. My mother, my father and my grandfather, Poppy, had come to Tampa to be there. I also had other relatives who showed up. I felt a lot of pressure. I was in my dressing room loosening up when I was told that it was time to go to the ring. As I walked there, I was in a state of total concentration. I blocked out the cheers of the crowd and well wishers. Jimmy was ahead of me. He climbed in the ring and opened the ropes for me. I climbed in and started shadow boxing. I saw Grover Robinson make his entrance. He was wearing a red outfit, complete with a cape. He looked like a black superman, and I was scared.

Jimmy had often said to me, 'Fear is like fire. It can burn down your house, or you can use it to cook with.' I chose the latter. The bell rang to open the first round. Grover charged at me and I used my legs to go side to side. I made him miss and all the while, I was pecking away with my jab. This pattern continued. I out boxed him until the eighth round. That was when I found out why his nickname was Torpedo. He caught me with a right hand on the chin. It didn't hurt me at first, but I had a delayed reaction to it when my legs felt a little wobbly. I grabbed him and tied him up. That was all I needed to get my composure back. He thought I was in trouble, so he let both hands fly. The bell rang to end the eighth round, and that was the first one he had won. During the entire ninth round, the Torpedo and I exchanged heated flurries. I would call that round a draw. The tenth and final round belonged to me, and I was awarded the decision. During my post fight interview, I expressed my willingness to fight Michael Spinks in a rather brash manner to say the least. They even had Karen on television in between the rounds.

After I was almost knocked down during the eighth round, my father actually had the nerve to walk up to Karen and in front of her sister Lisa, begin talking about how we shouldn't have sex within ten days of a fight. As if that weren't enough, he also asked her for details about our sex life. Now I knew where I got my nerve from.

The night was great. My mother had driven a hundred miles to get there, but she went out into the lobby before the fight started and wouldn't go back into the arena until it was over. The win put me back into the ratings, but not as high as I thought I should have been. It struck me funny how Ring Magazine didn't rate me, even though they had rated Robinson number six before our fight.

JAMES SQUANDERS A GOLDEN OPPORTUNITY IN ATLANTIC CITY

Salerno wrote in his memoir,

Alessi Promotions offered me an opportunity to fight 6' 4" Anthony Witherspoon from Philadelphia. The fight was in August, 1985, and I only had three weeks to prepare. The bout was to be at the Sands Hotel in Atlantic City, New Jersey. It was to be televised on Eye of the Tiger Cable.

In pre-fight interviews, James said,

I've had to do a lot of talking to get my career together. For a time, I wasn't finding fights on a regular basis, so I tried to gain attention. I've been fighting for nine years already, and I want a title fight. Somebody once called me 'the youngest old pro in the business,' and I think that's true. I'm really geared up for this fight because I want to show Atlantic City the best of James Salerno and keep the pressure on Michael Spinks. If Witherspoon wants to know where I'm coming from, it will be from his worst nightmare.

Salerno talked tough, but talk is cheap. As the events unfolded, they would reveal that James was not mentally prepared for that fight.

Salerno wrote in his memoir,

Jimmy, Jeff, Karen and I arrived four days before the fight. I didn't run or workout at all during those four days. Jimmy disapproved of that. I remembered reading in a book titled Fools Die by Mario Puzo that the management of casinos arranges to have pure oxygen pumped into the air conditioning to keep people awake. I couldn't sleep, so I gambled. I also had sex the night before the fight. This is something a fighter should not do because it takes the edge off you and makes you less touchy. When you get into the ring, you want to be touchy. If somebody touches you, you're ready to take a swing at them. But then again, I was the one who forced the issue, not Karen. Some people, especially women, will say that it's all in your head. From my experience, I have to disagree with that. Sex is the ultimate sacrifice prior to a fight. Depriving yourself of sex gives you an attitude. To me, sex is a misdemeanor. The more I miss it, the meaner I get. Jimmy Williams used to say, 'If you don't think the stuff that comes out of a man is powerful, just remember that they only need a drop of it to make a test tube baby.'

Having sex the night before was wrong because I became overly concerned about saving my energy. When Jimmy wanted me to warm up twenty minutes before the fight by hitting the pads, I didn't want to. In looking back, I had a loser's attitude before that fight.

We walked down the aisles leading to the ring. They gave my opponent's brother, Terrible Tim Witherspoon, a ten minute introduction. The bell finally rang to begin the first round. I came out jabbing and dancing, while Anthony Witherspoon was chasing and missing. This continued all the way through. Witherspoon finally did manage to get in a few hooks , but not enough to win, or so I thought. Jimmy Williams and George Frances, a trainer from England, were the men working my corner. Just before I left my corner for the tenth and final round, George said, 'I heard you do all that talking back in Tampa. Now get in there and fight.' He apparently thought that the scoring was extremely close, but I continued doing the same thing I had done all night. When the decision was announced, what I had done turned out to be not enough. I lost a split decision.

Salerno's record fell to 33 wins and six losses. It was his fourth split decision loss, and all of them had come on the road. Harry Grooms once told him, "James, you ain't with the power. You're not with a Bob Arum or a Don King. That's why you haven't been getting those decisions."

James wrote,

I wished there had been a trap door in the canvas that I could have disappeared through. The fact that the people doing the telecast had me winning on their scorecard was no consolation.

The newspapers in Tampa said I blew the fight because of my performance in the last round. The loss was devastating to my title hopes. Michael Spinks had vacated his three light heavyweight title belts because he had fought and beaten Larry Holmes. If I had won my fight with Anthony Witherspoon, I would have definitely been in line for a shot at the vacant championship.

After my loss to Witherspoon, Alessi sort of blackballed me. At least that's how it seemed to me. They put me on hold and didn't have a thing for me until six months later. I was training every day, but that didn't buy groceries. My original purse for the Witherspoon fight was supposed to have been $4,000, but after I paid all my bills, I ended up with less than $1,000. Alessi got their cut, plus I had to take care of manager, my trainer and my sparring partners. I had to find something to do for money. I started my own little landscaping business. I cut grass for small *businesses. It helped me out. I managed to get by for awhile doing that, but in the winter, the grass doesn't grow. I was out of luck when the cold weather started, and out of money. Karen and I started to get into fights. I never punched her, but she got me so mad one morning that I did some mean things. She was leaving for work and was all dressed. We lived on the second floor. Just as she was about to get into her car, I poured a garbage can full of water on her from the second floor balcony. She was drenched and furious. She came running upstairs yelling at me. Just as she stepped into our apartment, I hit her over the head with a picture of us that was in a glass frame. It shattered the frame, but Karen was no worse for wear, at least physically. I moved out a short time after that episode and got my own apartment.*

Alessi Promotions finally arranged another fight for me. My opponent would be a fighter from Tampa named Eric Holley. The fight would be televised by the USA Cable Network.

Holley was originally from St. Augustine, Florida, but lived and trained in Tampa. He had received honorable mention by Ring Magazine for 1986's Prospect of the Year. It would be his first ten round fight.

Salerno wrote in his memoir,

I used to spar with him. He was no boxer, but he could punch and he had an iron chin. He was also unbeaten at the time, with a 14-0 record and 12 KO's. I never had a problem in the gym with him, but this wasn't sparring. It was going to be the real thing. We wouldn't be using head gear or big gloves. Alessi billed it as the Battle of the Bay. I was given only a week's notice for the fight. I wasn't in the best of shape, but when they offered the fight, I couldn't turn it down. I whipped my body into shape with the help of Henry Grooms and Jimmy Williams. Holley had always stayed in condition. I was a little nervous the night before the fight because I knew that if I lost, my career was over. As I drove to the fight, all I could think about was 'the dreaded lawnmower.' That thought put me into the proper mood for a fight. I didn't want to be cutting grass for the rest of my life. After the bell sounded to begin the first round, I didn't come out moving like I usually did. I jabbed, but for most of the fight, Eric and I fought in the gutter. That's Jimmy's expression for fighting inside and doing what has to be done to win. Our heads clashed throughout the bout, and we both suffered cuts over both eyes. It wasn't a pretty fight, but I won by a unanimous decision. It upped my record to 34 and 6.

A REMATCH WITH LESLIE STEWART LEADS TO THE ULTIMATE BETRAYAL

James wrote in his memoir,

There was talk of a rematch with Leslie Stewart in Tampa and after a few weeks, the talk became reality. I couldn't believe it at first. It sounded too good to be true. I would be fighting the number three rated light heavyweight, and I would be fighting a rematch in my hometown. I knew I could win this fight. The first fight was in his hometown, with his judges. He had all the advantages, especially if the fight went the distance, which it did. He won a split decision which really left me bitter. I knew then that if I outpointed him, I would get the decision, take his number three spot in the world and get my long sought title shot. After all, it was going to be in my hometown with local judges.

I went into serious training for eight weeks. During that time, Karen was offered the job of public relations for Alessi Promotions. She accepted the job against my wishes. I told her that she could find herself being used as a pawn against me. She was tired of her job at the Salvation Army, though, and she said the job would open doors for other opportunities. So, she went to work for the same organization that had promotional rights for all my fights.

One day, Karen and I went to lunch. During our conversation, she happened to mention, 'Stewart wouldn't come to Tampa to fight you unless they brought their own judges from Miami.' I almost choked on my food. I said, 'What!' I got so upset that I said, 'I'm not fighting without neutral judges!' That ended lunch, and I immediately drove her back to work. After I dropped her off, Karen went straight to Brad Jacobs and told him what I had said about not fighting unless neutral judges were used. He replied, 'WHAT!! I can't believe you told him about the judges. Do you want to blow the whole thing?' Brad then coerced her into getting back to me and telling me, 'James, I was only joking.' She told me that very thing when I got home that night, and she assured me I had nothing to worry about. I dismissed what he had told me at lunch as just a joke and put all thoughts of the judges out of my mind.

I knew that the fight meant a great deal to my manager, Jeff Trager. I thought it was because he had paid an extra $3,000 out of his pocket for the fight. He insisted on me staying with for the last week before the bout. Jimmy Williams had me programmed to beat Stewart the best way we knew how. We were going to out box him, just as we had in the first fight. The only difference was that some Miami judges weren't going to be there to steal it from me, or so I thought.

On the day of the fight, I did a good psych job on Stewart at the press conference, then Jeff and I went back to his house, where I spent the time until we left for the arena. When we were getting ready to leave, Jeff said, 'I have all your equipment. Let's go.' This was unusual because I normally packed the bag I took to my fights. We arrived at the fairgrounds. A huge crowd was there. It was an attractive match, but a benefit was also being held for the daughter of Don 'Cowboy' Shiver, a local hero with a big following. All the proceeds that night were going into a trust fund set up for his little girl who wasn't going to have her daddy any more, at least her original one.

When the fights started, I was back in my dressing room relaxing. There were some quick knockouts and before I knew it, they were calling for me to get ready. Jimmy wrapped my hands. I put on my boxing shoes and trunks, and then I got greased up. I started loosening up and then Jimmy asked, 'Got your mouthpiece?' I asked Jeff, 'Where's my mouthpiece?' He told me he had packed all my equipment. He couldn't find it. This was a real nightmare for me because the mouthpiece is the most important piece of protective equipment for a boxer. It is supposed to prevent your teeth from being knocked out and keep your jaw from being broken. A properly fitted mouthpiece cost two hundred dollars. The mouthpiece itself was forty dollars, but the dentist would charge one hundred sixty dollars to fit it. While we were frantically looking for the mouthpiece, someone popped their head in the door and said. 'Be in the ring in five minutes.' I didn't want to fight without my mouthpiece, but I was thinking, 'I might never get a chance like this again.' Jimmy dug through his little black bag and brought out a super soft pliable object and inserted it into my mouth. It felt like a rubber band around my teeth, and I thought, 'How is this thing going to protect my teeth?' I smiled at Jimmy and said, 'Look at the positive side. I'll make sure he doesn't hit me in my mouth.'

As we walked out to the ring, the Kenny Loggins song This Is It was blaring over the loudspeakers. I was wearing red, white and blue trunks I had made especially for the fight. They were exact replicas of the ones the Apollo Creed character wore in Rocky.

At the start of our fight, Stewart didn't come out charging as I expected he would. He came out boxing, and that was fine with me. He was backing up and trying to out-jab me, but he found it was impossible to do that. By the fifth round, he had wised up. He finally figured out that he couldn't out box me. He then tried to take it to me, but he couldn't connect. I kept my jab in his face. I was making him miss and I was piling up points, and I was frustrating him. We got into a clinch and he ripped me with a good shot below the belt. I dropped to one knee. This allowed me to regroup. We finished the fight with a few good flurries. When the bell rang at the end of the ten rounds, I knew I had done it. I knew I had out boxed him and that they couldn't take it away from me this time. I looked across at Stewart and he was looking down because he knew he had lost. Finally, they read the scorecards. The first judge scored it 92 to 98. The second judge scored it 91 to 99. The third judge scored it 93 to 98. Each judge had the victorious fighter winning by a wide margin. They still hadn't come out and said which fighter had won. While they were reading off the scoring, I was walking around the ring thinking, 'I knew I beat him, but I didn't think I beat him that bad. I hope he doesn't get too discouraged.' Then came the real shocker. They announced that the winner by a unanimous decision was Leslie Stewart.

I went numb. Stewart was as surprised as I was that he had won. The crowd booed when he was announced as the winner. Everybody told me I had won as I walked back to the dressing room, but then again, your friends will always tell you that.

Words can never describe the heartache and depression that loss caused me. All the sacrifice, sweat and pain I had gone through had been for nothing but more pain. I didn't want to see my family or my girlfriend, so I went with Jeff to his mansion. As we drove there, I thought, 'I'm really losing it. I know I won, or at least I thought I did. How could they give it to him in my hometown? How could the judges vote for him by such a wide margin? I fought a better fight. I must be crazy or this is all just a bad dream.' After we got to Jeff's house, he offered me a drink and I accepted. He told me that he thought I had won. He began getting drunk and as he got boozed up, he brought me to his den and handed me $2,000. He said, 'I'm not taking my cut.' Then he said, 'I won $70,000 tonight betting on Stewart.' Now I knew why my mouthpiece was left behind. I didn't know what the hell to think. I just felt betrayed. I drowned my sorrows.

The next morning, I drove over to Karen's apartment. She confessed that the judges were handpicked by Jimmy Cavo, Stewart's manager. She told me about Brad Jacobs getting upset with her and yelling at her for telling me the truth. She admitted that she had lied to me when she said her comment about Stewart demanding Miami judges was just a joke. The next thing she said made me angry. She said, 'I don't think it made any difference.' She insulted my intelligence by saying that. Apparently someone thought it would make a big enough difference to force her to lie to me. At that point, I thought, 'Well, the damage is done.' And then I thought, 'If Karen knew about the judges, my manager knew it and didn't tell me.' If I had been told about the judges, I probably would have fought Stewart anyway, but my entire strategy would have changed to fit the situation. It would have been either knock him out or get knocked out.

I confronted Jeff with the truth. He said, 'I thought you would knock him out.' This was a lame excuse coming from a man who just happened to forget my mouth-piece and then when guilt got the best of him, admitted he won $70,000 by betting on Stewart. When I brought that up, he dismissed it as 'drunk talk.' I didn't know what to do. What Brad Jacobs had done was just part of the business of boxing, which I have never liked. What Jeff did to me was far worse. I didn't trust him anymore, and I had serious doubts about Karen.

JAMES FINALLY GETS A CHANCE AT A TITLE

James wrote in his memoir,

I forgave Karen for some unknown reason, but I was still in a state of depression. I drove back to Winter Park and watched the tape delay presentation of the fight on the USA Cable Network at my parents' home. Their announcers had me winning six rounds to three, with one round being a draw. I can't describe the sick feeling I got in the pit of my stomach, and I had that feeling for weeks. I felt so betrayed by my manager and my girl friend. I was still in this state of depression when I happened to walk into Brad Jacobs' office one day and he said, 'How would you like to fight for the vacant USBA Championship? Eddie Davis retired and the belt is up for grabs. Bob Lee, the president of the IBF/USBA, said you were qualified on the basis of the highly disputed decision loss to Stewart. You would be fighting somebody named Prince Charles Williams.'

This all sounded too good to be true. I said, 'Okay, Brad, what's the catch?' He replied, 'Well, the only real catch is that this guy in New York named Johnny Bos actually arranged it, and he gets $500 off the top. That is, if you want to fight.' I said, 'Wait a minute, Brad. Isn't Alessi Promotions supposed to be getting me the fights for their ten percent.' His answer was, 'Look, James, do you want the fight or not?' I said, 'Of course I do. How much money is involved?' He said, '$4,000.' I had to give Johnny Bos $500 off the top, then Alessi Promotions got ten percent, then my manager got 20 percent and Jimmy got 13 percent. I got what was left, which wasn't much. So, what else is new. I had been fighting for peanuts all my life.

I was also to be given three round trip tickets to Indianapolis. The fight was to be held in Market Square Arena as a co-feature to a WBA title fight between Marvin 'Pops' Johnson and Jean Marie Emebe. Both fights would be televised on syndicated TV. I said, 'Brad, isn't four thousand peanuts for a twelve round title fight on national TV?' He said, 'Think of the opportunity.' That is the line boxing promoters have used for ages to get boxers to fight for peanuts. I took the fight because I was in a desperate situation.

The promotion was billed as the "Indy 175" because the card consisted of six fights with the last two deciding the USBA and WBA titles at the 175 pound weight limit.

James wrote,

Jimmy Williams was excited about the idea and the more I thought about how good a USBA championship belt would feel around my waist, I became excited too. Karen was great before this fight. She made good meals for me, didn't worry me with anything and even took care of most of the bills. Jeff, my manager, was nowhere to be found. Since I had three round trip tickets, I wanted to let Karen use one. When I told Brad this he said, 'If I don't go, you don't fight.' I went over his head to Phil Alessi. Alessi sat behind his big desk and said, 'I want Brad to go so he can look after your best interests. I didn't have the money for another round trip ticket, so Karen stayed in Tampa.

When we arrived in Indianapolis, I couldn't eat anything all day because I had to be right at 175 and one half pounds. I noticed in the papers that Williams was getting good write ups and his name was in front of mine on the poster. I then came to the conclusion that I had been brought in as an opponent. I even voiced this feeling at the pre-fight interview. I said, 'You just think I'm a good opponent and I feel that's all I was brought here for. Well, I'm gonna surprise you.' At the weigh in, I met his manager, who was a woman. She was hanging out with a black woman who was wearing glasses. I thought the black woman with glasses might have been Prince Charles Williams' mother.

I was a little edgy the night before the fight. It was a little chilly in Indianapolis and it was hard for me to break a sweat. I went through a self induced mental exercise that I had learned from Jimmy. Instead of magnifying your opponent in your eyes, you simplify things and put them in the simplest forms of reality. A man can only hit you with the two blunt objects at the end of his arms. He can only throw one arm at a time. There are laws of nature, laws of gravity and laws of boxing. The laws of boxing are unwritten, but they still apply

During my conversations with Sal Salerno, he mentioned an odd thing that happened on the morning of the fight. Sal said,

James was within the weight limit when the weigh in was conducted on the day before the fight. Nevertheless, the local boxing authorities decreed on the day of the fight that my son had to lose a pound and a half for some reason. He was forced to spend time in a sweat box. It is a tribute to his remarkable stamina that the last minute drying out process didn't affect him.

James Salerno wrote in his memoir,

In the dressing room before the fight, Jimmy was putting Vaseline all over my body. It was a sort of pre-fight ritual. They say it helps prevent cuts, but I always thought of it as war paint. It offered very little protective value, but it helped my psychological state.

At the opening bell, Williams rushed out of his corner, winging with both arms. I was content to just move side to side and make him miss. Defense doesn't win fights, but I figured he couldn't keep the pace up for long. When the first round ended, I knew he had won that round, not so much for hitting me as for putting up an all out effort. At the start of the second round, he charged at me again. I tied him up and when we broke, I made the near fatal mistake of pushing off with both arms extended in front of my body. Williams quickly took advantage of this opportunity. He stepped in and fired a right uppercut underneath my extended arms. It caught me right under the chin and snapped my head back. It dropped me for a couple of seconds. I quickly rose off the canvas. The referee wiped off my gloves and then motioned for us to fight. At this point, Williams was moving in to finish me off, but I escaped his lunges with side to side movement. When the bell sounded to end the second round, I went back to my corner. Jimmy said, 'Are you okay?' I answered, 'Yeah,' but I knew I had been tagged real good. I was trying to remember where I was. At first I thought I was in Atlantic City, then I thought I was in Tampa. I knew that wasn't right because I looked at the lighting and thought, 'This can't be Tampa. The lighting is different there.' I was too embarrassed to ask Jimmy where we were. I had also forgotten that I was fighting for the USBA title. The one thing I hadn't forgotten was how to fight. The third round for me was nothing but jab and move. By the end of that round, I finally shook off the cobwebs. All I knew was that I was fighting the guy standing in front of me. All the hurt had transformed into anger. My anger had transformed into retaliation. In the fourth round, I started connecting more and more with the jab. Williams' pace had slowed considerably. He saw I wasn't going anywhere except back after his ass. In the fifth round, I snapped his head back with a right hand that drove him to the ropes. I threw another right to his chin that snapped his head back again. This time, his mouthpiece was sent airborne into the fourth row. The tide was beginning to turn when the bell rang to end the fifth round. In the sixth round, my jab was finding its mark more and more and Williams' face was swelling up. I connected with a right hand shot that turned his head around and buckled his knees. He fell back against the ropes and was visibly hurt. Another right hand found its mark and put his mouthpiece into the crowd again. Then, the bell rang to end the sixth round. In the seventh round, Prince Charles tried to box with me, but to no avail. At this point, I figured that he had only won the first three rounds, but he did have a knockdown to his credit. I had no doubt I had won the last four rounds. In the beginning of the eighth round, I was out boxing him, and he was still an ineffective aggressor. In the ninth round, I crashed another right hand over the top off his lazy left jab and put his mouthpiece into orbit for the third time. In addition, his two front teeth had been knocked somewhere out into the crowd. Williams was just trying to survive at the end of that round. By the tenth round, his mouth was bleeding profusely and his front teeth were no more. My jab was adding more to his disfigurement. At that point, we were both pretty spent, but I still out boxed him in the last two rounds. When the bell sounded to end the fight, I knew I had won, but that only lasted until the judges' scores were announced. Prince Charles had won by a majority decision.

I couldn't believe it. I just fell to my knees in my corner and then a split second after the decision was announced, I saw the same black lady with glasses who had been hanging out with Williams' manager. She was running up the steps to the ring with the championship belt and she fastened it around his waist, then hugged and kissed him. I later found out that she had been sitting with that belt in her lap for the entire fight. I thought, 'That lady isn't his mother. She's one of the top brass of the USBA.'

It was another heartbreaker that made it two in a row for me. Jimmy was also numb. It seemed that no matter how hard we worked, they would find a way to steal it from us. I later found out that the promoter, Russell Peltz, had a contract for promotional rights to Prince Charles Williams. The promoter also picks the judges and if the promoter doesn't like the way they judge, he doesn't use them anymore. This means that the judges and their wives do not get free vacations to fly to different cities and get paid for judging a fight. I think Perry Mason would call this 'indirect intimidation.' I received a purse of $4,000 for the fight. After I paid my bills, I was left with $1,800.

Sal Salerno raised another interesting point when he said,

There are usually post fight interviews with the winning boxer. In this case, there was no such interview with Prince Charles Williams. I honestly believe they skipped the interview because Williams looked horrible with his eyes swollen shut and teeth knocked out. Where I come from, a decision should be given to the fighter who causes the most damage to their opponent.

John Hayden has watched video of the fight several times. He concluded,

James could have destroyed Prince Charles Williams if he had really wanted to. I believe he was trying to pace himself. In my opinion, he just didn't throw enough

combinations. Jimmy Williams can be seen on the video giving instruction in the corner between rounds, and you can hear him say, 'James, I want you to throw a jab, right hand, left hook.' James just wouldn't throw that left hook. He didn't throw many hooks throughout the entire fight. But it's easier said than done. I wasn't the guy in the ring, and I wasn't the guy who was tired.

The video also shows what a wonderful person James was. At the end of the fight, he immediately went to Prince Charles' corner instead of celebrating and going back to his corner to be with his people. He went to the other fighter's corner to hug him. You can see Jimmy trying to get him away from there, and James goes back to his corner and meets with Jimmy for a minute. He still returns to Prince Charles' corner, though, and puts his arms around him. He thanked him for a good fight. That's the way James always was. Even if he kicked your ass or you took something from him, he still acknowledged you. This was a great quality about James, and he inspired me to be the same way.

A BRIEF PERIOD AWAY FROM THE RING AND THEN A CHANCE TO GO TO ITALY

Losing a controversial decision to Prince Charles Williams left James in a depressed state. He wrote in his memoir,

At that point in my life, I just wanted to get away from boxing. I had been a professional for ten years and it was draining me mentally. I started hanging out with Bill Compton and the local surfers. I even dyed my hair blond. I accomplished one thing. I finally lost my fear of sharks.

During this time, James made the Orlando papers because he landed a 16.2 pound snook at Sebastian Inlet. He caught the fish with a twelve pound test line and used a red and white bucktail.

James wrote about another dangerous experience he had which was much more dangerous. He Stated,

I'm a firm believer in the saying, 'The thrill and excitement derived from any given event is in exact proportion to the risk involved.' One Sunday morning, I decided to go fishing with Dom Polo's brother, Joe. We were in my old rusted out truck and were driving along at about 65 miles per hour. There was a slight fog. It was six in the morning, so there was a slight dew on the road. All of a sudden, Joe yelled, 'Look out!' At that moment, a truck that was in the right lane pulled a u-turn in front of us. He saw us at the last instant and cut back to the right. When I responded to his last minute antics, I lost control of my truck. We avoided the other truck, but we had spun around and were traveling backwards at 65 miles per hour. I'll never forget that feeling of complete helplessness and having no control over what would happen next. Those three to five seconds felt like an eternity. I could remember everything. When my vehicle finally spun onto the side of the road, it flipped. Joe shit his pants and got out of my truck first, then he helped get me out. I had been slammed against the driver's side door. Joe was shaken up a little. My truck was demolished. If you had seen it, you would have thought nobody survived. I found out later at the hospital that I had a shoulder separation and a chipped clavicle bone.

I met a man in the emergency room who set me up with a lawyer from Winter Park named Russell Troutman. They got a settlement for me. The entire settlement came to $10,000, but Troutman took $2,000 and the friend I met in the emergency room received $1,000. Karen called him an ambulance chaser. If it wasn't for *him, I wouldn't have seen the lawyer and gotten a red cent.*

I had to rehabilitate my shoulder. He was based out of Maitland. Within three months, my shoulder was stronger than before the accident.

James was fit enough to return to the ring, but he had no one to arrange fights for him after his relationship with Alessi Promotions had come to a stormy end. The breakup was caused by an argument over money, a subject Salerno had no knowledge of. For as long as he had been a prizefighter, he had never questioned what he was paid. In the long run he would have been better off letting the matter slide. Now, however, he was broke and he was desperate. James wrote,

After reviewing my contract with Alessi Promotions, I came to the conclusion that they owed me money. It really wasn't that much. It amounted to a thousand dollars. I brought that to the attention of Mr. Alessi. He told me, 'Get a job.' He acted like it was a big joke. He walked away from me, but I chased him all around his bakery waving my contract in the air. He finally said, 'See Brad about it.' When I talked with Brad Jacobs, he said, 'I don't feel like we owe you the money.' He had forgotten to review my contract after my loss to Witherspoon. The contract stated that if I had more than one loss during the term of the contract, it would constitute breach of contract. The split decision I lost to Witherspoon was the only loss I had while the contract was in effect. I was frustrated from trying to deal with Brad Jacobs, so I returned to Phil Alessi. I was finally told to sue them. I had enough of being lied to, so I hired, a Tampa lawyer, to review the contract. I ended up suing Alessi Promotions, which was still Karen's employer. Before long, Karen quit and went to work as part of the management for Pinellas Square Mall in Pinellas Park that had been built by Edward De Bartolo. Karen believed in justice and if I were wrong, she would have been the first to admit it. She knew that I was right. If they had just given me the thousand dollars I was willing to settle for in the first place, I would never had sued them. After I spent the money to file the suit, Phil Alessi told me he would give me the thousand dollars. I replied, 'Okay, I'll settle for the thousand, but you'll also have to take care of my attorney's fees.' He said, 'I'd rather spend three thousand dollars and blow you out of the water.' What a guy, huh?

By this time, James had severed all ties with free spending Jeff Trager. This proved to be a wise move. James and his parents were unaware of how the thirtyish entrepreneur was making so much money. It was later stated in federal court records that Salerno's manager had been involved in a drug operation. He was alleged to have procured multi kilogram quantities of coke from Colombians and other suppliers. After receiving the cocaine, runners were used to transport the drugs to Gary Starnes, who was based in northern Illinois.

Starnes would then sell the cocaine and forward the proceeds to Trager. The two of them lived life in the fast lane off their cocaine proceeds. They attended the 1984 and the 1986 Super Bowls and went in style. They hired private jets and flew to major boxing matches in Atlantic City and Montreal. They purchased a car wash in Florida. They also bought real estate in Florida and buried some of the money they made from drug trafficking on the properties.

It all came crashing down when one of their suppliers, Charles Froschauer, was arrested on cocaine charges in 1979. Even though Starnes and Trager selected an attorney for him and paid the lawyer fees, Froschauer eventually ratted them out. He told the Feds that the two were "together all the time," were "like one" and continued to distribute cocaine until at least 1987.

The court records stated that in the spring of 1987, Trager's Colombian connection fronted Jeff eleven kilograms of poor quality coke. The stuff was so bad it smelled like oil. Trager shipped it up to Starnes in Illinois. Starnes and an associate sold the coke, but didn't turn any money over to Trager. Gary told Jeff that the police had seized the shipment. He sent Trager newspaper clippings of a recent seizure as proof of his story. Jeff was put in a bind and had to pay off the Colombians out of his own pocket. This created a rift between Starnes and Trager that ended their partnership. Jeff no longer supplied Starnes. Starnes went to a new supplier who turned out to be a Federal informant.

James had no knowledge of this. He took Trager at his word and never really delved into how a man in his early thirties could afford a mansion in Odessa and a lavish lifestyle. There's an old saying; "If something appears to be too good to be true, it isn't." Jeff Trager was not the genuine article, and he ended up betraying James. By 1987, he was no longer part of Salerno's life. The fighter was in the midst of turmoil and his career was on hold.

Salerno wrote in his memoir,

In the midst of all this confusion, Johnny Bos called the apartment one night. He had a one of a kind Wolfman Jack voice. He said, 'Salerno, I thought you beat Williams and Stewart. Hold on for a second.' After a minute went by, Johnny said, 'Salerno, you still there? I got Italy on the phone.' The next thing I know, I'm on a three way conversation with what sounded like Wolfman Jack and Bruno 'Three Fingers' Finelli. Johnny had me talking to a big promoter in Italy named Umberto Branchini. Branchini told me that he would love to have me over there in the fall for some boxing matches. Since Jeff had not stayed in contact with me, I was a free man again as far as I was concerned. Karen knew that if I was ever going to work as a boxing trainer, it was not going to be in Tampa. I made arrangements to meet Johnny Bos at the Sheraton Hotel in Tampa to iron out the details and see where he was coming from.

Johnny Bos was a native of Brooklyn who was easily recognized because of his Fu Manchu and dark shades. He was an eccentric who never learned how to drive and never wore a wrist watch. He stood 6' 3" and weighed well over 255 pounds. He was big in size and in reputation within the boxing world. He was considered "part matchmaker, part manager and part booking agent." Johnny once described his role by saying, "I manage the managers." He was inducted into the Florida Boxing Hall of Fame. He died in 2013 at the age of 61.

Salerno wrote,

The next morning, I drove to where he was staying and banged on his door. A black girl walked out and for a while, I thought I had the wrong room until Bos yelled, 'Just a minute, James!' He got dressed and met me in the lobby. He bought me breakfast and said, 'I won't accept your money because I already made money off you.' That was just what I needed; an honest wise guy. After breakfast, we started playing Trivial Pursuit. He played like he made the machine. I got down to business and asked him, 'Look, Johnny, what's your angle? You're not doing this for nothing.' He replied, 'I make my money off the Americans I send over to fight you. You see, you won't be fighting against the people in Itally, but for them. If a fight happens to go the distance, they won't steal it from you like they have been doing to you in America. Besides that, you will be living at the beach. There will be beautiful girls everywhere and the best food in the world. You'll probably be a heavyweight after living there awhile. It's a resort town.' They wanted me over there the first week of September, 1987. That was only a few months away.

I started back doing road work. I heard through Karen that Mark Breland and Henry Tillman were coming to train in Tampa for awhile. I went down to the Alessi Promotions gym. I met Joe Fariello, who was Breland and Tillman's trainer. He asked me if I wanted to spar with Tillman since he had a tough fight coming up. I said, 'Sure, Joe. I'm not a sparring partner, but could you help me out a little?' He said, 'You must have that bad habit.' I didn't understand what he meant. I said, 'What bad habit?' He replied with a smile, 'You like to eat.' He understood and helped me out. I hated asking for money for sparring. I had been used to paying guys for sparring with me. After not fighting for a year, I was as poor as a church mouse. I couldn't even pay attention or spend the evening. This went on for about two weeks, then Phil Alessi came charging in the gym. He started poking me in the chest with his index finger and screaming at me to get out of his gym. He caused a big scene. I brought up the fact that Joe Fariello wanted me there to help him and that was the only reason I was there. He got even madder and the madder he got, the cooler and calmer I became. I said, 'Phil, I think this shows incredibly bad taste on your part to make scene in the middle of our workout.' I had never seen Phil Alessi so mad before. Before things got out of hand, I did as he asked and left.

Phil Alessi was abrupt with James, but in all fairness, Salerno was no longer part of Alessi Promotions and the gym was private property. The trainer and the fighter did not have the right to make up their own rules about who could be there. It was clearly time for James Salerno to move on.

JAMES' ITALIAN ADVENTURE

Salerno wrote in his memoir,

September tenth rolled around and Johnny Bos made arrangements for me to leave for Italy out of Tampa. The trip to New York was no problem. The big trip over the Atlantic was another story. The time changes got to me. I had virtually no money, but I had been given a round trip plane ticket just in case things didn't work out. When I finally arrived at the Milano Airport, there was no one there to pick me up. Finally, a little guy came up to me and said, 'Salerno?' I said, 'Si.' Luckily, he was the right man.

He brought me to Umberto Branchini's office where I met Giovanni Branchini, the son of the Chief Beef of boxing in Italy. That lasted about fifteen minutes. The little guy with the moustache then took me out to eat. Nothing was said between us because the only Italian words I knew were 'pizza,' 'spaghetti' and 'lasagna.' We then drove to a huge railroad terminal and I was put on a train to Rimini. The trip seemed to take forever. I looked out the window and all I could see was barren land and corn fields. I felt like I was going to a Soviet labor camp.

When I finally arrived in Rimini, a guy who looked like a KGB agent met me. He spoke very little English. He drove me to the resort place Johnny Bos had told me about. The building I was taken to looked good on the outside. He introduced me to my roommate, who was named Gimmi. He was huge, had a wild look about him and resembled a cicus strong man. The KGB agent said, 'This your room' in broken English, and then both he and Gimmi left.

I decided to take a shower. I couldn't find any soap or towels, things I had taken for granted during ten years as a professional boxer. I tried to make the best of things. There was no hot water and I was forced to dry off with a dirty wool blanket. At that point, I was cussing to myself and planning what I was going to do when I got my hands on Johnny Bos.

The next thought I had was, 'I might wake up in the middle of the night and find my new four hundred pound roommate sitting at the foot of my bed, staring at me, nodding and smiling. I've been screwed by Bos and the way things were going, I don't trust anyone and I'm not gonna get screwed twice.' I then walked to the nearest store and purchased the biggest switchblade I could. I placed it under my pillow that night and slept with my hand on it.

Daylight was a welcome sight. After I got up, I ran with the other boxers. When we were finished, I told their trainer, who spoke English, 'I'm sharing a room with 'Big Gimmi' and it just isn't a workable situation. The room smells like something died in there. It probably was his last roommate.' Thankfully, my complaint led to my getting my own apartment.

When gym time rolled around, they had me spar with Brutus aka Big Gimmi. We were in a tiny ring no bigger than the combined size of four phone booths. At the start of our sparring match, the big man charged at me as if he were shot out of a cannon. He caught me off guard. I survived and realized that I was not in as good condition as I thought I was. I had placed myself in a situation where it was sink or swim.

After about a week, I got to spar with Francesco Damiani. He had won a silver medal at the Los Angeles Olympics in 1984. He was a super heavyweight as an amateur. I moved and jabbed and kept him missing until we finished. At the conclusion of our sparring session, he lifted his eyebrows and said in broken English, 'You goo-edd, Salerno.' After a month, I had gotten back in shape. Big Gimmi couldn't hit me with a handful of rice.

They arranged my first fight with somebody named Bobby Thomas. He was from West Virginia. I thought, 'This is crazy. They bring a guy from West Virginia and a guy from Florida all the way to Italy to fight each other.' I didn't really care who I fought. I just wanted to get a fight and get the feel of the real thing again.

The fight took place in northern Italy in a beautiful city called Valle D'Aosta. It was on the undercard to the European Heavyweight Championship bout between Damiani and Anders Eklund. I had some doubts before the fight because of my year layoff, but when they called me to the ring, I was ready. I had broken a good sweat, which was something I had failed to do in previous fights. I wasn't ever going to be caught cold again, like I was in the Prince Charles Williams fight. When the bell rang to start the first round, I had a little trouble finding Bobby Thomas with my jab because he was a southpaw, but my newly discovered right hand was landing. I had him wobbly after the second round. When the third round started, conditioning became a factor. I got in some good body shots and he began to fade on the ropes. After a few more punches, the referee stopped the fight. I was declared the winner by a third round TKO.

After the fight, I went to my opponent's dressing room and got to know him. He turned out to be a genuine person. He had the potential to possibly win a title if the situation were right. He wasn't in the best of shape. I asked him why he took the *fight. He said he was broke. He had taken the offer on only three day's notice. It made me ponder the reality of becoming a journeyman fighter, or what is referred to in America as an 'opponent.' It made me feel lucky that I barely escaped that label. For once in my life, I felt as though I was being looked out for. After an eight hour flight over the Atlantic, it would take any human being at least a week to get used to the time change and the jet lag. When Bobby Thomas arrived, he was the 'enemy.' If you are the enemy, the people who are supposed to accommodate you before the fight and after are always late or sometimes never show up on purpose. They will never admit to that. They will just come up with some lame excuse. When Bobby told me about all of the inconveniences that 'just happened,' I put two and two together and came up with five on my own. I am a gladiator, but my heart couldn't help going out to this guy. He was a Rocky Balboa with a southern accent and blue eyes. His disabled father taught him how to box on the farm. I felt bad inside. I only wanted honesty from boxing, not an advantage. I felt that I couldn't win even if I won. I love victory, but the taste of victory is so much sweeter when all's fair.*

I rinsed my trunks of the blood and sweat and gave them to him. I said, 'When you wear these, you better be in shape!' He took them and smiled. He assured me that he would be in shape for the next fight he had. He guaranteed he'd wear the green and white trunks I had given him. I also made a promise to him. I said, 'When I win the world's championship, I will give you a rematch in your home state of West Virginia.' In boxing, promises are broken daily. Prince Charles Williams made me a verbal promise of a rematch, but I never heard from him. I don't hold that against Williams. I don't blame him for not wanting to lose his title. Bobby Thomas and I shook hands and said goodbye.

I went back to training camp in Rimini and I finally started to get back into condition after two months. I was having fun sparring with my roommate Big Gimmi. I gave him bloody noses four out of five days of sparring. I began to attract the attention of the old Italian men who would pass the time by watching the fighters in the gym. They would watch me and then murmur among themselves. There still hasn't been any talk of a contract, though.

Unlike other sports, when you get tired in boxing, you can't tell a coach, 'I'm tired. Send somebody in.' When you get tired in boxing, the only thing you'll get from the crowd is shouts of, 'He's tired! Knock him out!' Up in the ring, you're virtually naked. You have no pads, no shirt, no helmets and it's one on one. If you're not in shape or haven't been honest in training, it will be exposed by your opponent in the midst of battle.

I have to admit that boxers as a whole are easy prey for smooth talking managers and promoters who use them at their disposal. They are like cattle being led away to slaughter. Many will put in years of chasing an elusive dream that will never come true. They will end up as old, broke ex-pugs who will have to resort to some kind of manual labor to survive. That is the cold, hard reality about boxing. To the elite few who break through to the big time and big bucks that come with it, every hardship was worth it. Only the strong survive. The people who say that boxing gives a poor kid a chance to fight his way out of poverty are the same people who take advantage of him and who shun the mere mention of a boxers' union to make sure they have something to help pay the bills when they are through boxing. Every other big time sport has unity. Why can't boxing have it? It is because of the economic strangulation that most all boxers have to deal with. Even if there were a union, you would always have boxers crossing picket lines to fight for peanuts.

All I can do is let the fear of failure keep my wheels turning toward success. After eleven years as a professional, my faith is as strong as ever. I just thank God that I turned pro as early as I did. If I hadn't, by the time I got boxing smart, I'd have been too old to think about being champ. I don't think that I'm at my peak mentally or physically. Once you think you are at your peak, there is only one direction left to go and that is down.

As far as my religious beliefs go, I'm a Catholic, but a Christian first. Jimmy Williams would say, 'Don't be like a lot of fighters who make the sign of the cross up in the ring right before they fight. They are just fooling themselves if they think God loves only them and not their opponent. I firmly believe God helps those who help themselves. I confess that there have been times I have been Satan himself, but my conscience finally turned me around. Jeff Trager once told me. 'You remind me of a preacher in an old western movie who would ride from town to town on a mule, toting his Bible in one hand and a shotgun in the other.' I also believe that to whom much is given, much is expected from. If I see someone in trouble, I'll go out of my way to help.

Before I left for Italy, I talked to Dom Polo. He said, 'Tell them you want a $50,000 cash signing bonus. You'll sign for three years. They get 35 percent and you get 65 percent. You pay for trainers and all expenses out of your end.' He added, 'Look, even if you never box again, you'll be ahead of the game with $50,000 in the bank.' My father spilled the beans to Johnny Bos, and Bos told me, 'Forget it. If you start talking that much money, they'll put you on a plane and send you home.' I had to lie to Bos and say, 'I was only kidding.' I knew Bos was in cahoots with the promoters in Italy. He had probably told them, 'You can get Salerno for nothin'.'

I had a fight scheduled for December 11, which was a Friday night. When I arrived in Livorno at the hotel where I was staying, I saw a bunch of fighters walking around in the lobby. I tried to catch a peek at who I was fighting, but I couldn't see anyone who was about my size. They were a bunch of lightweights. There was one heavyweight. He looked like a twin to the Drago character played by Dolph Lundgren in Rocky IV. There was no one in my weight class.

Later that night, Umberto Branchini arrived. He gave me the scoop that my original opponent didn't show and then he introduced me to the guy who took his place. It was the heavyweight I had seen walking around the lobby.

His name was Andre van den Oetelaar, and he was from the Netherlands. When he shook my hand, he almost broke it. I was thinking, 'There's no way in hell I'm fighting this guy.' A few minutes later, Andre handed me a postcard that had his picture printed on it. The only reason I could figure why he did that was so I could write a last letter to my mother and tell her how I wanted my possessions divided. She would also have a picture of the man who killed her son in the ring.

I started a conversation with him. He spoke broken English. I found out that he had knocked out former European Heavyweight Champion Alfredo Evangelista in three rounds. I asked Umberto, 'Why am I fighting a heavyweight?' He replied, 'He'll be no problem for you as long as he doesn't hit you.' That was supposed to make me feel good? Then he tried to comfort me by saying, "The guy is slow.' I knew it was a lie, because I had heard the same lies from promoters before. I didn't protest for several reasons. The first was that I was in the best shape of my life. The second was that I wanted to show Umberto Branchini that I was willing to fight anybody. The third was that I wanted to impress him enough to get him to agree to pay a $50,000 bonus to have me sign a contract with him.

That night, I stopped by Umberto Branchini's room before I went to bed. He was sitting up in his bed writing up boxing papers for the next day's fights. He was dressed only in his pajamas. Another fighter walked in to get some last minute information. Before the fighter left, he and Branchini hugged and kissed each other on the cheek. When the fighter left, I said, 'Umberto, I've been here for three months and according to Johnny Bos, I was supposed to have three fights before Christmas. I was supposed to get two thousand for each fight, and I'm counting on that six thousand dollars.' He replied, 'Don't worry. We first have to build you a following in Italy.' I dropped the subject of money. I then said, 'Umberto, I trust you.' I bent over him, kissed him on both cheeks and hugged him. After that, I really felt Italian, although I don't think I'll ever get used to kissing whiskers. Then I said goodnight and left.

The next day, I was a little edgy all the way until about three hours before my fight. By that time, I had my nerves under control. While we drove to the arena, I found out that my fight would be the last one. When we arrived, I went to the dressing room all the fighters used and stretched out on the only table there. I had a good three hours to wait, so I tried to get some sleep. I was lying on my back with my hands wrapped. I was in full boxing gear and was covered with grease. I closed my eyes, but I couldn't really sleep. By the time I was just about fully relaxed, someone was knocked down or knocked out and I could hear the crowd roar its approval. That got my adrenaline flowing again. I lay there wishing they would hurry up, but then the voice of experience said, 'Just stay cool.' I tried to relax again. Jimmy Williams would say, 'The hardest thing about fighting is waiting to fight.' He would compare it to when you were a kid and they sent you to the principal's office for a paddling. The worst part was the wait. When the paddling was finished, you would say to yourself, 'That was nothing.' Jimmy would also say, 'A coward dies a million deaths and a man dies only once.' That's true, but everybody gets a little scared, if not for anything else, scared of losing.

Somebody was supposed to have come back and let me know twenty minutes in advance before I was to go on. This would give me ample time to break a good sweat. But there was an early knockout and they came running in the dressing room yelling it was my time. I didn't care what time it was. There wasn't going to be a fight without me. I jumped off the table and started doing exercises and throwing punches like crazy for about five minutes. I finally got a drop of sweat to roll down the side of my cheek. Ready or not, they wanted me NOW. I marched out to the ring and climbed in. I was continually moving, trying to break more of a sweat. I gave my opponent the same mean look he was giving me during instructions. When the bell rang for round one, I came out like a mouse in a snake's cage. I knew that if I was stationary, I was prone to be bombed. I got my jab going and kept him reaching for me. He was falling short because of my constant movement. The round came to an end with him in hot pursuit of me. I had won the round with my jab. In the second round, he caught me with a right hand and knocked me into the ropes. He not only was big, he was fast. He shook me a little, but I avoided his lunges and I kept my jab in his face. I went back to my corner and my corner man asked me if I was okay. I said, 'Fine.' In the third round, my jab was finally softening the tissue around his eyes and I managed to sink in some good body shots that slowed his attack. My jab had him cut, and I had something to work with. In the fourth and final round, I landed some good rights to his chin that made him cover up. My jab opened another cut. I followed that up with a good flurry and a left uppercut to the stomach that had him sucking air. The ref stopped the fight and had the doctor take a look at my opponent's cuts. That was it. It went down as a TKO in the fourth round. I had won.

Salerno continued to fight in Italy. On May 31, 1988, James took on a Montana boxing legend in Milan. He fought Marvin Camel, a 6' 2" southpaw cruiserweight with a 79" reach. Camel was an interesting fighter. He was born in 1951 and had his first pro fight in 1973. His birthplace was Ronan (pronounced "RO-NAN"), Montana, a town or only 1,500 people. His father, Henry Camel, was black and his mother was a full blooded Native American who belonged to the Salish tribe. His father had taken up boxing while serving in the United States Navy and went on to fight some professional bouts. Marvin grew up on the Flathead Indian Reservation.

Camel fought 180 amateur bouts and won 140 of them before turning pro. He captured the very first world cruiserweight title, and it took two bouts to do it. He fought Mate Parlov in Parlov's hometown of Split, Yugoslavia on August 12, 1979. The fight went the full fifteen rounds and although Camel clearly outfought Parlov, the local judges ruled the contest a draw. A rematch was fought in Las Vegas on March 31, 1980, and Marvin Camel emerged as the WBC's world champion. Marvin also won the IBF cruiserweight title in February, 1983. He remains the only world champion to come from Montana. He was among the first class of those inducted into the Native American Hall of Fame.

James defeated Camel by a TKO in the sixth round when they fought in Milan. Camel's final pro record is 45 wins, 13 losses and 4 draws.

Salerno's last fight in Italy was held in Verbania, Piemonte. He fought Jose Seys, a southpaw cruiserweight from Roeselare-West Vlaanderen, Belgium. Seys was a two time Belgian light heavyweight champion. James lost the fight because he was disqualified in the third round. Jose Seys was born in 1958, but passed away in 2007 at the age of 43.

Months went by and still there was no contract offer from Branchini. James was fighting for room, board and some walk around money. He finally had a showdown with the boxing promoter. Before the meeting James wrote in his memoir,

If they don't go for my deal, it tells me that they are not as serious as the Italians in America. The $50,000 would pay off my mother's house. It's as simple as this, if they don't do the things they promised, I couldn't do anything about it. But after they pay me what I want and I don't perform, they will have me killed. I understand the risks, and I would die for what I believe in... My Mother.

Umberto Branchini didn't accept James' proposal, and Salerno never received a large signing bonus. He continued to stay in Italy for a few more months. While in Italy, James met a very wealthy woman. She was overweight and not very good looking. She begged him to marry her, but he turned her down. It was time for him to go. His Italian adventure was over.

All in all, the time James spent in Italy was interesting, but not lucrative. He was provided with a plane ticket home, but arrived with no cash in his pockets to speak of. By then, he had broken up with Karen Piche.

He was looking for new opportunities on the horizon. He tried to goad George Foreman into a big money fight while Foreman was on the comeback trail, but that didn't work. He was hopeful of being hired as a trainer and possibly getting some more fights. His wish would be granted, thanks to a legendary heavyweight.

JAMES WORKED WITH BOXING LEGEND
FLOYD PATTERSON

James was drawn to boxing in the first place by Muhammad Ali, and Ali became a part of his life. It was almost inevitable, though, that Salerno would form an association with undisputed heavyweight champion Floyd Patterson because they shared some things in common. They both emerged as contenders at very young ages, they both fought at less than 190 pounds and their greatest commonality was that they were both sensitive individuals. Patterson was described as mild, sweet, retiring, reclusive, impassive and ascetic. James was sensitive in a different way. He was attuned to how others perceived him, was easily hurt by their criticism and had to construct defense mechanisms in order to cope with it. Salerno was described as a loving, compassionate man who became a master of disaster in the ring. Floyd Patterson was said to be a man of peace who loved to fight.

Patterson won an undisputed world heavyweight title at the age of twenty one, making him the youngest man to ever accomplish that feat. He was also the first heavyweight to regain the world crown. He was trained by the legendary Cus D'Amato.

Floyd came up the hard way. He was born into a poverty stricken family in Waco, North Carolina and was the youngest of eleven children. He experienced a troubled childhood. His family moved to Brooklyn, New York, where he refused to go to school and became a petty thief. At the age of ten, he was sent to the Willwyck School for Boys in upstate New York. He was there nearly two years and credited that institution with turning his life around. He learned how to read and write and was encouraged to take up boxing.

When Patterson was fourteen, he began to be trained as a boxer under the direction of Cus D'Amato at the renowned trainer's Gramercy Gym in Manhattan. Floyd fought 77 amateur bouts and eventually won a gold medal at the 1952 Helsinki Olympics. He developed his own style. He would carry his hands higher than most boxers and kept them in front of his face. Sports writers called his method the "peek a boo stance."

Floyd Patterson turned pro in September, 1952 and his career lasted until September, 1972. He fought his last bout at the age of thirty seven. It was a rematch with Muhammad Ali for the NABF heavyweight crown. Floyd lost that fight, but his pro record was 55 wins, eight losses and one draw. He was inducted into the International Boxing Hall of Fame. He also served on the New York State Athletic Commission from 1977 through 1984.

James Salerno began working with the champ as a result of a relationship that his father had developed with the former two time heavyweight champion. In explaining how that came about, Sal Salerno said,

Shortly after James' fight with Prince Charles Williams, I received a call from Floyd Patterson. He began the conversation by saying, 'Mr. Salerno, I watched the fight and there is no question in my mind that your son won that fight. It's easy to do anything in victory. It's in defeat that a man reveals himself. Your son is quite a man." I thanked him for the compliment and then asked him what was on his mind. He said that he wanted me to come to his home in New Paltz, New York, so that we could discuss James' career. I told him that I had some business meetings scheduled near that town in the coming weeks and that I would pay him a visit.

I went to New Paltz, visited with Floyd, his wife and family, and spent a couple of days at his forty acre residence. He had an adopted son named Tracy Harris Patterson, who he was training to become a professional boxer.

When we got down to the reason for his inviting me to his home, he explained that he wanted to have James help him train his stable of fighters, which included his adopted son Tracy. He also said that he was a boxing promoter and he could get some fights for James. This would be a great help because James had been forced to go to Italy, since no other promoters in the U.S. seemed willing to work with my son after he left Alessi Promotions. I told Patterson that I would do what I could to persuade James to work with him, once my son got back from Italy.

Salerno went to work for Patterson in 1989. The two time heavyweight champion was based in New Paltz, which is a college town in upstate New York. It is west of the Hudson River and just south of the Catskill Mountains. Patterson's residence occupied forty acres along Springtown Road. A blacktop driveway rose for almost a hundred yards between tall pines as it led to a two storied, white shingled house. James lived in town and worked in two story barn on Patterson's property that had been converted into a gym. There was a regulation boxing ring on the first floor. Stair led up to a loft that was like a balcony overhanging the first floor. The loft contained a couple of heavy bags, a light bag, two full length mirrors and a dressing room with steel lockers. It was a fine facility.

James learned a great deal by being around the champ. Patterson once said to him, "You know, the writers would often bring up that I was the fighter who got knocked down the most. Whenever they did that, I would say, 'But I also got up the most." Among the fighters James helped train Tracy Harris Patterson and promising Canadian heavyweight Donovan "Razor" Ruddock.

Tracy Harris Patterson went on to win world titles as a super bantamweight and as a super featherweight. Ruddock's career had been sidetracked by a rare respiratory illness, but he was on the comeback trail He scored upset wins over James "Bonecrusher" Smith and Michael "Dynamite" Dokes. Razor Ruddock went to face Mike Tyson in two ring wars. Which ruined the careers of both boxers. The Tyson fights took everything out of Ruddock, and Iron Mike was not the same after those two bouts.

In addition to working with Patterson's fighters, James resumed his boxing career. His first bout under his new affiliation occurred on November 3, 1989, when he fought Rick Enis in Poughkeepsie, New York. Enis came into the fight with a record of 19 wins, 17 losses and one draw. He was a 6' 0" 190 pound fighter from Richmond, Indiana and was known as the "Midwest Mauler." He had played football on both the collegiate and professional levels. Enis had been a fullback at Indiana University and had been on the Denver Broncos roster for a brief period. The contest was an eight round cruiserweight bout. It went the distance, and James was awarded the decision on points. An eight round rematch was staged three weeks later on November 24, 1989 in Binghamton, New York. The fight again went the distance and this time, James was awarded a unanimous decision.

James fought again in Binghamton on February 8, 1990. It was an eight round bout, and his opponent was a heavyweight from Lima, Ohio named Andre Crowder. Crowder was almost four years older than James. Salerno won by a TKO in the final round.

James appeared in Binghamton for a third time on June 23, 1990. His fight was part of an undercard for an exhibition bout between Larry Holmes and Terry "Lawman" Anderson of Tampa. Anderson was a 6' 3" 220 pound heavyweight with a 76" reach. He had been on the marine corps team that James had trained. He had won his first fifteen pro bouts before Levi Billups upset him in Stockton, California by a fifth round TKO. The Billups fight was intended as a tune up for Anderson's fight with Renaldo Snipes at the Felt Forum in Madison Square Garden. When Terry Anderson faced Snipes, he was knocked out in the tenth round.

The promotion was the brainstorm of Frank Florio, who was Floyd Patterson's partner in Florio-Patterson Associates, Inc. of Wappingers Falls, New York. Holmes agreed to fight Terry Anderson for fifty percent of the net profits, plus $5,000 for expenses. In addition, Holmes was to be paid $1,500 for a sparring partner and his band would perform for $2,000. James served as Holmes' sparring partner. He stayed at the Larry Holmes Commodore Inn in Phillipsburg, New Jersey, which is just across the river from Holmes's hometown of Easton, Pennsylvania.

James fought Aaron "Indian" Brown on the undercard of that show. Brown was a heavyweight from Oklahoma City, Oklahoma who had taken on Alex Stewart and Tommy Morrison. He had lost by a TKO in the first round to Stewart and had lost a six round decision to Morrison. James Salerno scored a victory over the heavyweight by a fourth round TKO.

Unfortunately, the promotion lost money. Holmes ended up with only $5,000. He sued Florio and Patterson, and there is no record of him ever collecting. The debacle caused the breakup of Florio-Patterson Associates. Floyd had little to say about it, other than, "We had some rats and had to clean them out."

On December 7, 1990, James fought Andrey Rudenko in Berlin. Floyd Patterson worked his corner. Salerno chopped up Rudenko's face with his jab, but even though his opponents was all beat up, the fight was declared a draw. Sal Salerno said,

James called me after the fight. He said, 'Dad, if you ever get a chance to see a film of it, you've got to watch that fight!' He told me he should have been awarded the decision because he had really beat the guy up. He also said, 'Rudenko is very strong. He's another guy who could have played the Drago character in Rocky IV.'

James continued fighting in 1991. In recounting that portion of Salerno's career, Steve Canton, a permanent board member of the Florida Boxing Hall of Fame, stated,

He fought Wali Muhammad on February 4, 1991. Muhammad had a point deducted from him for a low blow and two more points deducted for biting James while in a clinch. The fight was televised on Sports Channel America, and the TV camera caught a close up of the fraction for all to see. Nevertheless, Muhammad denied the incident saying, 'Why would I bite him... I'm a vegetarian!' Wali Muhammad was awarded a split decision in spite of his dirty tactics.

Four months later, on June 11, 1991, James had one more big opportunity. He was former cruiserweight champ Dwight Muhammad Qawi on the USA Cable Network's Tuesday Night Fights. It was a real crossroads fight which could have propelled him into his long coveted world title chance. Qawi was a formidable opponent who would eventually be inducted into the International Boxing Hall of Fame. In a good action fight, James lost a ten round decision.

Salerno's fight Qawi was the story of his career. He could be counted on to go the distance, but unluckiest fighter of all when the judges' votes were counted. This is why James should be regarded as the greatest fighter who never won a championship.

The 1990's would turn out to be a time when both James Salerno and Floyd Patterson would have life altering experiences. Patterson once said, "Boxing is like being in love with a woman. She can be unfaithful, she can be mean, she can be cruel, but it doesn't matter if you love her. You want her, even though she can do you all kinds of harm. It's the same with me and boxing. It can do me all kinds of harm, but I love it." Patterson served as chairman of the New York State Athletic Commission from 1995 until April, 1998. He led a successful campaign to have the state of New York mandate thumb-less boxing gloves. This type of glove quickly became the norm and accomplished a great deal in reducing eye injuries. Unfortunetly his term ended in a sad way. While giving a deposition, he experienced short term memory loss. He couldn't remember the names of his two fellow commission members, his secretary or his office routines. He resigned the next day. Floyd Patterson's demise in 2006 at the age of 71 was likely the result of a form of brain damage known as dementia pugilistica; a condition resulting from his fighting career.

A little more than a month after his fight with Qawi, James' boxing career was ended because of a motorcycle accident. It occurred late at night on July 15, 1991, three days after James' thirtieth birthday. He was riding along a stretch of Delaware highway. He was given no warning of the danger that was in his path.

The highway was under construction, but workers had left a big open ditch in the pavement when they went home after a long day. They had failed to properly block off that section of road or place warning signals. James rode his bike into the hole. He was lucky that he wasn't killed.

He lay injured for some time until a Delaware state trooper arrived on the scene. Salerno had to be air lifted to Christiana Hospital in Newark, Delaware. He wasn't admitted until 1:15 A.M. on July 16.

His most visible injuries lacerations to his left cheek and left forehead. His most serious injuries, however, were to his lower back and the portion of his spine contained within his neck. These injuries left him with constant back problems for the rest of his life. He would also have to deal with neuralgia in the form of recurring stabbing, burning pains in his lower back. He would have to avoid twisting motions and could lift no more than fifteen pounds. James Salerno's fighting days were over.

James Salerno's professional record was 41 wins, 11 losses and a draw, but the big pay days James expected when he was a teenager never materialized. He spent fourteen years sacrificing his body for peanuts. Jimmy Williams and I spent some time figuring out how much money James made from boxing. His highest purse was $6,000, with an overall average of $2,000. He grossed a little over $100,000 for 53 bouts and netted less than $40,000. He certainly didn't fight for money. It was a labor of love for James Salerno. While discussing this part of Salerno's life, Jimmy said,

I knew the great saxophone player Charlie 'Yardbird' Parker. Like James, he was an unbelievable talent who was paid very little for what he did so well. Both of them were true artists who were willing to give their best even if there was no money to be had.

Larry Barfield said,

James didn't have the body of a boxer because he was so wiry, but he was amazingly strong. Jimmy Williams said his legs were just as good as Muhammad Ali's. James could dance for fifteen rounds if he had to, and he could still do that even if he were totally out of shape.

Sal Salerno summed up his son's boxing career by saying,

The proof of James' boxing greatness is that four heavyweight champions called upon him at various times to participate in their training camps. Muhammad Ali, Smokin' Joe Frazier, Floyd Patterson all knew they could learn something from him. He could put on performances that would help even the great ones become better.

PART FIVE
THE YEARS AFTER THE BOXING ENDED

JAMES DISCOVERS RAP MUSIC

Sometime around the end the 1980's, James Salerno heard an LL Cool J recording. It was a style of music known as "rap." Just as when he saw Muhammad Ali on television as a child, James thought, "I can do that." He would spend years creating his own rap style. James stated,

With rap, I'm sitting on buried treasure. I had this going before Vanilla Ice. I used to write poetry, and rap is poetry put to a beat. I want to do both... fight and rap.

It just wasn't in the cards for James to be a rap performer while he was boxing. It took several years for him to produce his CD. He performed under the name Italian Ice. The CD was titled, Assorted Flavors. It was well received. One of the featured tracks is The College of Hard Knocks.

THE COLLEGE OF HARD KNOCKS
I became a pro fighter at the age of fifteen
With visions of glory to rule the boxing scene.
The promoters all said I could go far
And in a few years, I'd be a star.
When I was young, I learned how to box.
I'm from the College of Hard Knocks.
My fire always burned for a girl named Maggie Thomas.
I swore in my soul and made her a promise.
To do what it takes to earn her name
I'd fight my way to fortune and fame.
She said in my head she thought there were rocks.
I'm from the College of Hard Knocks.
I'm educated on the block
And time's running out on my clock.
When reality hits, it chills to the bone
That after all this time, I'm still alone.
Time is the thief that goes by silently,
The calendar of youth that went by violently.
I've come too far, too far to stop.
I'm from the College of Hard Knocks.

JAMES AND LARRY BECOME
RENEGADE LANDSCAPERS

James and Larry Barfield headed along different paths after Salerno went to Miami Beach in 1979. Barfield became more involved in music and joined of a band as a vocalst and gutar player. After the group Survivor scored with their smash hit Eye of the Tiger, Larry performed a cover version of the song at an Orlando nightclub. He came onstage in boxing trunks and shoes and with his hands bandaged. His vocal performance brought the house down and was worked into the band's act.

Larry moved out of the Barfield home. He was sharing an apartment with his girlfriend and performing with the band. He had serious substance abuse problems. It was an unsustainable situation. Matters came to a head when he got into an argument with his girlfriend and she locked him out. He was under the influence when he put his right hand through the glass portion of the front door. The hand was injured so badly that it required microsurgery.

Larry Barfield's fighting career should have been over, but a shady character named Stan Tomasello talked him into training for pro fights. In October, 1985, Tomasello arranged a four round bout for him in Daytona Beach. Larry was matched with a black middleweight named Allen Briscoe. Bob Barfield sang the National Anthem before the start of the fights that night. Larry stopped Briscoe and won by a TKO in the third round. Larry's hand hurt him so bad, though, that he realized that he was lucky to get through the fight. That was the end of his ring career.

Tomasello was involved in drugs, and he hired Larry to accompany him on runs to Miami with large quantities of cocaine in the car. Stan was also involved in high jacking operations. His father was an important organized crime figure in Chicago. High jacked merchandise from the Midwest was sent down to Orlando because it was a trucking hub and it had a huge number of warehouses. Stan Tomasello was well connected to that operation.

Tomasello was also very active in amateur boxing. An amateur named Dwight Albin who fought on some pro am shows at the Orlando Sports Stadium became involved with Tomasello. Dwight said,

Stan organized underground amateur bouts that were held in Tampa's Ybor City. A ring was set up in a bar, and there were between 150 to 200 people present. There was lots of betting going on. The fighters were given high jacked merchandise instead of trophies. A kid would get a TV set that they could sell to somebody for $60.

Stan became my manager. He had me fighting under the name Rocky Fabrizio. Everything fell apart for him. His wife divorced him. He wound up in jail and might be dead by now.

Dwight Albin's pro record is 12 wins, ten losses and two draws

Larry's drug problems became so bad that the other members of the band literally dumped him on the doorstep of his father's home. He couldn't stay there because he wasn't ready to settle down. He had heard that James was working for Floyd Patterson in New Paltz, so he headed in that direction carrying only a suitcase and his guitar. .

When Barfield arrived at the motel where James was living, the two friends had a joyous reunion. They immediately left on a fishing trip. It was just like the old days. The most important thing to them was having as much fun as possible each day and worry about tomorrow when it comes.

By this time, there was no doubt in James' mind that he was going to make millions with his rap music. Larry could be a big help to him. Barfield was enthusiastic about the idea, but he reminded James that it would take money to produce a CD and launch a career. They found the answer to the money problem one day while driving around in James' pickup.

Salerno suddenly realized that none of the lawns in the northeast were manicured. He pulled up in a neighborhood where people were out watering their lawns. James and Larry immediately attracted their attention. They wondered what the two young men with the pickup truck were doing there.

James took his edging tool out of the truck and put a new blade on it. He did this as conspicuously as possible. The edger didn't need a new blade, but it got the people's attention. Everyone knows that sharp tools make a huge difference.

Larry picked up another edger, and then he also made a show out of putting a new blade on it. He took one side of the street and James took the other. Barfield knocked on a door. When a woman answered, he said, "Good afternoon. I'm Larry Barfield. I'm with Salerno Brothers Landscaping and Ground Maintenance."

"We already have a landscaper."

"No, Ma'am, we're not here to sell landscaping. As you can see, your edges have not been taken care of. You're losing about six inches of sidewalk."

Larry cranked up the edger and did a little trimming with it. He then said, "Do you see what a nice, distinct line it makes? Edging will give your lawn beautiful lines and make all the difference in the world."

The woman asked, "How much would it cost?"

"Twenty bucks."

"Twenty bucks?"

"Yes, Ma'am. After we do the edging, all you have to do is pick it up. It rolls up like carpeting. If you've got any bare spots, this is like sod."

"All right, go ahead." The woman was sold, and she was the first of many customers.

In recalling those times, Larry Barfield said,

Edging was like coining money for us. Going into a neighborhood and manicuring ten or fifteen lawns in an hour at twenty dollars apiece became routine. We'd be knocking on doors and at the same time, we'd be listening. If either of us heard one of our edgers fire up, we knew we had a live one. If one person in the neighborhood bought the deal, we'd reel in their neighbors on both sides and across the street. We'd be getting twenty dollars from one house after another. James also handled a chainsaw very skillfully. He was great at up selling. It was no problem for him to remove tree limbs at twenty dollars a pop.

One time, we were driving back from Atlantic City. We had been gambling all night and had lost all our money. I said, 'James, we gotta get some credit cards or do something. We don't even have enough money to pay the toll up ahead.' He replied, 'Our credit cards are in the back of this truck.' He meant our edgers, and he was right. He found a neighborhood, we went door to door and within a few hours, we had almost a thousand dollars. The edgers were better than credit cards because there was no monthly bill.

James and Larry seemed footloose and fancy free, but they were operating outside the law. Barfield was without a driver's license after having surrendered his because of a DUI. Salerno's truck had Florida tags, but he carried no personal liability insurance or licenses for his landscaping business. There was a period when he lacked a valid driver's license driver's. They had to be very careful at all times, because they were just a heartbeat away from getting into serious trouble. They were renegade landscapers.

There was the time they were in Daytona Beach and neither James nor Larry had valid license. They were in James' Nissan pickup. The Gulf War had just started. James got a brainstorm. They had one thousand bumper stickers printed up that read "Saddam Sucks." They sold them for three dollars each or two for five dollars. The first thousand sold easily, and so did a second thousand. In the midst of their selling frenzy, Larry was driving down busy streets and James would be hanging out the passenger window and hollering to passersby about the bumper stickers. All of a sudden, a police car pulled up right beside them. It turned out they wanted to buy bumper stickers, and James sold them two for five dollars. While the transaction was taking place, Larry was scared to death that one of the officers might have asked to see his license.

Their windfall didn't last long. James and Larry ordered a third thousand but the war ended too quick and they were left holding them. Easy come, easy go.

James got in over his head on one occasion when he took on the job of removing a tree. In recalling the incident, Larry Barfield said,

He put in a bid to cut down a huge tree that was right next to a house. I asked him, 'How much would we get for the job?'

'Five hundred bucks. Three hundred for me and two hundred for you.'

I said, 'James, I can do ten yards in an hour and make $500 bucks.' He said, 'Man, this will be simple. It won't take hardly any time at all.' I had to admit James was good at dropping trees, but I had seen the tree. It had a huge base and a limb that stuck out at a weird angle. I said to him, 'I don't care what happens. I'm not going to that gig.' He said, 'That's fine man.'

I planned on staying in our hotel room and watch movies all day, but that morning, James said, 'Hey man, last chance or I'm gonna go up to Home Depot and pick me up a Mexican.' James was good at selling to me too. He also said, 'It'll just be snip, snip and we're done; two hundred for you and three hundred for me.'

I thought, 'If it goes down like he says it's gonna do, I'll make two hundred bucks. But if it don't, this should be something funny to watch. I'm not gonna miss this for the world.'

The house was owned by a little old lady. Her son lived there, and he was a karate instructor. We bought orange cones to use to divert traffic from our work site and we tried to look professional, but we weren't licensed or insured.

James was sawing away and putting on quite a show. A crowd of people from the neighborhood were watching us. I could've probably signed autographs. I was standing out by the road, directing passing motorists around our work site.

James cut one part of the tree just the right way and it would've dropped on target, but Mother Nature was against us. All of a sudden, I heard a loud snap. I saw the tree twist as it dropped, and it hit the corner of the house. It ripped all the gutters out. It could have gone through the house but didn't. To this day, I say, thank you, God. It shook the ground when it landed.

The son came charging out. James' face was as white as a ghost. I was dying inside. I thought, 'Oh shit!' There was debris all over the lady's yard and some of it had even landed out in the road. James said, 'We'll be right back.'

The old lady's son jumped right into James' face and said, 'You aren't going anywhere!'

James then pulled out his wallet. He removed a couple of items and said, 'Here's my driver's license and my car insurance card. Hold onto them. We're gonna be right back.' He handed the pieces of identification to the son.

We were in deep shit. We really didn't know what to do. James headed the truck to a lawn mower place we had passed on the way to the old woman's home. After we pulled into the parking lot, we went into the place and ran into a guy who was there to buy some oil. It turned out he had a professional quality wood chipper.

James didn't know him from Adam, but he went right up to him and said, 'Hey man, you gotta help me out.' He begged the guy to help us. He was so desperate that he agreed to give the man all the money we were to be paid. He assured him that he would instruct the homeowner to give him the entire $500, just for the use of his wood chipper. The man went back with us, and James and I busted our asses all day cleaning the mess up while he operated his machine. At the end of that long day, I was scratched up, drenched with sweat, filthy dirty and exhausted. Finally, the old woman paid the man with the chipper and we were allowed to leave.

I sat in silence all the way back to the hotel, infuriated at the thought of having done all that work for nothing. James was like a little kid. If someone was mad at him, he would wait until he thought it was all right to say something, but he would eventually have to say something. I was in no mood for any conversation. I was exhausted, I had scratches, I was drenched with sweat and I was filthy dirty. James began to say, 'Larry...'

I cut him off with a loud SHHHH! JUST SHUT UP!'

He meekly pulled back, saying, 'All right, that's cool, man.'

I had calmed down by the time we got to our hotel. Two beers later, I felt civil. James piped up and said, 'Hey man, let's go the Red Lobster. It'll be my treat.' I said okay. I figured I'd get something to show for the miserable day. I didn't even shower or put on clean clothes, which I normally insisted on doing before going into a Red Lobster at night. After all, you never knew when you'd run into some girls. James had a different attitude. He would show up at Red Lobster day or night in his filthy work clothes.

By the time we were seated, we almost too exhausted to lift any knives or forks. It was 9:30 and we hadn't eaten all day. The waitress took our orders. She asked me what kind of dressing I wanted on my salad, and I said bleu cheese. She said to James, 'Would you like soup or salad?

'Salad.'

'Dressing?'

'Yes.'

I said, 'Yes, James? What kind of answer is that?'

He said, 'Dude, I'm exhausted.'

As tired and discouraged as I was, I cracked up.

It had been a day when everything had gone wrong for the renegade landscapers, but it produced moments that gave James and Larry belly laughs for years. It was the day Salerno learned how impossibly difficult "snip, snip, snip" could sometimes be.

GOING DOWN SLOW AND HEADED
TOWARD HIS LAST DAYS

After Larry Barfield decided to settle down and lead a normal, everyday life, James was left all alone. His health was also deteriorating. He was on medication for his back problems, but he had constant severe pain in his neck, his shoulders and all the way down his back to his hips. The pain made it very difficult for him to get any sleep. He would try sleeping on the floor. Sometimes that helped, but many times it didn't.

Through the efforts of his father, James was in and out of drug rehabilitation programs. There would be some improvement for a while, but then he would revert to his old habits. He once told his father,

I have pain to deal with, and I'm always feeling low and feeling depressed. I know I shouldn't smoke the crack, but if I do, it will turn all that around and give me a good feeling. For a little while, I'm happy. When the good feeling is over, I'm miserable. I fell lower than a cigarette butt on the ground. That's why I have to keep smoking crack. I'll feel horrible if I don't keep doing it.

During 1999, James was participating in a rehabilitation program in Jacksonville through Gateway Community Services and from all outward appearances, seemed to be doing well. They arranged housing for him at the Comet Apartments at 550 Comet Street. Sal would check in on him and see that he had enough food. He was working with an organization that offered several different programs. He was also helping out with the local PAL program by teaching boxing skills to kids. He had earned a lot of respect from the Jacksonville Police Department. He worked off and on at landscaping. Sal was unable to see his oldest son as often as he would have wanted because of an assignment in Texas. Things appeared to be going well for a change, but James had been using crack cocaine long enough to become very skillful at concealing his habit.

The drug scene in Jacksonville had become meaner as the 1990's came to an end. Increasing border policing south of California and Texas had resulted in increased seizures at the Port of Miami and the Port of Everglades. Jacksonville's relative equidistance from several major cities made it a natural transport and trade hub for crack cocaine and other illegal substances. There was a big change from what had gone on before because instead of crack heads dealing in order to support their habits, the business had become controlled by organized dealers who would resort to violence. They would not hesitate to engage the services of young kids, if need be.

In May, 1999, James received a settlement for the accident that occurred in Delaware back in 1991. Rick Baker was his attorney. He had known Rick since they were kids. Baker called James' mother and said, "He needs help, Joanne. The money he's getting is going to go somewhere that's not going to do him any good. I'm telling you he needs to into a rehab program. I'm not allowed to deduct the money he owes you from the settlement, but I'll tell him that he has to go and see you about it." James only netted $50,000.

He went to see his mother and paid her the $10,000 that she had loaned him. Joanne said, "I could tell that he didn't really want to pay what he owed me, but he ended up giving me the money."

James blew through the rest of it. His habit had gotten bigger and bigger. In In the past, when he was out of money, he would go to see his parents. His mother was more likely to cave in than Sal. It was difficult for Joanne to turn James down because he appeared to be in great pain because of his forced withdrawal from crack cocaine. More often than not, the mother would give her addicted son some money. She couldn't bear to see him in agony. He always thought he could go to her and she would bail him out.

James' official residence at the time was a low income apartment complex that was part of a program for people who would otherwise be homeless. Many of the tenants had drug issues. At that point in his life, he had reached rock bottom. All of his friends were druggies. He was reduced to begging on the streets. The police brought him in several times. They told him he couldn't continue doing it. They warned him by saying, "We're getting complaints." A white woman served as a resident manager of the complex where James was residing.

It got to the point that Sal had to go to Jacksonville because James had been picked up for begging. The authorities would not release him unless a close family member appeared on his behalf. Many of the police looked out for him, but James was placed on probation and told that he could not leave the county until it was served.

During James' last visit to his parents' home, he said to Sal,

Dad, it's not just me. You can talk to anyone who takes drugs and they will tell you it is all about escaping from the real world. The drugs make them feel good. Forget cloud

nine, you feel like you are cloud one hundred ten. You have the world in the palm of your hand. You are happy. It is all about feeling good.

During this same time, James was also staying on what could be described as a houseboat or a small yacht that was owned by a man named John Woods. James was negotiating with Woods to buy the boat from him, once his settlement came in. Woods told James that he would not tolerate any drugs on his vessel. Their relationship ended when Woods found marijuana in James' pockets.

James attended Larry Barfield's wedding on June 26, 1999. Larry was surprised that his old friend was able to be there. In recalling that day in June, he said,

James seemed genuinely happy for me. I had sent him an invitation, even though I knew he was trouble with the law in Jacksonville. When we talked on the phone, he had mentioned that he was on probation and wasn't allowed to leave the state. I sent him the invitation strictly as a memento he could keep in his scrap book. I spent the week before the wedding at the home of one of my brothers. Around eight in the morning on the day of my wedding, I received a call from the church where the ceremony was to take place. They said a strange man was sleeping in a red Nissan pickup truck with a Florida plate that had been parked in their lot. I blurted out, 'James is here!' I assured them that I knew the man and there wouldn't be any problems.

I couldn't believe it, and I was so touched. My mom lived right up the street from the church. She went right over and brought James to her house. She kept asking him, 'Why didn't you come to me? You know you're always welcome.'

Everything was quickly straightened out. It was a great weekend, and we had a blast. I took some time to have a serious talk with my old friend. I tried to recruit him to work at one of the outlets in my employer's chain of furniture stores. I told him, 'James, you'd be excellent at it. You can sell ice water to Eskimos.' Unfortunately, he didn't take me up on it.

I did notice one disturbing thing about him. He was slurring his words badly. In my honest opinion, he was showing signs of brain damage. I truly believe it was caused by all of the hits he had taken while boxing. He did an enormous amount of sparring during his seventeen years as a fighter. He looked good, but it was the first time in my life that I saw a look of fear in his eyes. My mom said, 'There's fear and sadness in his face. I've never seen that before.'

No one had any idea that James' life would end just four and a half weeks later. It was ironic that the same suit he wore to Larry's wedding would be the one he would be buried in.

THE KILLING

Fifteen years have passed since James Salerno met his tragic end. It remains a cold case. There is no longer any effort by the Jacksonville police department toward finding the answers to questions about who hired the hit man and who pulled the trigger. This chapter contains information from the official police report. It also includes a version of what happened that was pieced together by James' old friend Larry Barfield. Much of it is speculation, but it is very close to the truth.

It was 10:00 P.M. on August 1, 1999. James was behind the wheel of his red 1988 Nissan pickup truck. He was approaching forty, had filled out to 210 pounds, but was still on the lean side. Two males were in the truck with him. All three men were white. The only other things they shared in common were being addicted to crack cocaine and leading useless lives. Birds of a feather flock together and they operated on a buddy system. They had an unwritten code that they would share their coke with any of the three who happened to be out of money. They had recently done some serious partying, financed by the settlement James had received a few months before. He had finally been paid for the case that had resulted from his accident in July, 1991. He had been generous with his two party pals and it didn't take long for them to burn through the cash. Now he was at less than zero because he had not only spent all he had, but had managed to run up a tab in the thousands with their main supplier.

Larry Barfield said,

He had failed to meet his deadline for coming up with the dough, and that had placed him in grave danger. James was James, though, and he still thought he could talk his way out of it. He had always been a very persuasive guy who could sell ice water to Eskimos, so he believed he could sell his coke pusher on the idea of giving him just a little more time. No one ever accused James of being a realist, and he seemed incapable of comprehending that the dealer meant business. He was actually surprised that the dealer suddenly became unavailable to him. He had always been far too trusting, so it didn't dawn on him why the dealer was avoiding him. Suddenly, everything seemed to turn around for the best when his two drug buddies told him that the dealer had agreed to meet him in unit number twelve of the Comet Apartments. When they told him about it, he felt reassured that everything would be straightened out. After all, he was a good customer, and drug dealers are all about money.

As Salerno wheeled his small truck into a parking space of the apartment complex, he looked over at his companions. They didn't say anything, but the looks on their faces gave him a false reassurance that everything was good.

After he parked his truck, one of his companions supposedly said, "We'll wait for you down here. It won't take long. Then, we'll go get high."

He was perfectly at ease in his certainty that the worst of it would soon be over. He had never stiffed any drug dealer and he had mentally drawn up a list of family members he was going to try to get some cash from. The guy he owed the money to would get every penny. It wouldn't be the first time he had talked his way out of a jam. Every time something bad happened to him, it always seemed to lead to something good. It was like the time the Florida Highway Patrol placed him in shackles and flew him to Tampa because of all the tickets. That led to his meeting Karen Piche. He smiled at that memory.

Larry Barfield added,

He had left his keys in his pickup because he trusted his pals. He had no idea that they had set him up. His assassins were probably paid with free dope from the man James owed the money to.

After shooting James, the kid ran down to Salerno's red pickup and hopped in the bed. Three of his buddies who had acted as lookouts jumped in with him, and they began to hoot and holler in celebration of the kill. One of James' drug buddies was behind the wheel and he sped away from the parking lot.

Warren Wade was the tenant in apartment number eleven. He heard the gunshot, and then he heard someone bang on his door and say, "I'm shot." When he opened the door to his apartment, he saw the Nissan pickup speed away. He immediately called 911. After making the call, he walked out of his apartment and saw James Salerno lying on the ground. Wade checked James' pulse on his left ankle. There was none. The man was dead, so he waited for the rescue people to arrive.

The apartment James was to have met the dealer in turned out to be vacant. The police conducted a canvas of the area. Detectives spoke with three other tenants of the Comet Apartments. Each of them told a little different story. Bill Burdges in apartment number six said he heard what sounded like two shots and a man say, "Oh no, no." He then heard a vehicle speed away. Michael Bradshaw in apartment number one said he heard some noises outside and then a few seconds of hollering. He said he didn't see or hear anything else. Melvin Carter in apartment number fifteen said that he heard a shot and then he heard somebody yell, "Someone shot me!" After that, he heard someone running up the stairs. All three of the tenants interviewed were shown a photograph of James, but no one knew him or could identify him, even though he lived in their sixteen unit apartment building.

Salerno's Nissan pickup matched the description of the vehicle leaving the scene. The truck was found at 1000 N. Liberty Street. It had been abandoned with heavy right front side damage and a flat front tire. The windshield had two cracks in it. Detectives stated, "The cracks appeared to have come from two separate impacts, possibly from individuals inside the vehicle."

An autopsy was performed. James had one gunshot wound on the right side of his upper chest. He also had some blunt trauma to the back left part of his head, which was described as a contusion. The trajectory of the bullet wound was from Salerno's front to his back and slightly downward from right to left. The projectile had gone through James' upper aorta and through both of his lungs. There were cocaine metabolites in his urine at the time of his death.

No suspect was ever identified and all leads were exhausted. After all the evidence was processed, the case was suspended on January 31, 2000. It will continue to be a cold case until new leads can be developed, and that appears unlikely.

THE AFTERMATH

Two days after the shooting, a white woman who managed the Comet Apartments called Sal. She had his number because she had met him previously. The father knew that she thought the world of his son. It was clear from the way she was talking that it was not easy for her to make the call.

She had probably agonized over doing it for the two days it took her to finally pick up the phone and dial the number. It just didn't seem right to have to tell a father that his son was dead. When she finally worked up the courage, she got off the phone as quickly as she could. She was petrified at the thought of saying the four words "Your son is dead."

Once she got Sal on the line, she began to freeze up and did a poor job of getting to the point. She said, "Mr. Salerno, I'm sorry I didn't get to you sooner. I was so devastated by what happened to James. I didn't know how to even say it to you, but I knew I had to call you after I found out what happened." The way she handled things made it even worse for the parents.

Joanne was sitting there watching Sal as he took the call. She had no idea of what was being said. When he realized what the call was about, Sal wondered how he could possibly tell her what had happened. Joanne kept asking, "What's wrong? What's wrong?" She could see that her husband was acting strange while he was on the phone.

When she finally got the message across, Sal began to choke up, and then he broke down. He tried to speak, but it was hard for Joanne to make out what he was saying. Finally, she realized that he was mumbling, "James was shot and killed."

The news hit her like a bucket of ice cubes in the face. She and her husband clung to each other for dear life and cried for over an hour. As they recounted all of this to me, Sal said, "I never shed so many tears in my life."

When there were no more tears left in them to shed, they began to think rationally and talk things out. They recalled how many times they had talked about the possibility of James dying because of an overdose. Sal brought up a comment James' friend John Wolfe had made when they were in Delaware, going door to door, looking for work manicuring lawns. They had taken a room in a cut rate hotel. Wolfe had said to Sal, "James was holding his drug usage to a nighttime thing, but now he's gotten into the habit of slipping off during the day and heading back to the hotel to get on the crack pipe. I have a feeling that one of these days he's going to O.D. and never come out of that hotel room."

Sal finished said to his wife, "It would have been much easier to accept his dying peacefully because of an overdose than to hear that he's been murdered in cold blood by a stranger and that he suffered before he finally went." Joanne agreed. The thought of it caused her to find some more tears within her, and she began to weep again.

The nightmare did not end with the killing. Four days after the phone call from the apartment manager, a Jacksonville police detective came to the Salerno home for an interview. He left his card, but gave little information.

The task of making funeral arrangements for their oldest son was just too much for the parents to deal with. It was left to Rick Baker to make the arrangements. James was in an open casket. Matt Salerno delivered a eulogy in which he spoke of his brother's compassion. Hundreds of people attended the Roman Catholic service and then followed the hearse in their cars to the graveside ceremony. As an honorably discharged veteran of the United States, James was buried with full military honors. This included three volleys of shots being fired in honor of him. His head stone was supplied by the United States Marine Corps.

Sal's father loved James. The parents never told the grandfather about what had happened. The old man lived to be ninety nine. He died in 2000, the year after his grandson's death.

The Orlando Sentinel, which had extensively covered James' boxing career, made no mention of it in his obituary. All it stated was that he was a landscaper. I have been told that information for obituaries is normally supplied by funeral parlors. I still don't think that was a good enough reason.

His old friend Larry Barfield said,

There was sadness, and then a relief which followed the shock of hearing what happened. I was very worried about him when he attended my wedding. I'm sure that he was showing signs of brain damage. I believe James would have had a hard life had he lived another ten years. By then, the dementia would have really kicked in. He probably would have ended up living on the streets. I think God protected him by arranging for him to be taken home quickly. .

Jimmy Williams was unable to attend the funeral. Jimmy explained what happened to me when he said,

I was in Oregon working with light middle weight champ Winky Wright when James was killed. We were preparing to fight Fernando Vargas on December 4, 1999. The bout was going to be held at the Chinook Winds Casino in Lincoln City, Oregon. When I finally returned to Florida over four months after the murder, someone told me about it. I was terribly hurt at the news because I felt I had failed to perform my duty by delivering a eulogy at his funeral services. I immediately called Del Vonza, an old time cop in Jacksonville whom I had known through my work with the PAL. Del told me all about it. I went to see Sal as soon as I could. My emotions got the better of me and I shed a lot of tears.

Memories of James still haunt me. He was like a son the Lord had given me to raise. I still think about what might have happened if James had not been taken from me to be turned into a professional at fifteen. I can assure you his life would have been far different. By being placed in a world of hard men who carried their pride on the outside, he was never given a chance to grow into a man who seeks the help of the Lord and finds his value within him. That is why what happened to James is such a tragedy.

The parents needed closure, but that was not to be. Sal made four trips to Jacksonville to meet with the police. At first, they tried to evade his questions. It was obvious that they looked upon it as a case of one burden on society being blown away by another burden on society. Jacksonville was in the grip of a huge drug problem at the time. The authorities saw little to be gained by pressing an investigation. As long as regular people were not hurt, who cared what the animals did to each other? They didn't come right out and say that to Sal because they had too much respect for him. Finally on his fourth visit, Sal was told by a sympathetic officer, "The truth about what happened to your son is so bad that it is far better for you not to know it." The father realized he was going to get any more from them, so he finally let go of it.

Many people in the fight game remember him with fondness. Hall of Fame referee Bryan Garry said,

I sparred many rounds with him inside the 'oven' on West Cypress Street in Tampa, home of the 'Alessi Boxing Stables,' during the late 1970's and early 1980's. Since I was in great shape and had been seriously training for many months, Jimmy Williams allowed me to work with James. He was an excellent technician, with quick combinations and wonderful footwork, combined with a great defense. I refereed many of his pro fights. I always liked James and his father and thought that he could have been a world champion. What a sad ending to a very happy go lucky human being! He will be missed.

Larry Barfield said,

To James, everything was good. There were no bad times. If he had won a ten million dollar lottery, he would have bought a huge house for all his buddies to hang out in. We could all play football, play guitars, go to the beach and hang out with chicks.

James' brother Matt paid him a marvelous tribute when he said,

I am at ease with his passing only because I knew that my brother seemed to have a harder time than most in dealing with the harsh realities we call everyday life. He was a hair away from being the next Muhammad Ali, but ended up doing landscaping or whatever it would take to feed himself. He never had a bank account, and could not deal with disappointment. Again, he thought like a child. I loved my brother. He could not have been a better brother to me. He taught me how to fish. He taught me the value of spending time with those you love. He showed me how important it is to tell your parents and those in your life who are close to you that you love them, without reservation. He reminded me constantly not to take life so damn seriously. He believed, 'Have a great day today, have a blast tonight and do exactly what you want to do tomorrow… it may be your last!' James Salerno is the undisputed champion in my world as he was to everyone who had the pleasure of being his friend, or had been on the end of one of his many practical jokes.

IN CONCLUSION

There is a great deal to be learned from the story of James Salerno. He rose from being a tall string bean of a kid with ADHD issues to reaching the cusp of a world boxing championship. He was screwed out of decisions several times, but never whined to the media about it. There's something to be said for that. The most important things to remember about him were that he was a generous, compassionate, loving man who used his music to send a message of racial harmony. He could fill an opponent's face with leather, but he was a true sportsman who always thanked the man he faced for giving him a chance to fight. He was a character who possessed character. He is remembered fondly and will never be forgotten. He is a legend, and legends never die.